Parents with Inconvenient Truths about Trans, Volume II

T0356850

Parents

with Inconvenient Truths about Trans

Volume II

*More Tales from the Home Front
in the Fight to Save Our Kids*

Edited by Josie A., Dina S., and Florence M.

Foreword by Az Hakeem

PITCHSTONE PUBLISHING
DURHAM, NORTH CAROLINA

Pitchstone Publishing
Durham, North Carolina
www.pitchstonebooks.com

Copyright © 2025 by Parents with Inconvenient Truths about Trans

All rights reserved.
Printed in the United States of America
First edition

The views and opinions expressed in the parent essays in this volume are those of the authors alone and do not necessary reflect the official positions of Genspect. Nor do the views and opinions expressed in the parent essays necessarily reflect the views of the publisher, editors, or other parent contributors to the volume. As a collection of stories by parents from a wide range of personal and professional backgrounds and with a wide range of experiences and viewpoints, this volume is intended for informational purposes only, and the publisher, editors, and contributors disclaim any liability or responsibility for any errors or omissions in the information provided.

The names of some individuals in this book have been changed to protect their privacy. All parent essays in this volume were previously published on the Parents with Inconvenient Truths about Trans Substack (pitt.substack.com). With minor exceptions, they are replicated here as they appeared on PITT to preserve the voice of each parent, to highlight that each parent's story is unique despite the many commonalities across the essays, and to reflect the immediacy and authenticity of each parent's choice of words. For links to the essays on PITT, see the "credits" section of this volume.

Library of Congress record available at https://lccn.loc.gov/2024044816
Library of Congress ebook record available at https://lccn.loc.gov/2024044817

ISBN 9781634312622 (paperback) | ISBN 9781634312639 (ebook)

This book is dedicated to Josie, Dina, and Florence's sweet children and loving husbands, and to all the parents who hold inconvenient truths about their children and young adults. We thank all the brave parents who allowed us to tell their stories and hope that their voices will help other parents navigate through this medical scandal.

Contents

Parents on Social Contagion and Indoctrination

Parents on Heartache and Tragedy

Parents with Medicalized Children

Parents on Desistance

Foreword

As a psychiatrist in psychotherapy, I have specialized in the psychotherapeutic treatment of adults with gender dysphoria for over twenty years. Indeed, in the United Kingdom, I am the only psychiatrist who has offered such a service, with most psychiatrists steering well clear of patients with gender confusion, except for a small minority who work in Gender Identity Clinics functioning as sex hormone prescribers and gatekeepers to surgeons offering physical castration and "'sex change'" operations. It has always been my opinion that it is not possible to change one's sex and that gender is a social construct, so one cannot operate on that.

For many years, I was led to believe that I was in the minority in my belief that there was something fundamentally wrong with a healthcare system that was colluding in what I, as a psychiatrist, believed was an "overvalued idea"—an idea or belief that a person holds with fairly firm conviction but that, with the help of a thoughtful clinician, can be made sense of. For example, a person's fantasy of being able to transform themselves might be understood as a magical way of escaping something.

In psychiatry, we are familiar with patients investing in overvalued ideas and fantasizing that physical solutions can be an escape from psychological distress. The critically low-weight anorexic patient believes that their life will be better if only they were able to lose even more weight despite those around them trying to make them see how such attempts will endanger their lives. We are familiar with the severely depressed patient who believes that they must bring a physical end to their existence via suicide in order to relieve mental pain. In both of these cases, the role of the psychiatrist, psychologist, and clinician is not to collude with the overvalued idea, to agree with the fantasized physical solution, but instead to try and help the patient by challenging their overvalued idea and treating the underlying psychological distress and disturbance. I have always wondered how, as a profession, we have found ourselves treating those presenting with gender confusion differently.

Being "gender critical" means being critical of current "gender ideology," which is an ideological off-shoot of social justice theory with roots in queer theory. Whilst many may be of the opinion that religion is dying in the Western world, I would argue that social justice theory and gender ideology are new religions gripping the West. Gender ideology argues against biology and science. It replaces scientific thinking with belief-based reality—what you believe to be true is true despite any scientific evidence to the contrary.

Surprisingly and worryingly, scientific, clinical, psychological, and medical institutions in the Western world, which until recently had prioritized evidence-based medicine, are now adopting gender ideology and have been captured by this new belief system. The belief system forms what we could understand as a cult, with cult-based thinking and beliefs drawing people in and keeping out those who do not believe.

Historically, there were only a very small number of people who believed they were born the wrong sex. This was formally called transsexualism as separate and distinct from those who did not believe they were the opposite sex but wanted to temporarily appear as the opposite sex for social or sexual pleasure; these individuals were referred to as transvestites, and there have always been a much greater number of transvestites than transsexuals. In my work, I have described eleven different subtypes of transvestites. Then there are the men with a sexual fantasy of having female sexual body parts. These men, for whom Dr. Ray Blanchard coined the term "autogynaephiles," are again distinct from transvestites (more about clothing and overall appearance) and transsexuals (more about social and gender roles with the wished-for bodily changes secondary to that). In my clinical experience, autogynaephiles are often clinically mistaken for transsexuals. Unhelpfully, thanks to the cult of gender ideology, the umbrella term "trans" has replaced the distinct terms of transsexual, transvestite, and autogynaephile, resulting in the general public believing that they are a uniform group of people—all the same—all "trapped in the wrong body.'"

Recently, we have seen a meteoric rise in children and adolescents identifying as being "trans" or "nonbinary." There has been an 8000x increase of trans-identifying girls. Today, every university and secondary school in the Western world almost certainly has a significant number of students identifying as having a gender dysphoria. So how do we account for this explosion of gender dysphoria in young people? It is not a viral contagion of pandemic proportions as we saw with COVID-19—of course not. No, it is a social contagion, for as those who are familiar with my work and writings will know, my clinical opinion is that "trans" is the new youth subculture, the new "cool." Up until recent generations, youth subculture was based in music and bands. The role of youth subculture—whether hippie, rocker, mod, punk, or goth (of which I was one, and probably to a lesser extent still am)—is to subvert everything we are told to believe as a child and rebel against the frameworks we have been given (such as rules and uniforms, appearance, and behavior) in the transitional period between adolescence and adulthood (by which time we have usually worked it all out—or are on our way to doing so). Generation Z is the first generation to grow up in a world with social media—which has taken over from the role music and bands once played for us in older generations. Gen Z youth subculture is not based in music or bands, which may make it less obvious to recognize it as a youth subculture. But if one looks at the youth identifying as "trans" or "nonbinary" these days, they look no different from the emos, goths, and punks who preceded them. The only difference being that, whilst in our day our parents and teachers either turned a blind eye, ignored, or discouraged such external manifestations of our youth subculture, these days those around them may be positively encouraging them and colluding with their gender ideological cult beliefs and convincing them that they have a medical condition that needs correcting by chemical castration followed by physical castration or mastectomy, bodily reconstruction, and a lifetime reliance on hormones.

When I sat in on the now infamous Tavistock Gender Identity Clinic for Children, I was horrified not only by the lack of critical thinking in the staff team and their collusion with the children's gender beliefs, but also by the attendant homophobia of such a position. Most gender dysphoric children, if let alone, end up being gay adults happy with their sex. At Tavistock, there seemed to be a belief that a trans outcome would be better.

I met parents whom I refer to as "transsexogenic," more recently referred to as "transhausen by proxy," who seemed overly invested in their child being the "wrong sex," actively pushing for clinicians to alter their children's bodies and taking their children to "transing factories" in pursuit of chemical and later physical castration. I was concerned and shocked. It was clear that some of these parents would have much rather have had a son or daughter rather than the daughter or son they had. I also wondered where the parents were who may not have bought into the gender ideology cult, but of course, parents grounded in reality were not voluntarily taking their children to the "transing" clinics.

Up until recently, such parents did not have a voice and were, in effect, "invisible." It is thanks to social media platforms such as X, formerly Twitter, that gender-critical parents of children identifying as trans have been given a voice and have found each other to offer mutual support and a collective voice. It is thanks to X that I have connected with other gender-critical clinicians, parents, and others. Together, we are gathering a voice to counter the widespread cult-think that is potentially destroying the lives of young people. My work with gender dysphoria has included a great many post-op regretters and detransitioners (26 percent of my gender patients) for whom the realization that changing their bodies was not the solution, leading to a post-transition gender dysphoria. All of whom asked, "Why didn't someone challenge what we were saying at the time?" With the huge number of children currently being placed on "transing" conveyor belts with no one able to question or challenge them for fear of being accused of transphobia or offering "conversion therapy," we can expect to witness a tsunami of young adult post-op regretters and detransitioners asking why they have been so let down by the society around them for not challenging them, especially the clinicians who facilitated the irreversible changes in them.

I have been following Parents with Inconvenient Truths about Trans (PITT) on their social media and know that they have been a lifeline for those increasing number of parents who are faced with the unimaginable situation of a beloved child who has been taken over by the cult of gender ideology. Schools collude with their child's erroneous beliefs and friends collude with their child out of support, while social media influencers and transactivists encourage their child to go further into the cult of gender ideology, even at the expense of the relationships they have with those who want the best for them and love them the most, their parents. As in all cults, these children and young adults are encouraged to sever ties with those who won't share their beliefs. But through the collective work of groups such as PITT, these parents have a voice that needs to be heard, for they have been silenced for too long. This is a valuable book that is a welcome addition to the ever-growing body of gender-critical literature that serves to counter the otherwise one-sided propaganda from the cult that is gender ideology.

Az Hakeem, FRCPsych, MSc
Consultant Psychiatrist & Group Analyst
Author of *DETRANS: When Transition Is Not the Solution*

Acknowledgments

All of our royalties from this book go to Genspect, an international organization that advocates for parents and supports detransitioners.

We'd like to thank all the parents who gave their permission for their essay to be in this book, and we are grateful to all the parents who have had their stories told on the Parents with Inconvenient Truths about Trans (PITT) Substack.

Scientific Parent of a Trans Kid, Victoria G., Maria G., Chris Carrier, Halley Morgan, Eliza B., Catty A., Jennifer Wesson, FHLmom, Julie B., Beth D., Erin Stone, Samuel Alfred, Daisy W., Gay Johnson, Mama Ain't Playin', M&M, Meghan O., John Moore, Stephanie P, Mary L., StoicMom, S. Dupont, Elliott Swimmer, Hanna V., Gigi LaRue, Anon TransParent, Michelle Allen, Michele and Sage Blair, Zelda Linda, Edel Weiss, Susan Zamecnik, Charlotte Johnson, Rachel's mom, Lisa D, Overit, Mamabearsunite.org, Stacy L. Williams, BarbCP, 2014_ROGDmum, John and Emily Gordon, Stan Masters, Suzanne P, Mrs. Miller, Chris Carrier, Lillian Sheriff, T. Zara, Julie J., Erin E. Kosta, Jenny Vaughn, Hippiesq, Ruth W. Simeon, Andrew P, Evi, Julie B., Sam B, Joanne S, C.A.B., Derek Duval, A. Palacios, Cara, Cindy W, Angela Alvarez, J Vee, Caroline S, Melody and Hugo D., NJ Mom, D.L. Campanile, Jea Rea, Una madre +, Struggling South African mom, Nicky J, Fathyma Parker, Evi, Erin Friday, Amy S, D.E.V., Rose Marie Patrick, Nissa, Mama Bear, Eliot M., Kevin Ingalls, Lioness, Ellas G, Jenny Poyer Ackerman, Sharon Lee, Talia, Kierra Hope, Angeles Green, Mars, A.M. Bear, Sofia Shevchenko, Keiko, Lynn Chadwick, Sam's mom, Lydia McLaughlin, BCarfi, Hanna V., Dr. Maggy Goldsmith, Andrea Dalhouse, Maria Palacios, Kelley Johns, Juliet Nevasta, Mary Downs,

Anika M, P.E.T., SK, Penelope R., E. C. M., Oxana Orlova, Mothers Grim, NJ Mom, Joy Flores, Bob Breslin, TigerMom, Forging Fatherhood, Vera Lindner, Mom who prays, Mungerilal, A Loving Mom, Mom from Minnesota, Greer Taylor-Ginsburg, D. Renda, Donna M., Jennifer Dellasega, Tatiana, Mechelle M., Kate Parker, Jolene Brown, CatCactus, Beth D., Martin, and Stacy Jones.

Preface

In this second volume of *Parents with Inconvenient Truths about Trans,* a compilation of stories and essays from the Parents with Inconvenient Truths about Trans (PITT) Substack, we continue our quest to show the world that the prevailing view toward the treatment of gender-confused children—that children who suddenly declare a transgender identity should receive immediate affirmation and drugs if not invasive surgical procedures—is flawed beyond redemption. The inconvenient truth is that medically treating vulnerable children who are experiencing culturally induced gender confusion is not lifesaving care—it is the opposite of care.

While much has changed since we first entered the scene in 2021, and even since the publication of the first PITT book in 2023, the United States continues to sanction the medicalization of children while the rest of the world is changing course. Sadly, our PITT Substack has seen a growing number of estrangement essays, but it has also received even more tales of parents pushing back against harmful school policies and government legislation, and more hopeful essays of children desisting and detransitioning. Our stories stand as a testament to the courageous, lonely, and often anonymous battles parents have been fighting against the biggest medical scandal of our time.

On a hopeful note, much positive progress has been made—thanks, in no small part, to the growing chorus of parents exposing inconvenient truths. For example, the American Academy of Pediatrics (APA) has announced that it will be conducting a systematic review of the evidence for pediatric gender-affirming care. Progressive countries like Denmark and Norway have joined Sweden, Finland, France, Australia, and the United

Kingdom in restricting medical interventions for children. Many detransitioner lawsuits are now in process in the United States against Kaiser Permamente, the APA, and other healthcare institutions; there are also lawsuits underway in the United Kingdom, Canada, Spain, and Australia. Parent lawsuits in the United States have also begun, and finally, some whistleblowers from within the gender industry are speaking out.

The release of the Cass Review in England has been a milestone in the fight to return to sanity around gender care. Based on a number of independent, systematic reviews of healthcare for children and adolescents with gender identity issues, the final report found that "there continues to be a lack of high-quality evidence" in relation to the use of puberty blockers and masculinizing or feminizing hormones.

The World Professional Association for Transgender Health (WPATH) is considered the leading global scientific and medical authority on "gender medicine," and in recent decades, its Standards of Care have shaped the guidance, policies, and practices of governments, medical associations, public health systems, and private clinics across the world. Newly leaked files from within WPATH revealed that the clinicians who have shaped how "gender medicine" is regulated and practiced around the world have consistently violated medical ethics and informed consent. Additionally, in December 2024, the justices of the U.S. Supreme Court heard oral arguments in one of the highest-profile cases of the term, *United States v. Skrmetti*. The case is a challenge to a law that Tennessee enacted in 2023 to protect minors from medical harm under the guise of "care."

Perhaps most encouragingly, the general public is starting to awaken to this scandal, especially parents. With trans-identified kids among their children's friends, and in every classroom, it's increasingly difficult, if not impossible, for anyone to think this could never happen with their kid. The increased incidents of parents speaking out at school board meetings is further evidence that parents are scared, angry, and emboldened to push back against an ideology that has insidiously infected schools around the world, eroding parental rights.

Our fight is far from over, however. PITT will continue to publish parent stories until the groundswell of support is overwhelming and gender ideology is, like lobotomies, banished to the annals of history and recognized as the colossal tragedy it is.

Introduction: What about the Parents?

Parenting in today's culture is extremely difficult, especially if your child has declared they are the opposite sex. A decade ago, when these cases started escalating among children and young adults, parents on the receiving end of an out-of-the-blue declaration of a trans identity had no real access to good information, and any online information that questioned the narrative was buried and unsearchable. Some fortunate parents stumbled upon Dr. Lisa Littman's work on rapid-onset gender dysphoria (ROGD), or Lisa Marchiano's 2017 article in *Psychological Perspectives*, or the website 4thWaveNow, or the organization Transgender Trend. Otherwise, parents were exposed only to reports of parents who had happily transitioned their children or to the unfounded threat promoted by activists that the alternative to affirmation was their child's suicide. We're thrilled that the parents who are new to this scene today have access to an abundance of information, including PITT, which provides an alternate viewpoint—one that is supported by science and embraced by medical communities abroad.

Unfortunately, despite growing data and reports to the contrary, the common perception remains: children can be born transgender and parents who stand in the way of their transitions are bigots or abusers who will inevitably, if not stopped, drive their children to suicide.

Today, the battleground is shifting to schools. Increasingly, parents are emboldened to push back against the myriad activist teachers and school districts that, taking advantage of conflicting and vague state guidelines, have exceeded their mandates and are now teaching gender as an article of faith, couched as science or embedded in anti-bullying and "be kind" campaigns.

Over the last ten years, gender ideology has thoroughly infiltrated most public and private schools, starting as early as the elementary level. Grade schoolers are introduced to alternate pronouns and asked to declare theirs. Teachers share books with gender ideology content and transgender-identified characters make a regular appearance, even in math lessons and other school subject matter, thus normalizing the concepts at an early age. It has also become popular for schools, in a clear conflict of interest, to enlist outside companies or consultants to teach sex ed and gender ideology to students. Most disturbingly, in a direct affront to parents' rights, activist teachers and school administrators in many schools collude with each other and students to keep students' trans-identification a secret from parents. To many parents, even those without trans-identifying children, this is a step too far.

PITT is doing its part to document and bring awareness to the plight of modern parents in the hopes that we can work together for change. We are the first generation of parents confronting this particular challenge: that, with the help of the government, schools, and the medical-industrial complex, our children can be converted to a new faith where one can and should choose their own sex. And this is the first time that democratic nations have encouraged a movement that aims to separate parents from children, in the home and in the classroom. Much of this is the inadvertent consequence of the Age of Technology. Our children are being deprived of their childhoods through the internet and omnipresent devices that serve to addict and control them. We are the first generation where the boogeyman has been invited into our homes, free to prey on our children at will. As Suzanne O'Sullivan explains in her book *The Sleeping Beauties: And Other Stories of Mystery Illness*: "That is Western medicine's culture-bound syndrome—we make sick people. We medicalize difference, even when no pathology is available to be found. Sometimes, we are right to do so, but we are also wrong more often than people realize." Similarly, Lee Daniel Kravetz, in *Strange Contagion: Inside the Surprising Science of Infectious Behaviors and Viral Emotions and What They Tell Us about Ourselves*, writes: "So, rather than look at each type of social contagion in isolation, I'm left considering the possibility that we have witnessed the merging of highly communicable traits, catchable phenomena mixing together as a perfect storm, 'strange' contagion compromising many common phenomena silently passing between people. Perhaps this is not the result of any one type of social contagion—thought, behavior, or emotion—but a terrifying consequence of all of them together."

Parents today are confronting the perfect storm—puberty in the time of the Internet, amplified by COVID-19 lockdowns. In our view, the explosion of interest in gender ideology—together with the popularity of the non-scientific, faith-based idea that people can be born into the wrong bodies—is the biggest threat to the safety of our children's generation. It is damaging our children's psyches and provoking mental distress in wide swaths of our society. Our hope, by publishing our stories, is that this threat will fizzle out before it causes even more damage and seeps into the next generation. As Ethan Watters explains in his book *The Globalization of the American Psyche: Crazy Like Us*, "The diversity that can be found across cultures can be seen across time as well. Because the troubled mind has been perceived in terms of diverse religious, scientific, and social beliefs of discrete cultures, the forms of madness from one place and time in history often look remarkably different from the forms of madness in another. These differing forms of mental illness can sometimes appear and disappear within a generation."

In these difficult times, we are doing the best we can, and fortunately there are more experts emerging every day that are sympathetic to our plight. Psychiatrist Dr. Miriam Grossman is one of those friends. In her book *Lost in Trans Nation: A Child Psychiatrist's Guide Out of the Madness*, she describes a Zoom meeting with dozens of ROGD parents:

> Your child is struggling with an issue you don't understand, there's some conflict at home, and you want guidance. You can't stop worrying about your child—what to do, what to say, what about school, internet, new friends—it's consuming, I know. But I'm not going to speak about your kids today, I am speaking about you. From what I am seeing in my office and in the parent groups and reading in PITT, you parents are traumatized and it's time we start talking about it.

> Like your trauma, your grief is disenfranchised. There's no recognition, so you are isolated without support. You're driven underground, living double lives, using fake names, but you've done nothing wrong—it should be the gender evangelists, therapists, and doctors who should be hiding.

Parents, you are grieving, you have a multitude of losses. They must be named and recognized. Others may trivialize your grief or even blame you for it. They might say you brought it on yourselves. I know this is done by family members, trusted friends, and doctors. I cannot imagine how that feels—another trauma on top of all the others.

We also have the support of a growing number of detransitioners, such as Luka, who, in a message on Instagram, tells parents:

It's important to remember that only telling someone yes, and telling someone yes you're valid, and only affirming them, and only saying yes, is not an act of love. That's not what love is, love is not giving into every whim and only saying yes. Love is putting up those boundaries and saying no and having to keep someone safe even when they might be upset at you for it. Because only saying yes and only going down one path, and only affirming, isn't love, it's enabling, and I feel that's just something that parents need to understand with this.

We love our children and hope that one day we will be vindicated for saying "no" to them—or at least for not reflexively saying "yes." As psychoanalyst Stella O'Malley, founder of Genspect and an outspoken leader and advocate for parents, writes:

When the history of this unfolding medical scandal is written, there will be a chapter that details the terrible treatment of the parents by a world who refused to see what was really going on. The stories that emerged from the parent groups I facilitated were harrowing. These loving and engaged parents, who had the natural and noble desire to seek the best treatment for their distressed children, were vilified, isolated and dismissed as bigots during their family's most vulnerable time. I'm relieved to see the parents have finally found a way to get the truth out there, however we must learn from this so that this doesn't happen again.

Parents will not stop fighting to save our children's future. This ideology is stealing the brightest minds and sterilizing a whole generation. It needs to be stopped but, in the meantime, please take care of yourself. This life is all we have. As difficult as this time is for parents, it's always useful to look at what you have learned from this Orwellian experience and to try to find the positives in your life.

This medical scandal will end, but until gender ideology is history, we will continue to tell our stories—even if many of us must do so anonymously or pseudonymously to protect ourselves, our families, and our children. Thank you for reading them! However, before jumping into the parent stories, which we publish here with few edits, changes, or revisions to preserve the authentic voice and communication style of each individual, we'd like to close this introduction with an essay by a detransitioner who has some advice for us parents—and who reminds us that we can't ever give up on our children.

"Back from the Other Side"
An essay by a detransitioner

Being the parent of a trans child of any age is probably the most dreadful and soul crushing experience a parent can go through.

When any tragedy hits a child, parents are usually surrounded by family members, friends, medical teams, social groups and institutions that provide help navigating this difficult journey. But when you are the common-sensical parent who is not jumping on the trans band wagon, who is not buying the trans narrative, who asks the right questions, exposes the inconvenient facts and urges caution regarding gender affirming practices of all kinds (or should I say more accurately mental illness affirming?), you become the villain of the story. And those very folks and institutions that used to be there for you now label you as an intolerant hateful bigot who wants their kid to die. As a result, you get socially ostracized and alienated from your own kid.

You might think that I'm speaking out of experience. I'm not. It's a nightmare I never had to go through. Being a parent today, I can only imagine what it must be like.

Because I actually come from the other side—I was a transgender kid. I'm the one who once inflicted the pain.

Now I'm one of those detransitioners. And I'm one of those now loathed by the trans community because I'm helping to bring down the house (which was made of hay to start with).

At a young age, I thought being a girl was the source of all my inner turmoil. Though it was before trans became trendy, the social contagion, and the TikTok trans influencers, I lived in the self-delusion of being a boy for most of my youth. I didn't talk to my dad for years.

Then I very slowly reconciled with the reality of being a woman, my TRUE self, my God-given gender—and I extricated myself from the insanity.

No matter how deep your pain is, how hopeless your situation or your kid's situation might seem, there is always hope. Don't lose it.

Gender confusion is not a mindset that trans individuals never question, even post transition. Deep inside, there is always that constant nagging feeling that we may be living a lie, that we may have made a mistake. That's why we need trans support groups. That's why we push back vehemently and sometimes violently against any real or perceived opposition. We don't want to hear a word against it, from anybody or else we scream at you, we cancel you, we cut off relationships in some kind of survival tantrum. We live in a state of constant insecurity and second guessing about ourselves even though we'll never admit it.

Gender confusion is a mental anguish that encroaches upon every aspect of your life, sucking your very existence out of you. It's a pernicious disease that distorts your vision of the world (which is why those who love us can't get "through" to us until we're ready). It rips your identity and your relationships apart and makes you behave in reckless and unreasonable ways.

Though at first we might go through a honeymoon phase of blissful delusion, it's only temporary. The illusory feeling of peace we might experience fades away eventually.

Very often, we are enabled by our "glitter" family who silences, replaces and erases our real family.

We expect that this new family will fulfill our every need and bring us lasting peace and happiness. Except they won't. Because that "family" is made of people as sick, confused and unhappy as we are. But we're oblivious to it.

That's where you, parents, come in. No matter how long we have been gone, physically or emotionally, no matter how far we've gone in terms of hurting our body or our mind, never give up on us. Because if you do, who do we have left?

The number one issue detransitioners face is loneliness. Their birth family is often gone and the trans cult hates them.

We are where we are because we believed destructive lies. Don't follow our example.

When your trans kid tells you he/she doesn't love you, he/she hates you, will never see you/talk to you again, doesn't want anything to do with you, etc, etc, please don't believe it.

We are only regurgitating the nasty mantra of the cult who stole our hearts, minds and bodies.

What we're really telling you is: I'm sick, I'm lost, I'm desperate, my life is spinning out of control and I'm scared because, deep inside, I know the flimsy house of cards I'm stuck in is inevitably gonna come crashing down.

Of course, we are all different. We have different stories, different paths. But overall, the quest and the mindset of trans people are eerily similar.

One day, history will remember you parents as courageous visionaries who fought the politically correct culture of transgender insanity out of love for your children, respect for your intellect and clear understanding of scientific realities and biological facts.

It may not feel like it today but you're still a family. One with temporarily suspended relationships. It will not always be like that.

There is hope. Don't lose it. Never say never when it comes to complicated and delicate sexual and gender identity issues.

Always speak the truth but with tender love. If you're gonna affirm something, let it be that your child will always be your son/daughter and there is nothing he/she can do or say that will make you love him/her less.

Then stand your ground. And wait.

One day, the struggles of life and the insecure fragility of the fake gender identity might bring him/her back to you.

It's exhausting to continually battle and make sense of the constant dichotomy between biological reality and gender fantasy in the nitty gritty of everyday life. I know something about it ...

When that day comes, let there be no lecture, no judgment. Just welcome your child back, knowing that the healing will take as long as the delusion lasted.

In the meantime, take good care of yourself. You are as important as your kids.

Make yourself get out of the constant worry, the excruciating pain you feel. I know it's easier said than done but it's not helping. Neither you nor your kid.

Pick up a hobby or a sport, go for a run or a hike. Volunteer, run for school board or city council so you can be a voice against trans indoctrination. Follow detransitioners to get inspired and encouraged. Use your gifts and talents to help them (morally, financially, legally …).

Don't let your kid bring you down. If anything, for their sake. They'll need you when they wake up. When I left the trans cult, I was glad that my family was still there for me. And though imperfect, that was the somewhat stable element in my out-of-control life.

Live today as the great day it is because it's the first day of the rest of your life and it can bring amazing changes.

Take courage, miracles do happen. I'm a living example of it.

As a conclusion, I want to leave you with the 10 truths/facts I realized and ran with when I left the trans life:

1. There are only two genders, male and female, a few rare anomalies, and a plethora of glorified mental disorders.
2. Being a woman or being a man is not an identity, a feeling, a costume or a cosplay. It's a biological reality and a birthright.
3. Men (chrom. XY) cannot be women. Trans "women" are men. Women (chrom. XX) cannot be men. Trans "men" are women.
4. Nobody is born "in the wrong body". I am not a mistake that needs to be fixed. I'm perfect just the way I was born.
5. Happiness is never found in mutilating my body or permanently altering appearance. Removing healthy body parts and/or adding fake ones is neither healthcare nor lifesaving affirmation.
6. Demanding spaces and opportunities free from individuals of the other sex (there are only two) is not bigotry or fascism. It's a matter of safety and fairness.
7. Pseudoscientific lies that fly in the face of facts-based science and biological rules are just that: lies. Puberty is not a disease but a normal stage of life. Women don't have a penis. Men cannot menstruate or get pregnant …
8. There is no such thing as "misgendering". The same way you wouldn't "affirm" a person suffering from anorexia or schizophrenia, you

shouldn't "affirm" a person suffering from gender dysphoria by using their made-up words and pretend names. It's not a sign of respect, it's just abetting and partaking in the mental confusion.

9. Transitioning is never an efficient and lasting solution against suicide ideation. The occurrence of suicide is higher in number and frequency post-transition due to the transition having failed to bring the sense of relief and joy that was expected.

10. Life is not irreversible. A mutilated woman is a woman, nonetheless. A castrated man is a man, nonetheless. Even when your body has been savagely messed up by (presently) irreversible, and gruesome surgeries, you are still a valuable, precious human being.

There is ALWAYS hope. Life manages to sprout from the ashes of mistakes and tragedies. Relationships seemingly broken beyond repair can be mended. Life might be different. Life might need to be reinvented, to be reborn. But it's still life. And it can be vibrant. And it's in your future.

Parents on Family

1

Maybe I'm Suffering Too

Today, I'm going to talk about ME and NOT my gender dysphoric child. By nature, I'm not a very selfish person. I hate even saying that, as it takes away some sense of humility.

But today, I HAVE to be selfish. I HAVE to talk about ME! For the sake of survival and for YOUR sakes, because we need to be heard. Because we too are suffering terribly, not just our dysphoric children. By we, I mean mums and dads and everyone else who is watching this disaster unfold to those we love so dearly. By we, I mean us who are being silenced and crushed to death by this giant bully which is the transgender religion. So this is ME…

I am currently in a state of crisis. I think about suicide some times, about a rope taking me away from all this unbearable and piercing pain. Even about doing it spitefully, just to cut off my nose to spite the trans ideology. To show them that we too could be statistics and that we too are suffering. Where is our affirming care, that acknowledges the damage this is doing to us? We too are vulnerable after all! Parenting is also a spectrum. Some days we are strong and have wisdom to do well, but there are days where our fragile selves crumble under this immense pressure and we fail to summon up any courage. Days when we are weak and do the wrong thing or lack any parental control and feel frozen in helplessness.

I am alone in this battle. I can't share with friends or family out of shame and fear and, for those in my immediate circle, the immensity of

31

this wrong is not appreciated. I am a mother, being pushed to the limits of her sanity and overwhelmed with such heavy sorrow. Every way I look is darkly clouded and the light of hope growing so dim, that I feel trapped in a parallel universe cut off from reality. I am crazy to feel like I need to be locked up in a white room, that it is me who is mad. That somehow I have just lost my senses and that the whole world is fine! That I'm just not accepting of everyone's subjective reality, because I am a hateful lunatic. Facts seem to fly in the face of everyone around me, Truth is now nothing but an old construct fading away into distant memory, created only to oppress and destroy. And for me to hold onto this, is apparently a telling of my oppressive and unprogressive true nature.

Well they are right ... I am going crazy! Living amidst this dissonance is splitting. I am not looking at this dialectic from afar, void of personal involvement. I, like a tree struck with lightning, am caught right in the middle of it and it has split my heart in two. My mind can barely fathom the trauma this is and I am left shocked and bizarrely near catatonic.

My days and months slip by, like potato peels sliced off and thrown into the bin. It's been almost a year in this nightmare and where has my life gone? What has happened to all these days? I know I've spent many of them in tears, sobbing uncontrollably from the depth of my soul. I've spent others painstakingly going through statistics, facts, history of John Money, Socialism, dialectics, Hegel, Politics, effects of hormones, doctors lists that aren't affirming (there aren't many, trust me) and mostly, I've been praying to God to give me strength… asking Him to help my child and begging Him to stop this nonsense and to utterly destroy this evil cult that spreads like a rotting mold. I've also, not to tell a lie, been trying to bargain with God to do whatever It takes to save my child from this THING!

I've not much left to give to my other children at the moment. Every day, when I go to work or have to go shopping, I just put on my fake face and trudge through the hours like an empty shell. I aimlessly meander through life with not much in my head, very disconnected from earth in a dreamlike state, to be found in the murky waters of my current traumatized mind. Can I ever come back from this? Where will this end? How far will my child take this? How much can I endure? When is enough, enough? I've never felt so much hate towards a group of people as I do right now towards those who are allowing this! Please God, help me forgive them, because this murder in my heart for them is great! Another thing about Me right now—when I am home, I am in CONSTANT damage control mode and it is exhausting … checking for any new signs all the time, asking questions constantly, sneaking peeks at laptops and chat sites, plotting to thwart and avoid any bad influences, coming up with schemes to study at appropriate places to distract, throwing facts and truth to attempt to interject the lies, shouting defensively when being called hateful and arrogant, breaking down when being told I am no longer anything but parent by birth, watching with love as I see my child slip away and then soaking up moments when we finally connect and have a laugh or a brief moment of genuine love. All of this runs off pure adrenalin and it is wearisome and taking its toll. I am becoming forgetful and simple, withdrawn and empty. My heart feels encaged in a slow inflating compression balloon and the squeezing is suffocating. Most days, I have this nervous feeling in my stomach, like something is in there, in the pit of my belly, writhing and twisting any hope I have into a dubious ball of grave despair… it grows and climbs up my stomach wall and into my mouth, making me want to throw up.

This is when I am left in complete hopelessness. This is when I go inward and to a dark place. This is when I wish myself away and imagine death as a pleasant reward of this bleak world. This is when I wonder if it is at all possible in today's age, with all it's cctv footage and social media devices, to truly disappear from my life. Maybe I could go live on a remote island in a tent and pretend this life I have now never even existed. Perhaps just slip away, like you do when you fall asleep!?

This is when I have nowhere else to go but inward and upward, as I have to find strength from somewhere to keep going. I have to be strong for my other two kids. I have to be there for my suffering child to help him through this, to lead him out of this, to be here when it's all over. And so this is when I look up, to the Only One who is good. The Only Truth I have known of late that hasn't been dispelled. And the Only One who loves more than we do and has given us a way back to peace and joy. I look to the One who was pierced and say "Your Will not mine!" and I surrender my child to Him and say "This is YOUR child, do what You will and give me the wisdom and strength to endure this trial". This is when I open the Psalms and see the trials David went though, during his most difficult days and yet turned to Him and was filled with Hope once more and it fills me too with hope. This is when God Himself picks me up from the floor and says "Stand Up! You are Not alone! I Am here with you!" And this is when the moments of hope begin and God, I believe You are True. I believe You hate this evil more than we do. I believe this serves a purpose to bring about Your justice! May your Will be done and may Your justice be swift. And may You protect Your children and bring them back to the Truth!

So, in one of my rare and hopeful moments, I say this ...

The Truth WILL come out in the end.

2

Who Is Thinking of the Parents?

I recently had a lovely dinner with some mom's from my support group. As we were talking someone mentioned when this whole Trans thing blows over, something along the lines of "will they think of how this hurt us parents? " I started thinking in all this child centered agenda of the push for acceptance of your child announcing their new gender identity. Who is thinking about the parents? The government isn't thinking of the parents with their new push to "gender affirming care." AKA genital mutilation and double mastectomies and hormone drugs for kids. Doesn't seem like caring to me. More like Eugenics. My state of California dosen't care about us parents as Governor Newsom passes SB107 that makes us a gender affirming sanctuary state. A cash cow for everyone with their hands in the cookie jar poised to profit on confused kids and their homophobic parents.

The schools aren't caring. When they secretly call your daughter or son by another name, gender and pronoun behind your back. They do this hiding behind of the law AB1266 that gives them rights to usurp your parental rights. They don't care about the love and care you put into choosing your child's name. Therapists don't care when you come to them for your child to seek care for their confusion and mental destress. They actually tell the child you the parent are the problem because you won't affirm them in their delusion. The Trans activists don't care. They tell your kid you the parent are the toxic one. The transphobe the bigot. Because you believe in the reality of biological two sexes. The doctors don't care because all they see are dollar signs. The glitter moms who buy into the lie don't care. They think you should just give up your child to the alter of the gender gods for body sacrifice.

You know who is a caring about the parents? I found out early on when I got snarled into the net with my daughter one year ago. I was totally new to Twitter. It was a gay man named Mr. Menno. He cared. He cared enough to send me a tiny account of 6 followers a video of mom's talking about their journey with this Trans phenomena. He told me to " buckle up for the bumpy ride." Then it was a Radfem named Kara Dansky she showed me she cared about me as a parent. Then little by little more and more Gender Critical people from all over the world, ROGD parents, gay men and women showed me they cared. Then something happened in March of last year. I posted something about women's rights during women's history month. Posie Parker took notice. Because all of a sudden over night I had gone from 600 followers to 1600 followers all showing me they cared. Then a mom named Lynn who lost her son and daughter to this cult showed me she cared. She took the time to talk with me on the phone and she invited me to join her private parent group. I am no longer on Twitter because when you speak the truth the permanently suspend your account.

Then I joined a private local group for parents like myself a group of loving moms of ROGD kids. They showed me they cared as we sat in the shade of a old tree in a park. Sharing our stories our tears, our fears and our deep love for our kids. Now one of these moms I call friend and a few more have come into my life from that group have showed me they care. A radical feminist lesbian Joey Brite showed me she cared. She is now my friend. Detransitioners have showed me they care. "When Richie the young British man who was rushed into gender surgery told me "keep calling my daughter by her pet name." He showed me he cared. When a teen who used to think she was Trans shared with me her story of how she thought that she was Trans and how she stopped. She showed me she cared.

With so much caring I am still pondering the question "who will care for all of us parents who have lost our kids to this cult of ideology of gender identity?" We will. We will band together. We will unite with gay people, women and men who are thinking critically, policy makers that hold the line in reality and speaking loudly that no one is born in the wrong body. That Trans is a lie and it isn't real.

We will pick up our broken pieces and patch them back together. Humans are resilient like that. We will move forward, forever changed. We will recall we were on the right side of history. All the people shouting into the canyon as they say of the echo chamber. The echo is being heard one voice at a time. Bouncing back at us. Letting us know we are not alone. All those voices screaming Trans is lie. That's who will care for the parents.

3

The Silence Is Killing Us

I was born into an activist family. I am not afraid of standing up for my views and being in the minority. For many years, I have fought for LGBTQIA rights and been dismissed or attacked for it but I have always openly fought for what I believe in.

Until now …

I find myself in an insidious position. I want to toyi toyi in the streets and scream from the rooftops about the dangers of gender ideology, the affirmative approach and men in women's spaces but, if I do, I will push my adult daughter further into her trans identity and more medicalisation.

Out of the blue, my daughter decided she was trans after years and years of severe mental health issues, social awkwardness and terrible loneliness. She was immediately affirmed and within months had started testosterone and was booked for a double mastectomy.

The advice I gave her to slow down and explore her identity more carefully before medicalising made me, in her eyes, a transphobic bigot with whom she was unsafe.

At first, I tried to fight it. I showed her all the literature cautioning medicalisation and the YouTube stories of detransitioners. I made my views very clear on Facebook and in articles I wrote to any media outlets who would publish.

I continually told my daughter that I would always love her but I could never agree with rushed medicalisation. I tried to hide my tears and devastation when her voice became deeper, when she grew hairy and started growing a beard, and when she had a double mastectomy. I still have to mentally prepare myself before I see her.

I was told by therapists and most other people that it was important to keep our relationship going at all costs. I still sometimes wonder if that is the best advice. Is it not more loving to fight for the best for your child, even if they hate you?

Our relationship has improved over time and a huge effort on my part, although the hurt I feel because of her rejection of me, and the pain and fear for her future, makes it very hard.

For a while, I thought I could still fight the ideology by writing articles where I could, and posting on social media.

But I changed my mind. I know that so much of my daughter's identity and rush into medicalisation is a reaction against me. Because of her mental health difficulties and our very close relationship, she has had great difficulty separating from me. The trans identity seems the only way she can do it. The harder I fight, the harder she pushes.

It leaves me in a helpless position but I know I have to stop fighting publicly for a while. I am still trying to talk to people individually (especially influential people) if they will listen.

I am keeping up with news about gender issues but I don't share any more articles on Facebook. I don't write any more articles for newspapers and magazines. It is killing me. Our children will only be safe when this ideology and its dangers are exposed and yet if I try to expose it, my daughter will go more deeply into it.

Many of my friends and family are activists on the left. I thought, when they saw what was happening to my daughter, they would be enraged and fight against it. I was so wrong. Most of them are too terrified to go against the woke ideology. They still believe or pretend to believe that by supporting the ideology, they are supporting human rights. I was once like them, blithely supporting something I knew little about. It took personal experience and a little research to find the shocking truth.

When people are going through difficulties, they say they would not wish their trauma on their worst enemies. Forgive me for my terrible thoughts, but in my lowest moments, I wish this upon everyone around me because only then will people wake up and understand—and only then they will start doing something about it.

I am angry, I am hurting, I am lonely and I am feeling helpless. I know there are many other parents in my position. How will we fight this, if fighting pushes our children in the opposite direction, and when so many of those who could fight it, won't?

4

In It for the Long Haul

I am in it for the long haul. A mother walking a marathon, carrying a burden—the truth about the dangers of transitioning.

I have been walking through this space now for 7 years. My daughter may have been embroiled in gender ideology and its social contagion for longer than that even. I must choose my questions and choose my moments, upsetting or offending her may lead to the closure of other possible moments when I want to raise the subject.

That is why I have turned to other parents, walking this same marathon, for help and support.

In our parent support group meetings, people acknowledge the length of time they have been involved in standing and holding firm about their views on the dangers of transition.

We speak of the years we have spent and wasted in this unknown abyss, and bring our concern and comfort to others who have just been dragged in with us. We are sorry and glad you are here, we tell them. You are not alone.

Isolation is a major factor for some of us, so our support groups become a lifeline—the only place in our lives where we don't have to watch what we say or worry about being judged. We share many experiences in common and at the same time we give each parent who wants to chance to tell their own story, to share their hurt and bewilderment, their frustration and anger, as if they were the first and only to feel this deep hurt and betrayal.

We share our anger at people qualified in medicine who condescendingly tell us and the public that our children, rather than receiving a listening ear and psychological support, should instead be affirmed in their wish to put themselves in danger. We know our children and we were children. They, as we were, are entitled to mess up in their childhood and teens and to learn lessons. They should not be permitted to make decisions that will impact them physically, emotionally and psychologically for the rest of their lives, which they may come to regret.

For 7 years I have been walking on eggshells, reading frightening evidence of the consequences of her wishes. While my daughter has socially transitioned, there are still moments when I think she has seen the light and understands the dangers of wearing binders or the outcomes of a mastectomy or taking cross sex hormones. Then we meet and she refers to herself with male pronouns and I know it's not over.

Now that she is an adult I am finding ways to let go. I am also giving myself permission to speak more to her about her perilous plans. It's time for me to share this burden, not just with other parents, but with my daughter—she needs to hear it and, hopefully, to understand.

I am forever grateful to each and every parent I have encountered since I found myself here. I am very sad and so very glad to be among you.

5

The Opposite of Love

Can you imagine your own child changing sex?

Just try for a moment to envision what it might feel like if what has happened to the PITT parents happened to you.

It feels like the death of your child—and yes, this is strong phrasing but, in the moment, it is honest.

Imagine not being able to recognize your own child's voice—not because you have haven't seen each other, but because it's been changed by testosterone.

Imagine not seeing your child for years. Not being able to touch them or hug them, or give them a kiss, to celebrate together, take trips, enjoy dinners together.

Imagine calling your child's number to find you have been blocked. Then finding out that your child had blocked his or her grandparents as well.

Imagine if this trans movement, which some have called a civil rights movement of our time, had irreparably broken and changed your life forever.

Imaging wanting to die to relieve the pain.

Imagine feeling all of this, suffering, screaming and begging every-one for help, while young people give breathlessly excited interviews to the equally excited and breathless media about their newfound political, nonbinary identities.

Imagine being terrorized and blackmailed by Trans Rights Activists, while the world, the media, even your neighbors and family either look away or actively support the other side.

Thousands of loving mothers and fathers have lost their beautiful children, loved ones or relatives to this powerful, state-sanctioned Cult. It has touched millions more. Try imagining that this has happened to you, and you will see why our resistance is growing and will never stop until we bring down this so-called civil rights movement that is actually a cult.

6

Trans: The Family Destroyer

There is a trans mental health crisis, but not the one you think.

The emerging crisis is the mental health of parents who find themselves fighting against the tide to protect their children.

I have spent the last year swept up in the madness that is gender ideology. Throughout my year in trans, I have come into contact with dozens of struggling parents that are also swept up in this madness. Most people somehow think that trans is an immutable state of being. It is not.

I'm happy to report that my child's big pronouncement of trans has faded into the background, and he's back to being his old happy, healthy, nonconformist self. Thank God. This only happened because I refused to be pressured into the affirmative approach. When parents stay grounded to reality and don't affirm, generally the kid grows out of it. Undoubtably this is the best outcome—for kids to grow up feeling comfortable with their natural bodies, avoiding a lifetime of medicalization and mental health struggles. For some reason though, our society doesn't currently see it this way. The fact that often people "desist" (stop feeling trans) is carefully obscured by media and activists, because it calls the whole system into question.

My child's successful navigation out of his identity challenge was only possible because of the extraordinary parents and mental health clinicians that are working together behind the scenes to support other parents and to protect our kids. What they are doing comes at a huge cost to sanity and mental health.

I have yet to meet a family, where one or both parents hasn't had a complete mental collapse following their child's announcement. Many have contemplated suicide, some seriously. Many parents, moms especially, have had to seek out mental health therapy and anti-depression or anti-anxiety drugs to cope with daily life, in a world where there is a physical threat to their child AND all of society, seemingly, is aligned against them. I am one of those parents that needed to Xanax myself into oblivion for a period of weeks just to cope with daily life. Strife between parents is also common, breaking down marriages and sibling relationships.

Why are the parents losing it? Because in this movement, our confused kids, having been indoctrinated in the false belief that they can literally become the other sex and magically fix all of their problems, will seek out and easily obtain drugs that will chemically castrate them, break down their bones, and degrade their brain function. They can do this without any gatekeeping, without our permission, and without any real mental health screening or therapy.

The family unit is under siege, as parents wrangle with life or death decisions for their children, with no evidence-based information available, and tons of public pressure. Children are given a parent-ectomy; told to reject their loving parents and to trust outsiders that do not have their long-term best interests in mind. Some of these children are seriously mentally ill, with other conditions that may be the root causes of their trans identity feelings, but they cannot get real mental health help—only a shove toward hormones and surgery. It's appalling.

This mental health crisis for parents is real and immediate. It's time that we, as a society, take a step back to decide—is the activist agenda of normalizing cross sex hormones (with known harmful effects) and body modifications to defend the lifestyle and protect "treatment" options for a few, worth harming thousands of individuals and many hundreds of American families?

No, it is not. The sacred bonds of family are at stake, along with the mental and physical health of our children. Parents are starting to fight back against the biggest threat to children's mental and physical health that we've ever encountered. We are rising up to put a stop to indoctrination in our schools, and to defend our parental rights. Parents pushed back against big tobacco, driving under the influence, Juul and eCigs. We can do it again. But not without some help and support for us first.

7

I Thought This Would Be Over by Now

I thought this would be over by now. I really did. You're smart. Really smart. And a staunch feminist—like I raised you to be.

But it's been over a year now. And it's not over. Not even close. And it's killing me. Bringing me to tears day after day as you deny reality and set yourself on a path of self-denial and self-destruction.

You know that you were always a feminine kid. Stunningly beautiful as a toddler and young girl. Strangers gasped at your looks. You were that pretty. You were wild too—running away from me and jumping off playground equipment while your twin brother stuck close to me and yelled for you to come back.

I never dressed you in girly clothing. But you loved wearing them on special occasions. I'll never forget the vision of you in the frilly costume you wore for your skating recital—with makeup, a shiny tiara and a huge smile on your face. You reveled in your strength and beauty and accomplishments. I did too.

Then it all came crashing down. Some friends decided not to be friends with you anymore. You were so sad and confused. You asked me what you'd done wrong, and what you could do to get them back. You said you'd change. You said you'd do anything. Anything. I tried to console you but you were inconsolable.

Then COVID happened. We were in lock down. You bonded with a few friends who remained, the ones you called your best friends in the fifth grade. One had an older sister who was trans-identified and began identifying as trans herself. Another got caught up in online trans spaces and decided she was trans as well, and omnisexual.

One day you sat down on the couch next to me, very serious, and said you needed to tell me something. All of eleven-years-old and with your big, blue, naïve eyes looking up at me, you told me you were pansexual. After that, on a nightly basis, you began showing me all of the sexuality and gender flags and quizzing me and your brother, even your grandparents, about the different genders and sexualities. You wanted me to take an internet quiz to determine my gender and sexuality. And you seemed confused when I told you I didn't need take a quiz to know who I was.

I didn't take any of it seriously. I was stupid and naïve. I didn't understand the zeitgeist. I'm an older mom, after all. And a single mom by choice. So, for more than a decade I'd been working full-time and spending all of my time raising you and your brother. I didn't have any spare time or energy to engage with the wider world.

Then the summer between sixth and seventh grade you had your first panic attack. And in seventh grade you became absolutely consumed with sex and gender. Once back to school in person, you embraced, and were embraced by, a friend group full of kids who defined themselves as somewhere along the rainbow, including several who declared they were trans or non-binary. Some of whom began using different names. You made and lost friends who temporarily joined this friend group but decided they weren't trans or non-binary after all.

Mind you, we live in a small town. Your entire class was about 120 students. It's simply not possible that such a large cohort of kids, including those you'd known for years, can all claim to be trans.

I remained stupid and naïve to what was going on in the world.

And so you also began talking about being trans. And perhaps changing your name. You demanded they/them pronouns. And you were miserable; sinking deeper and deeper into anxiety and depression. I took you to a therapist—the only one I could find who took our insurance and was willing to see you in-person. She was young—half my age—and still in training. And I got you to a psychiatrist who put you on an anti-depressant. She questioned whether you had been sexually abused. Had I exposed my children to any boyfriends? The parent-blaming had begun.

To be clear—I hadn't had any boyfriends. When I decided to have children on my own, I decided to give up dating altogether so I could focus on my family. But maybe that was a mistake—not exposing you and your brother to a male role model in the house. You had your grandfather and uncles and adult male cousins. But was it enough?

I started blaming myself too. And I haven't stopped. Because if I had done something wrong, then maybe I could do something right too? I could fix it and make it all better. I want that more than anything. I'd do anything, change anything. I want you to love and accept yourself and understand that you're perfect just as you are.

But you don't. The summer before eighth grade, at twelve years old, you told me you were a demi-boy. And omnisexual. You demanded to be referred to as my son and sobbed when I wouldn't, because you're my daughter. You assumed a different name and yelled at anyone who called you by your given name, even your grandmother, who is nearly eighty years old now, who was there the day you were born. She cut your umbilical cord and heard me call you by your name in the delivery room. That was the first word I ever spoke to you.

And you were miserable. Utterly miserable. Still are.

But you kept with it. You went through eighth grade constantly at war with yourself and the world. Crying and complaining any time someone called you by your name or referred to you with she/her pronouns. You adopted he/they pronouns. You ran with the boys' cross-country team. And you tried using the boys' bathroom.

I consulted with experts and educated myself about what's going on in the world of gender. So different than the second-wave feminism I grew up with in the 70s and 80s. I found you a new, more experienced therapist and a new psychiatric provider who understands the social contagion.

You've been getting better psychologically, and you're coming off the medications.

You've had a boyfriend for almost a year. You're still gorgeous after all. But he says he's gay, and you insist you're in a gay relationship.

And you're more convinced than ever that you're a boy because you feel like one, even though you can't explain what that means when I ask. You talk about how much you hate your breasts and your female body. You hate having periods (don't we all?)

You talk about having your breasts removed and taking testosterone once you turn eighteen.

At the same time, you're just a typical teenage girl. You spend your days making jewelry, gardening and pressing flowers, learning to knit, and obsessing about friendships and the people you like and those you don't.

Your brother now calls you by your chosen name, and sometimes your grandparents and other relatives do too. And each time I hear it, my heart breaks.

I still won't use that name. I associate it will all the dysfunction of the past few years. And I don't call you he, or my son. Because you're not.

You're my daughter, and you always will be. And I love you more than you can imagine, and I always will.

8

I Was Robbed Multiple Times

First it stole her appearance: her beautiful long blonde hair, her brightly-colored dresses and skirts, her crystal-blue eyes and vibrant smile. It left her looking like a homeless person, with unkempt hair, baggy, ill-fitting clothes, poor hygiene and dead eyes.

Then it stole her outlook and world view. Someone who was once a high-achieving and positive student leader morphed into a sullen, angry victim who came close to failing high school courses.

Next it stole our happy family dynamic. We were a fun, close family that enjoyed traveling together, playing board games, watching movies. Now the atmosphere is tense and guarded.

It stole her ability to receive and give affection. Gone are the days of snuggling on a couch, hugging her tightly, and physically letting her know that I am there for her. She winces, cringes, and gets angry when touched.

Then it stole the joy of the milestones of adolescence: middle school graduation, performances in school plays, high school graduation, and prom were all clouded with weird outfits, public pronouncements of her "new name" and avoidance of her d@$d name, awkward conversations with other parents, and not even wanting to take photos because looking at what she's done to herself is overwhelming. I'm left with photos that break my heart every time they appear on my phone or screen saver.

It stole the past. Her "lived experience" requires me to deny mine. To her, there is no daughter, no sister, no granddaughter, no emerging young woman in this household. She never ACTUALLY liked dress up or princesses or makeup. I had no right to name her what I did. Eighteen years of child rearing, of sacrifice, of unconditional love, mean nothing. There is no past – just her present identity.

It stole my present. Instead of focusing on taking care of my aging parents, surviving menopause with health and humor, and just living in the moment, I was left with worry, with anger, with guilt, with fear, with desperation. I fall asleep praying for her rescue and wake up wondering if the day might bring some new bombshell about her identity.

It may very well steal her future. She is on the cusp of throwing away her health, her breasts, her ability to have children, her whole history – just to cosplay an identity she will never truly become. For every word, every mannerism, every reaction, everything about her is female. Try as she might to manspread, wear size 32 men's pants at 100 pounds, artificially lower her voice, and "act like a man," the body does not lie. When she lets her guard down, or she's excited, or stressed, or emotional, the body returns to its natural state of being: female.

It has been a long, slow, painful series of thefts. I can't identify the perpetrator. It is elusive, relentless, sinister, and stealthy. It wears me down. There's very little left to steal from me – except my memories, my convictions, and my hope. I will hold onto them until my last breath.

9

From the Father
of an Adult Trans-Identifying Daughter

After several years of struggling with our daughter on the trans issue, we have officially been relegated to "personae non grata" status with our own child because we recognize the immutable reality that our daughter's sex doesn't change simply because she wants to live her life in accordance with trans ideology, which she has adopted, and now identifies as a male.

There are few people that understand the topic of trans as an ideology. Even fewer people understand this ideology from the perspective of a parent whose child has been inculcated in it. Our current culture is split between those who unquestioningly support and promote a lifestyle that denies reality yet seem to be willfully ignorant of the upper hand they enjoy in our society and those who refuse to kowtow to what ultimately is a destructive ideology at the social and personal level and are publicly excoriated for it.

We, the parents of trans-children, know our children. Not everything they believe requires that *we* change our viewpoints.

In the case of our daughter, and perhaps many other trans-identifying daughters, there seems to be a combination of issues including lack of personal identity, anxiety, depression, social expectations and great offense at one's own body when puberty hits.

All these issues are complicated by porn-misinformed socio-sexual issues which surround the biological phenomenon of a girl becoming a woman. Social media exacerbates all these conditions. There also seems to be an overlap with trans-identification and being on the Autism spectrum, at least for some. (There is significant on-spectrum behavior on the male side of my family and considerable anxiety-depression on the female side of my wife's family. Fortunately, our adult son, while exhibiting these same traits somewhat differently than our daughter, does NOT identify with the trans-community.)

A trans-positive ideology, perhaps even an agenda, is pushed throughout the nation in elementary schools, television and social media. It is reinforced via legal means, not to mention sociological pressures. Those who disbelieve the previous statement ought to attempt opposing trans-positivity, which is merely a part of the LGBTQIP+ sociopolitical agenda and see what reaction they get.

Trans individuals accuse "non-believers" of "erasing people like them" if we oppose the ideology they have adopted. This seems to reflect a lack of personal identity and extreme ideological tribalism. While we do not want to "erase trans people", we do want to eliminate the social promotion of what is a fringe ideological movement and its elevation to practically religious levels of belief.

The underlying anxiety and depression associated with trans-ideology seem to be caused by an inability to adopt the social behavior expectations of what they feel is required for their sex. At the least, there is a sense of "unwillingness to participate" in all the sociocultural expectations associated with their biological sex.

We know the pain of watching our children destroy their own lives. But we are NOT alone. There are more of us than most would believe. We are stronger when allied than we could ever be individually. This is why our voices are so opposed.

Refuse to comply. Refuse to be silenced.

Parents with Estranged Children

10

The Runaway

I lost a kid. My sweetest, baseball playing, hockey playing kid. The one that wanted to go places with me all the time. Sunsets, errands, whatever. She got great grades. Excelled at sports. Graduated from a very rigorous, all girls, college prep highschool. She very much wanted to go to college.

Technically, she is not a runaway. She is 18 and in my state you can't be considered a runaway after age 16. The morning before she left she insisted on making pancakes for the whole family. She made them very often for herself and, if there were leftovers, she would give them to me. This time she made a big deal about wanting to make enough for everyone. And she did. She kept them coming until everyone was full and there was still some left over. Her sister's pancakes had some hair in them. Her sister is especially sensitive to hair in her food. Maybe my runaway did this on purpose to make some kind of point? I'll never know.

That evening she wanted to see the sunset—a common family activity for us, but one we'd been doing less and less recently. She made sure we went that night. She usually wanted to get ice cream on the beach but this time she said that she would rather not miss any of the sunset, so we did not. She usually wanted to go home as soon as the sun set, and I usually argued for us to stay until it completely faded. That night she didn't say anything about leaving.

We got home late because it was near mid-summer. We chatted in the kitchen and somehow got onto the subject of games we used to play, like chess. We realized we had not played chess since she was nine years old. She said, "Let's play now." I said "It is late, let's do it tomorrow or soon." She said, "People always say that and then never get around to doing it. Let's play now or we might never do it." So we did.

She only needed a brief refresher on the game. We played and—she won! I wasn't being very careful and she took my Queen early on and then, very skillfully, finished me off. She was so excited. She took a picture of the board with the pieces in the finishing spots.

The next day was a Sunday. I woke up early but she didn't. Since she always slept in, I chose not to bother her. Finally, about noon, I asked loudly, "Are you up?" from outside her door. When she did not reply, I opened the door and found a note on her bed. It said that she was leaving and would not be coming back. Don't try to find her. She hates us both - her mother and me. She said she was an asexual non-binary person. I had to look up "non-binary." I'd heard of it of course but wasn't sure what it meant.

After investigating a bit, I found out that there were at least three and maybe a dozen other girls in her class that were all trans or non-binary or something of that ilk. All born female and now shedding that label while declaring they hate men. Oh, and ACAB. Google that.

Also after the fact, we learned that a number of these girls were following a TikTok/Instagram/Youtube, trans influencer. We found out that this influencer person actually came to our town and visited with a number of girls from the school. We believed s/he set things up for our child to have a place to go. Other girls, when they heard about our child leaving home, confessed that they were encouraged to run away too. Only ours did though. There was no previous indication of any gender confusion. That note on the bed was the first indication that she now wants to be called "he" or "them." S/he changed her name to "Grey."

Since she started dressing herself, she only wore dresses—never even shorts much less pants. She paints her nails all sorts of silly colors. When she ran away she took all of her stuffed animals.

She wanted and got a $600 prom dress and had her long, thick beautiful hair done special at the salon for the prom. She took almost no clothes or anything except her ice skates, the stuffed animals and the prom dress! While she is 18, this seems like something a 12 year old would do.

11

The Wolf at the Door

It was right around the time the Ocotillo flowers blossomed 7 years ago that you announced you were non-binary. You were 17. Two years later you were calling yourself trans, convinced you weren't female and never had been.

I often wonder where that story began. Our family fairy tale was dreamed about and crafted long before you were born. The way we planned it, there were no witches or wolves, no tricks, no punishments, no shaming moral at the end. We had written the wolf right out of the story. It was a story of closeness, healthy minds, and healthy bodies. We imagined it would undo centuries of unhappy endings.

Maybe it began when you were 13, and we discovered you had been secretly cutting and starving yourself, urged on by online anorexia and self-harm forums? I remember watching the unfettered ease of your movements leak away, get tighter and more restricted. No more cartwheels. Your body closed in on itself. Despite our plans, the wolf stole your playful, innocent freedom and told you your body was a thing to be despised. The beast at the door was just a puppy, whining, looking up at us with innocent eyes. We believed it could be tamed. We were naïve about the cunning of wolves.

Maybe all the years of quirkiness caught up with you, the social struggles and loneliness too much to bear. Was it the betrayal and stupidity of friends? The pain of unrequited crushes? Were you ashamed to tell us life felt too hard sometimes? Your beloved face with the dazzling smile turned away from us; the smile faded into a blank stare lit by the blue light of a screen. You were captivated by your phone and computer, while I fantasized about smashing them to bits. Those devices appeared insignificant compared to all the years of love we gave you, but they sauntered in right under our noses and took our place. After years of trusting our thinking, you looked to us no longer. We had stupidly opened the door and offered the wolf a place by the fire. We believed love was stronger than any wild animal. We were fools.

In your high school years, we laughed a lot together. We drove you to art and dance classes. We took long walks in the desert. We said "I love you" multiple times a day; we goofed around, making up stories about our cats. Together, we analyzed the social dynamics at your school; we analyzed the world, we analyzed life. We helped you make college plans; you learned to drive. You sometimes called me your best friend. One sweet night we sang karaoke together with our arms entwined. I told myself the secrecy and the outbursts here and there were just normal developmental friction. The agonies of middle school were behind you, so I let myself relax. The wolf rested by the fire, tail wagging, seemingly tamed, and posing no threat. When I worried, I told myself it wasn't intuition, just anxiety.

I was wrong.

Were you already gone then? Already making secret plans? The phone and computer were taking you places I didn't even know existed. Wildernesses and wastelands filled with predators. The friendly wolf was not friendly at all. It leapt up overnight, it multiplied into a pack, and the pack expressed its true wolf nature: it was not to be tamed and it was out for blood. The wolves circled, snarling, and lured you in. They wanted all of you.

For a short, painful while you stood undecided: you avoided us, and you clung to us; you pushed us away and pulled us close. I tried to learn that awkward dance. I called you back, I stood waiting with arms open, I tried to catch you when you fell, I loosened my grasp when you resisted. The wolves were right there at the edges of my vision. They were getting meaner; they were getting wilder; and they howled with excitement as they closed in. Through their sharp teeth, they whispered lies, telling you it was we - your parents - who were the dangerous ones. They slunk around the margins, their eyes focused on you. We told ourselves all the years of closeness and love were stronger than any wolf pack. We told ourselves your common sense could see the wolves for what they were.

We were wrong.

Soon every conversation was fraught, every different opinion an affront, every minor issue a huge fight. The spirits of curiosity and friendly banter, always present in our home, withered and died. Nuance was long gone. It was a slow-motion slide downward as you searched for something undefinable within yourself, yearning for an easy answer to a hard question. The wolves dangled this imaginary answer just out of your reach, tempting you further on. Like the fairy tales we used to read, you wanted the Magic Pebble, the perfect spell, the sorcerer's wand to enchant your way out of discomfort. To our sorrow, the places you searched for magic instead offered its opposite. Your misery grew. Your discomfort was amplified. Your mental health deteriorated. Off you ran, panicked, following the wolves into the thick forest without a backward glance. You left no trail of breadcrumbs to find your way back. Don't you remember that fairy tales always end badly? Don't you remember that the 3 wishes always backfire; the wizard is a fake; and there is always a price to pay for trying to obtain things you aren't meant to have? We forgot the most important lesson of every fairy tale: the wolf will never be your friend.

Your eyes and heart hardened towards us. When you shouted that you wanted your breasts cut off, I gripped the table to keep from collapsing. Horrified, I pictured bloody scars on your precious body—a body I had nourished and protected your entire life. Our concerns about irreversible medical damage from hormones and surgeries were deemed transphobic. We offered information, but you didn't want to hear about the health risks: sterility, cardiovascular complications, compromised bone health, losing the potential to breastfeed, losing sexual pleasure; a shortened life span. We didn't believe in permanent solutions to temporary problems, but you had one aim only: for us to pay to have your breasts removed and celebrate your new identity as male.

We told you we would never stop loving you, you had a home here forever no matter what, we would have any hard conversation, we would listen. You didn't want these reassurances. You said you'd rather die than live with us. I hardly recognized you. Your skin was sallow and covered in acne from the testosterone you were given after one short visit visit to the doctor. Once your providers heard you say you were trans, they ignored your eating disorder and poor mental health and passed out testosterone like Halloween candy. You were unhappy, lost, confused. You ran out in the middle of therapy, hung up on us, leapt out of cars, sent cruel texts. You said it wasn't your job to tell us what you felt. You called us names: Bigots. Transphobes. Friends and family joined the chorus, blamed us, turned their backs. Our support system disintegrated. You lied to us: a first. You stole from us: another first. Then you stopped communicating at all. I couldn't feel anger; only fear, grief, and anguish. The child I cherished and adored, the young adult who felt so much a part of me—you had become a stranger. My heart was shattered. My stomach ached. Your dad and I stopped sleeping. We cried with each other but could not really comfort each other. We were losing you. Worse, you were losing yourself. The wolves had won. They had you now.

I wonder… how did the wolves get you to stop believing in the truth of your own body? How long did you suffer with a feeling of wrongness, not knowing this was a normal part of growing up? Who lied to you, telling you your body needed to be altered instead of your mind? When did you decide the two people you had been running to for comfort and understanding for 20 years were no longer "safe?" Social media, your friends, your teachers, your therapist, your doctors, these Orwellian "experts" all convinced you your parents were the enemies, your suffering was special, happiness was to be found through hormones and surgeries. They said you would never be happy until you left us behind, they told you we were "toxic." We implored you to stick with us, but you left and, as you left, you said the words that broke our hearts for good: you would never be back. Your brother watched it all from the sidelines, traumatized. Watched his parents wilt, cry, lose hope. Watched his sister scream, threaten, and leave the family without a goodbye. With you went something vital, and no, we haven't gotten it back, any more than I could get back a severed arm. The storybook is ripped to shreds, the fairytale pages a crumped mess in the corner. We had imagined many possible futures, but never one in which we were disposable. Numb, I looked outside. The Ocotillo plants had dropped their blossoms; their branches were just thorns.

So here we sit, turning the pages of a different kind of story. It has no happy ending. It's a nightmare, a cautionary tale that scares the children.

It's a story that makes families check the window latches, look warily over their shoulders, and pull chairs close around the fire. This is the story where you learn it's too late to throw away the magic pebble—you've already been turned to stone. You learn you've already swallowed the bite of poisoned apple. You learn no one is coming to rescue you. You learn your wishes won't come true. You learn no spells exist to undo the curse, there is no hero's journey with a reward at the end. We locked the doors; we said no; we placed ourselves between you and the pack; we reasoned; we pleaded; we bargained; we loved you beyond measure; we held you close; we ran after you; we wailed in grief. But we could not tame the wolf.

12

Trust Transferred from Parent to Predator

Like so many teens that declare a transgender identity, our kind, gentle and very intelligent son is on the autism spectrum.

Beginning in his early teens, we noticed that something was causing great turmoil, but we were not able to get him to articulate what it was. When he graduated from high school at 16, we questioned whether it would be too soon for college but since two of his brothers attended a nearby college, we decided commuting with them would allow gradual change.

Life seemed to be going well during these college years. He was enjoying choir and making friends. We were feeling optimistic about his future. By his 3rd year of college, things still seemed to be going very well. Our son mentioned that his advisor had proven a great advocate for him, and made arrangements for me to meet with her. I had no inkling of how drastically our world was about to change.

As soon as I stepped into her office, she placed a five page letter in front of me that she and our son had arranged to present to me. The letter began with "Hi, Mom," a greeting I had taken for granted and one that I would later long to hear. His letter was written with the tenderness that was a consistent part of who he was:

"I have to let you know that I'm every bit as afraid of this hurting you and the rest of the family as I am of it hurting me, if not more so… Because what it comes down to is that I'm not your son, or anybody else's son, for that matter. What I am is your daughter. I'm a woman."

Giving me just enough time to read, his advisor knocked on the door and returned to her seat across from me. Following her was a small parade of characters—our son, an LGBTQ family coordinator, a licensed professional counselor, and a chaplain. I felt as if I was on trial as each one of them looked into my face to assess my response to the letter. I gently smiled and moved in the direction of the only one I wanted to see at that moment. We embraced in a long hug. I thought I'd handled the moment well under the circumstances, although I later learned that I had used his name and it hurt him deeply. No one had given me the rule book—the one called "Affirmative Care" that I would learn about years later.

This was in 2014 and resources on this topic were extremely limited. One of the first things I searched was "transgender and autism" as it seemed reasonable that they would be connected. I was quickly chastised by a Social Justice Warrior. We had dealt with other health conditions, why was I forbidden to ask questions about this one? Even more troubling was that I was demonized for doing so. I was deemed unsafe. One question that did get answered was that our son's help was coming from Tumblr.

We had made it a tradition to grab ice cream with our family on Wednesday nights, an activity we all enjoyed. We stayed in touch in other ways as best we could. On occasion, our son, now living with another young man on the autism spectrum, would show interest in being picked up (he had decided against getting a driver's license) on a weekend for a visit. I also made a trip weekly to help him with his grocery shopping. He was getting along well with his new roommate and making good progress in living independently. Shopping continued to be a bit of a challenge as there were still times that he would freeze up when there was a need for a decision. We were still working on these life skills but I was confident that he would get there and continued to encourage him towards his independence.

Six months after his "coming out", we were doing our best to keep the lines of communication open. I was thankful that he could communicate so well in writing and that we had this new technology through text to do so. One day, as I reached out to confirm a meet-up with him, I sent out a text but received no response. When I reached out to his roommate, I learned that our son hadn't returned to the apartment for the last few days. The roommate was surprised to hear my surprise—he had been under the impression our son was with us. He confessed that our son had "seemed off" recently, and raised the concern of suicide.

We immediately got to work tracking him down and were soon relieved to see recent activity within a video game that he played with his brothers—but we still didn't connect with him. On the following Sunday one of his high school friends successfully connected with him via a video game and relayed, "She's doing fine and will contact you soon. No need to worry." After several days passed, we reached out to this friend to followup. He didn't know much but relayed that, "She won't be returning to the apartment." We learned later that our son was nearly 2,000 miles away.

Entering his empty room was one of the hardest days of my life. As I climbed each step of his second floor apartment, I felt more and more like vomiting. Everything appeared to be the same as usual with nothing but his computer missing. It's as if life just stopped suddenly for him. His quilt from mom was still on the bed. The quilt that he made sure he always had, along with the thin feather pillow he couldn't give up, his Wii, notebooks from school, his favorite novels, loose change, deodorant … It just didn't make sense.

Then there were reminders of the battle he was fighting: over a dozen appointment reminder cards for a local counselor, an empty package that once contained women's underwear, a bag of makeup and jewelry (obviously a gift because it had gone untouched), unpaid bills from an endocrinologist and a small pile of business cards from various doctors. I stuffed a flood of thoughts that began to rush through my head into a mental compartment, the same way that I stuffed the belongings into bags. I then hauled the bags down to the car with the help of his roommate.

We have been in touch with the human trafficking hotline. Given the amount of red flags shared, they highly suspected that our child was trafficked. We were met with kindness, compassion, given a case number, but not much hope.

It will be eight years in May since we have heard from our son. The thing that angers me most is our culture is paving the way to have this happen again and again. The transgender ideology is tearing vulnerable children from the safety of their loving parents and leaving them wide open to be taken captive by predators.

13

What I've Learned This Year

Our daughter, now 27 years-old, dropped the bombshell letter of her "transition" to "manhood" on us last October. I visited her a few weeks later, and listened to what she had to say. The visit went okay, but I was dismayed to learn that she had recently begun taking testosterone. I knew that I had a small window of opportunity in which to exert any influence I might have left.

Over the next three months I sent her two letters. The third, I delivered in person. That visit did not go well. She did not like the relevant and probing questions I asked. About a month later she cut off all contact with us. My only ray of hope is that it appears she hasn't blocked our texts. We try to keep the connection open, dropping a neutral note from time to time so that, if she decides to turn to us again, it will be easy for her to do so.

I have been pondering lately what I have learned in all this. This is what I've come up with:

- I have realized that her estrangement from us began long before her proclamation of a trans identity. She had been withholding information about the depression she was experiencing post college graduation. She excluded us from her "questioning" period, turning instead to God-only-knows-who on the internet. **This might be what hurts the most—that she trusted complete strangers more than us.**

- I have realized that my **internal compass,** which has guided me for my entire life, is still intact. I *know* that her trans-identification is a very bad decision. I have no doubt that she suffers from autism or some form of neurodiversity (although none of her counselors caught this). I know that medical transition is not necessary. What she needs is to learn to accept and love herself.

- I have realized that **the movement to squelch free speech and scientific inquiry is alarming.** So today I have begun a letter-writing campaign, targeting leaders of companies or publications that have let me down. My first letter—to the CEO of Springer Publishing, which is retracting a scientific survey about ROGD because of activists' claims of "transphobia." Will it do any good? It will do *me* good. Will you join me?

- I have realized that **my identity cannot be wrapped up in hers.** I have a purpose in life and a meaningful job. I have another child whose relationship I value and a husband who loves and supports me. I cannot allow her to control my life. I turn again and again to Mary Oliver's poem, "I Go Down to the Shore": *"I say, oh, I am miserable, what shall—what should I do? And the sea says in its lovely voice, 'Excuse me, I have work to do.'"* I refuse to dwell in misery; I have my life's purpose to fulfill.

- Remembering another Oliver poem, "Don't Hesitate," which ends *"Joy is not made to be a crumb,"* I began keeping a daily journal of "crumbs" of joy. And sometimes they are indeed no more than crumbs. But **I have learned that I cannot always passively *wait* for joy.** I must seek it in places where I know I can find it—John Rutter's musical composition, *Gloria,* is another work of art I can turn to when I can't find joy elsewhere.

- I have realized that my daughter may not outlive me and my husband, that **we may have to survive the death of a child.** Despite the emotional terrorism perpetrated on parents, I know that it is unlikely that she will commit suicide. But heart attack, stroke, dangerous blood clot, early dementia…all of these are possible.

- I am giving much thought to **life's true transitions.** Everyone experiences loss—loss of innocence at some point in childhood; loss of loved ones or relationships and the pain that brings; loss of vitality or health in later life. Yet we can move beyond that loss to become someone new. I'm beginning to have a very different perspective on the notion of "resurrection."

Whether my daughter will return or not, I don't know. Even if she does, I will never be the same again. I am hoping and working to make the new me better.

14

Trauma That Leads to More Trauma

Who would have thought that a huge tragedy where I almost lost my son would lead to actually losing him?

My son was hit by a car when he was two and a half. He was strapped into his stroller, on the way back from a walk through the park with his babysitter, when a car turned right on red and struck the two of them in a crosswalk. The babysitter broke a few ribs and her arm. My son, still in his stroller, slid across the asphalt, skinning his face. It was a close call and, at the hospital, the doctors confirmed he had escaped with no physical harm beyond the face lacerations. But the experience left us all traumatized, especially him. He never left my lap that night, and he wouldn't sleep in his own bed for a year, and I have always sensed that that trauma stuck with him, deep in his psyche.

He received a settlement from the insurance company for a considerable amount of money, which I squirreled away from him until he turned 18. At the time I thought he could use that money to buy a car or for college.

At 15, my son announced he was transgender after showing no signs of gender confusion as a child. He is now 18 and still fully believes in this ideology. We truly thought he would outgrow it since he had been showing signs of desistance for years, and no outward signs of being "trans". But then he turned 18 and everything changed.

Guess what was waiting for him when he turned 18? **The insurance money.** He quickly started gathering documents and became very secretive. He'd been waiting and planning. He took the money, and he left.

He left his parents who love him more than anything in this world, the only house he has ever known, and two pets he adored. We don't know where he is and have not heard from him. We had always been close and I thought love would win. But I was wrong. The outside influences are too strong.

My son was almost taken from me at 2 and 1/2. I got 15 1/2 years back and for that I am thankful, but in the end, I lost him nonetheless.

15

The Crimes of the Mother

Her bedroom is empty, waiting for a visit I hope, but know she will not be coming any day soon.

This is the house she grew up in, in a nice neighborhood in the suburbs. Her view out of her bedroom window is of a large backyard with flowers and trees. We, her parents, have all the memories the house held for us, the ghosts of Christmases and family gatherings, so many birthdays and holidays, dinners and graduation celebrations, and just moments of playing board games and watching favorite shows on television.

I hear the echo of laughter and sorrow too, of lost family members and break ups with friends and boyfriends and all the anxiety and fear that goes into growing up. The tears and fights too, about braces, about grades, wants and needs, learning what is not possible and what is.

All the love poured into our daughter and all the memories that make up a life. The trips to the mountains and beach, the trips to places she wanted to go like Hawaii and Florida and even trips overseas. The ability to save and, with help from relatives, have her college education completely paid for to help ensure a future with promise.

Now this childhood home, with all those memories, all that love, is not "safe" anymore, according to our daughter. Because she has decided that she is literally a man.

The announcement that she was now a man came to us out of the blue during the pandemic, at age nineteen. We had never seen a hint of her having an issue with her body and she had no great reasoning for this when we questioned. Gender ideology is totally based on a "feeling" and, more worryingly, a whole belief system, very much like a fundamentalist religion or even a cult, that is absolute in what can even be asked. We don't know who influenced her on the internet or at college. But we know her deep anxiety and depression affected her her whole life. We know it was almost crippling at times, including having obsessive thoughts that would not end. She had told me one time when she was having anxiety attacks that it was so just so hard having her brain.

Now she considers me an enemy, and my crime is believing in reality, in biology and knowing she is female and will always be female. I continue to assert what I believe and know—that she can take testosterone to mimic what a man looks like but she will still be a female pretending she is a man. She can have her healthy breasts removed but she will just be a female who had her breasts removed. Changing sex is an impossibility.

She thinks my position means that I am denying her very existence, because she has been told by gender ideology that the only thing in her existence that matters, that has ever mattered, is her new identity of being trans.

We think she is on the autism spectrum but it mostly never interfered with her succeeding. She didn't fit in with the other girls a lot of the time and had trouble making friends. But, and there are so many buts, she never exhibited any unhappiness during puberty or about her body. She thrived in high school and became valedictorian and got admitted to an elite college. There were dresses and jewelry and prom and parties and all of the usual stuff that girls do. There were boyfriends and friends she loved.

Then the pandemic came right during her first year at college, her first year of separation from home. She was forced back home and it created more anxiety since there was no seeing of friends, and no boyfriends. When she went back to college there were new friends that called themselves trans or non binary. She came out as trans to everyone at college months before telling us anything and, of course every friend and every professor accepted this and started calling her by her new name and pronouns.

The only people who have told her the truth are her parents. We asked that she wait until graduation, because this was too much to add on to the pressures of completing college. She told us she wanted hormones and surgery including the very cutely named "bottom surgery" which is more like frankenstein surgery, and we were horrified. There was no waiting or talking, it was all an absolute. We were shocked, and we didn't say all the right things. But we believed we were fighting for her very life. And for this, we may never be forgiven.

Ever the dutiful daughter, she did as we asked. She waited on transition. She also lied when we asked about her identity at college, lied over and over to us, but still graduated early. Dumbly and sadly, I had believed she might be desisting because our bond was so strong, her love for her father and I thought, even me, the mother she now despises. Unlike the happy celebration after high school, there was no college graduation celebration. She cut us out of her life with no way to reach her.

She has cut off contact because we won't lie. Because we won't tell her that she can attempt to change sex without consequences that will affect her life for years and years to come. She doesn't believe that I, her mother, am telling her these things because I take my first and really only job as a mother seriously: To protect her from harm. That is supposed to be the motto of medical professionals, "first do no harm". But that isn't what is happening today in the realm of "gender affirming care". Our daughter is someone that needs therapy and that needs to find out ways of navigating the world as an adult, she doesn't need wrong sex hormones to pretend to be a man. But of course this is what I am told is the one and only answer by institutions like the American Medical Association.

If they knew my daughter, had seen her through every trauma and fear of almost twenty years, they would know that messing with her hormones could destroy her mind. It could destroy her already shaky sense of self, because she is someone that folds easily at criticism and strives for perfectionism. She will not find it easy to convince the world that she is something that she is not. But that is the path of trans medicine, the search for an impossible reality.

There is (at last) some debate about sex hormones and surgeries for minors. There are, horrifyingly, loads of young adults out there that are being harmed by this belief system. And that is all this is, because it is certainly not medicine.

So the live and let live attitude that is often parlayed because someone is over the age of eighteen and thus it's just a "choice" is infuriating to the parents of young adults. Young adults in distress, no matter other issues like trauma, anxiety, depression, autism, anorexia, and the vulnerability of being gay, are offered cross sex hormones on the first visit to a gender clinic.

Where will these young adults be at 30? At 40? No one remains 20 forever. Will their options to have children be forgone? Will they regret surgeries and permanent changes to their bodies that cannot be undone after often just a few MONTHS on cross sex hormones? Where is the evidence that long term medical procedures bring long term happiness?

Besides medical horrors, the other fear I have for her future is just as large. Who will she find to be her partner? She knows we would be fine if she was a lesbian but she has only wanted to date boys and now men. She thinks of herself as a gay man now. The absurdity of this and the naivete, that she doesn't understand that gay men want to be with other gay men.

She believes that somehow I, her mother, never knew her at all. There are so many guides on the internet, and therapists that undercut parents at every turn. The past never happened. She was never happy. If you even think for a moment that you are trans, you are! If you don't fit in and have doubts about your looks, you are trans. What young woman in this age of Instagram perfection has never thought they weren't beautiful enough?

If we go to a therapist, they will tell me that my daughter, who decided in all of six months during a pandemic, who had suffered from mental anguish her whole life, that the answer to every pain of her life is to somehow magically change sex and I must believe it, or I am hateful and I am wrong.

I know she is in pain and that thinking of herself as a man brings relief and comfort, I know that she has distress. I don't want her to be harmed by drugs or by thinking that because of not believing in her reality that I hate her true self. But I don't believe the answer is a lie.

I know that the entirety of society is now expected to lie and accept the unseen inner feelings of everyone we meet. I know this is not sustainable, anymore that taking wrong sex hormones for 20 years will have no consequences.

It seems everyone knows that somehow, prior to the internet, prior to internet porn and social media, trans-identified girls were a tiny tiny minority. And now I and everyone I know, have some girl in their family at age 12 or 15 or 20 deciding that they are really a man or some combination of "non-binary". And somehow, the non-binary also means that the breasts must go, be bound and hid, and that the female part is the part that is wrong. Something has radically changed in a short time. And how in any sane world is the only answer to this massive societal shift a needle full of testosterone?

Parents like me are in a living nightmare. The doctors, the schools, the governments, are all lying, seeming to imply it's as easy as turning a switch to change sex. That there are no long term consequences. That detransition is rare and everyone is happy forever after transition. That an inner feeling had for a few months trumps all biology, all her history and everything she has ever known and everyone that has ever loved her. All of that is the reality of trans ideology.

The emptiness is enormous for parents like us. We maintain our silence to relatives and friends because we don't want to be thought of as bigots. We speak in private groups only because we are so alone. But there are many, many of us, and so tragically, more every day. Something has to change. We are liberal and would like to tell all the institutions and politicians that "gender affirming care" just sounds nice and accepting until your child walks in the door and tells you that they aren't your daughter anymore. Then you are forced to discover the reality of drugs and surgeries and it isn't so simple.

Most of these people telling us what to do have zero skin in the game. This is our lives, every second of every day, and many good parents are trying to navigate the right thing to do for their precious child, whether they affirm completely or not. We are all trying to love our children and we need help and we need answers, not hollow slogans and endless culture wars. We need left and right and middle coming together to help our children out of a new nightmare that didn't exist twenty years ago. I have no doubt if my daughter was born 20 years earlier none of this would have happened.

When I hear her "deadname", I know she is not dead but that, rather, she somehow killed off her childhood and all her memories and connection to me and her family, I am sliced to the heart. The missing is endless and forever.

I pray (though I am not much of a believer) that she comes home soon and someday comes to forgive the crimes of her mother and understand that a mother only lies to save her child and not the other way around.

16

I Cry on the Beach

I cry anywhere I can be alone or where no one can see me, and in places where I never cried before. When I weed our vegetable garden in the warm sun, I think of how much Ricky might love a slice of the juicy watermelon we are growing. And I weep. As I keep my hands busy building things around the house, I pause between power drill spins to sob. When I go out for my jog, I occasionally choke up between breaths. On breaks while working, I stand, stretch, and snivel. On long trips, while I drive and my wife dozes off, I tear up.

Even on the beach where the two of us empty-nesters go to relax and reminisce, I cry. Though the beach is one of God's uplifting gifts to His servants; a place to swim, body surf, play silly beach games, enjoy cold drinks and fried food, a place that evokes tranquility even on a cold, moonless night or wintry storm, on it I now drop tears whenever my face is out of sight. I grew up on the coast and we were delighted that we could retire near a lovely beach where our children and doted-on grand baby could come visit. I remember lovable, playful Ricky as a child on the beach and how I would launch him high into the air so he could splash into the sea. He would squeal with delight and say, "Daddy do it again."

No more. That was 28 years ago. True, children outgrow those playful antics between their parents. But it is because they enter adulthood and understand that such are pleasant memories of bygone days. But that is not Ricky's mindset. He has openly and publicly disowned us as parents in favor of membership in the trans cult. He practices absolute obedience to all of the cult's dictates, which include alienation from and spite for "non supporting" parents. This cult has appropriated not only Ricky from us, but also the full love and affection of one of his older sisters and our beloved grandchild, our access to whom has been downgraded from action-packed visits to a snail-mail penpal style of communication.

This alienation is solely because we affirmed Ricky's true and natural destiny to embrace the challenge of manhood. Because we refused to lie to him and endorse his parody of a woman. Because we see his body as the Temple of the Holy Ghost, not to be defiled with blockers, fake body parts and genital amputations. Because we rejected the Current Thing.

We will have no walks or frolics in the ocean or sand with our grand baby. Only cards and letters. Not even the latter from Ricky.

Another reason to cry on the beach.

My tears irrigate seeds of action to impart the gravity and repercussions of this wicked movement—to tell my story as a warning for parents of children in the early phases of this affliction, and to help them fight.

Ricky's Early Years: All Systems Normal

Ricky was born in the early 90s. His older sisters, were born in the early 80s. His younger brother, Joshua, would be born in 1995. Ricky was a full-term baby. Due to some pre-birth complications, the doctors performed amniocentesis on my wife to screen for birth defects. The DNA results were negative for defects—they also showed that the fetus was male. I still have the original DNA report. I cannot wait to wave this at a judge telling me what pronouns to use. Let the black-robed non-binary tyrant jail me for it. Bring it on.

Ricky was a joy to behold and to raise. I have the countless memories, photos and videos to prove it. In contrast to the girls, Ricky and Joshua loved to rough-house, play soldier, jump on furniture, get dirty, race on their bicycles, and go on camping trips. Also unlike their sisters, they had to be coaxed and threatened to the bathtub and dinner table when it was time. What all the children had in common were a love for the beach, their grandparents, Sunday worship and the long trips making army moves. Not once did any child ever complain about the inconveniences and anxieties that came with the fourteen Army relocations.

Through the years up to tenth grade, Ricky showed a talent for soccer and making and re-making friends at every new Army installation that became our home. His school performance was mediocre—he hurried through homework and seemed okay with being an academic underachiever. He rarely acted up in school. Teachers loved his personality. He had a gentle voice which I suspect was one of the cracks that the hidden online satyrs were to slither into later like slimy lizards.

Before he reached school age, Ricky watched Barney on TV when he wasn't outside. At age eight he discovered Pokémon, and later Yukio. He spent a lot of time with the cards and games. This interest spread into anime during his pre-teen years. I would not have allowed these types of child entertainment had I known then what I know now.

High School: The Online Obsessions Begin and Dim the Light of Ricky's Mind

Shortly after I returned from my deployment in 2006, Ricky was spending a lot of time on the computer. He now disliked soccer and going to the movies with friends. We reduced his computer time, but he kept sneaking away to the base Youth Center to go on the computer. He had Meebo, Tumblr, Buzznet and MySpace accounts, which we thought harmless. I suspected that this was where the groomers started working on him and, by the time I found this out for sure in late 2007, Ricky had undergone a complete change in personality. Deep harm had already been done to Ricky's personality, identity, morals and worldview.

(This channel has featured this excellent deep dive of the snares presented by Tumblr and other teen-oriented microblogs. The author is a recovering trans man:)

In his new-found isolation, Ricky no longer made friends at school and spent all his spare time on the computer. There were no more puppy-love girlfriends, only girl friends with similar antisocial interests. Ricky adopted an androgynous style for his clothes and hair. He stopped wearing cool hoodies and sports t-shirts in favor of tight-fitting clothes. His handsome head, once covered with a short-cropped haircut, now sprout a pixie-style straightened cut. We were concerned, but thought it was just a phase.

Over the next few months though, moodiness and out-of-character sassiness increased. He tore up the family photos he had taped to his bedroom door and walls. Joshua started getting questions from his friends about his brother's "weird" clothes and mannerisms. Ricky's voice started to take on a lispy affectation. Suddenly he was polishing his nails. The boy who would not take even a teddy bear to bed as a toddler now walked around the house with a pink Pikachu doll and a Hello Kitty button. Around this time he also ruined a family trip and beat up the little brother whom he one time taught how to skim rocks on a lake.

Ricky's Same-Age Groomer Then and Now

In late 2007, I installed parental monitoring software on our family computer to see what Ricky was into. The gentleman who only a year before would dance with his mother, listen to soul music, and leap on the trampoline with his brother; was now polluted with online vices. The filthy kilobytes were like worms gnawing on the flesh of his young soul. Here is a sampling of his profile page and the codswallop what he was composing and peering at every day:

Now enter Brad, his online Bobbsey Twin. Today, Brad claims to be "Bradleigh." Ricky aped Brad, as the pair posted daily entries on these sites in the tradition of shock-phrase contests between two miserable, cynical 16-year-olds severely lacking in intellectual nourishment or spiritual perspective. Family loyalty was stomped to death.

Other posts were replete with obscene entries too disgusting to mention here.

Brad continues to influence Ricky to this day. He hosted Ricky at this home for many weeks. He contributed money to his recent "trans journey" body mutilation. His social media profile today makes the old one above look like choir boy material. Imagine a 32-year old man who populates his profile with photos of his half-naked obese self, and tributes to known satanists. An open follower of Anton LaVey. When people call the alphabet cult "satanic," it is no knee-jerk characterization.

Hack Therapy

Meanwhile, Ricky had become unrecognizable. When my wife saw her makeup and lingerie showing up in Ricky's dresser drawer, we took him to a therapist. He did not resist, but pouted in the car all the way to the therapist's office every trip.

This would become a three-year run of therapist visits that resulted in no progress. Nay, reverse progress. No diagnosis of the obvious Gender Dysphoria and narcissism that was torturing him. Depression and Suicidal Ideation. No parent-friendly ways ahead; only the occasional joint sessions where the psychologist would criticize our "backward" outlooks.

Lay people had little experience with this and little advice to offer. Some meant well, many offered adages, others were cruel. People said things like, "Oh, it's just a phase, it is kind of cool for the kids to say they are "bi;" and "Oh, my daughter thought she was a lesbian, but she got over it." Others blamed the situation on us and "offered" to take Ricky in themselves. Another close relative took offense at a comment I made and answered with sailor-shocking profanity. The parish priest scolded us for not forcing Ricky to Sunday services.

Senior Year of High School and After

So antisocial, inward, neurotic and persecutory had Ricky become that the mention of starting his senior year in high school caused him to tremble and beg not to attend. So we brokered an agreement with the high school that allowed him to complete his diploma requirements online. Normally, senior year is what all American teenagers look forward to. It is informal leadership of the school. A time to strengthen friendships and determine a course for the future. A time to enjoy adults from colleges competing for their applications and admission.

But not for Ricky. Senior year was to be dreaded. A choke point on the callow, make-believe, hedonistic virtual road he had constructed for himself and was determined to travel without us. A road where he would be free—not to pursue a responsible career and mainstream adult life, but to shut himself in rooms so he could record himself dancing around in woman's underwear to the music of Marilyn Manson, Lady Gaga and other ghastly noisemakers. He would write and publish cynical, self-absorbed prose. He would cement his belief that the whole world hated him because he was "gay and black." (He is half white.) He would give no help to his hosts in chipping in for rent, food upkeep, or even so much as do housework. He would ask us for money occasionally, which we would provide. We did not want him to take on homelessness.

After high school, he spent the next seven years physically living alternately with his sisters, online perverts, and us. Mentally he was still in the same virtual plasticene wasteland that preached the futility of normal life, the joy of superficial celebrity worship, and celebration of mindless stupidity. He hardly held any jobs and spent most of his time alone in a room or on couches, living his pretend life as a womyn online. Each trip outside the dwelling brought on "panic attacks." He was continuously emailing us for rent and food money, making empty promises that he would get a job and pay his own bills. It was hard enough work for Ricky to constantly pretend to be something he was not and never could be—a woman. He had no time for reality.

Some Signs of Hope—Only to be Dashed

So it went until he moved to DC in 2017 as a boarder and got a part time job in coffee shops in notorious neighborhoods.

Then Ricky showed some signs of proper adult behavior. We stayed in touch. He travelled to attend Joshua's college graduation. We exchanged phone calls, cards and presents for special occasions. We met for vacation trips. I took him to the racetrack and showed him the fine art and fun of analyzing horses. He held an assistant manager's job at a coffee shop and would often call me for advice. He would drop the voice affectation when he talked to me. He prayed with me on the phone. When the COVID lockdowns hit, Ricky lost his job and we sent him care packages and money and a new computer. Government money kept him afloat for rent, but he showed signs of coming through. We were happy with this improvement and bet on hope, not forcing functions. The real Ricky is a treasure locked up deep inside the deviate veneer of acquired alternative gender. We were hoping the Rainbow of God's Protection was taking its rightful place over the misused rainbow of boastful sinners.

He even shared reminiscences of his childhood which he said proved that we were good parents. Which makes the sudden changes in his attitudes and communications later all the more startling.

Ricky Fires Us When We go Look for Him

In June 2021, we stopped hearing from him. I texted him in vain, except once he responded, "Did someone die or something?" When he skipped the customary phone call to his mother on her July birthday, we started worrying. As he was at that time still on my cell phone account, I pulled phone logs and saw several calls to various DC welfare offices, psychologists and plastic surgeons.

Since this indicated he was still alive, I waited patiently for my chance to talk him out of this.

In September 2021, some in-laws alerted us that they had seen Ricky on a crowdfunding post asking for donations for his "surgical transition." In his narrative, he said he was a "black trans woman..asking for support from my surgical recovery." He described his "journey" consisting of years on HRT, which did not "align myself with my body." His next step would be breast augmentation. He said that due to the high rate of murders of black trans women, it was urgent that he "blend in with society" and any contributions would be life-saving.

He managed to collect roughly $3,000 of his $10,000 goal.

We took a road trip for a health and welfare check on Ricky in November 2021. We drove my truck for a ten-hour trip to the DC area to try to find our son. We stopped at another city on the way to look for our homeless in-law Barnabus. Though we were unsuccessful in finding or contacting either lost sheep, the trip was an education nonetheless. Sadly, Barnabus would die alone and destitute in the cold city streets last January. He and Ricky were close; or at least as close as an alcoholic and a narcissist could get. We were never able to confirm that Ricky received notice of his death.

We went to Ricky's last known address. The owner said Ricky moved out and did not say where he went. We tried calling Ricky a few times and he did not pick up. Finally, we texted him with our photo in holding this sign:

Ricky, we love you.

And with this text:

We are in front of your old house right now. Please tell us where you are.

He responded with this text:

"turn this phone off I got a new number I moved I do not want contact

Stop trying to find m (sic)

I don't want to be found"

As we drove away, this VM came up on my phone from Ricky:

"Hello, I'm calling to let you know I don't want contact with you. I don't want you to try to contact me anymore. You can turn this phone off. Um I'm filming this interaction just in case..um this is all being documented. Um. Just leave me alone I want to live my life…I'm happy. Um you had your chance to be a good parent to me and the chance is now over with. Um so please just…STOP! Just stop. Please."

Soon afterward, Joshua called us and told us Ricky had talked to him and said that he still cared about Joshua, but Mom and Dad were "dead" to him and that we were "terrible parents" and he was prepared to "take legal action" against us if we were to try to contact him.

Without a word, we headed out of DC. We were whipped for the moment. At least we communicated to Ricky and his uncle that we were willing to travel anywhere anytime to find them.

So, how could a penniless, unemployed, mentally ill young man like Ricky find the $50,000+ he needed to receive this depraved neutering procedure at taxpayer expense? The DC GRS Policy in force was the answer to this question.

DC GRS Policy: Government Gelding Blueprint

DC policy # OD-001-17, "Gender Reassignment Surgery Policy," was the law that enabled my son to receive the total castration process from the public kitty. The Department of Health Care Finance administers it.

In this policy, the authors concede that:

There is a "lack of clarity and absence of consensus among (our) sources about which medical and surgical interventions constitute comprehensive and medically necessary treatment for GRS (Gender Reassignment Surgery)."

"Although self-reported outcomes and observational studies have shown improved quality of life for some persons with GD (Gender Dysphoria), the evidence base for long-term GRS outcomes is minimal, largely qualitative and lacks bias protection measures such as randomization and control groups."

"The systematic review by Murad, et al., reviewed 28 studies that enrolled 1833 participants with GD. Despite this detailed analysis, knowledge gaps about optimal long-term therapy for GD persist."

"The peer review literature on treatment for GD… highlight the lack of information about the long-term efficacy of surgical interventions, particularly on mental health outcomes. In addition, research to date has not established definitive patient selection criteria for ancillary procedures, services and treatments for GD."

"[t]he quality and strength of evidence were low due to the mostly observational study designs with no comparison groups, potential confounding and small sample sizes. Many studies that reported positive outcomes were exploratory type studies (case-series and case-control) with no confirmatory follow up."

"Because of the controversial nature of sex reassignment surgery, (outcome) analysis has been very important. Almost all of the outcome studies in this area have been retrospective. More studies are needed that focus on the outcomes of current assessment and treatment approaches for gender dysphoria."

And the bottom line and kicker:

"DHCF acknowledges the absence of clear clinical, scientific and therapeutic guidance for optimal treatment of GRS. However, despite the limited evidence, DHCF is committed to facilitating access to specific forms of GRS for the Medicaid population."

Translation: With full knowledge that this cosmetic surgery has no useful track record and may harm more than help the patients, we don't care. We hereby allow, encourage and fund the indigent population of Washington, DC to undertake experimental, high-risk mutilation to keep the trans activists off our backs.

Outrageous. Authorizing such drastic procedures is nothing other than premeditated medical malpractice and surgical experimentation targeting poverty-stricken, mentally ill racial minorities. (95 % of non-elderly DC Medicaid recipients are "people of color.") Where are the SJWs on this one? Oh, but your son is an adult, you are saying. Yes, but a mentally incapacitated adult. His emotional age is 15 years tops, as he ceased maturing at that age. Such a person cannot objectively appreciate the second and third order effects of this gelding process, let alone rationally evaluate the tsunami of government-supported pro-trans propaganda.

DC had some help putting together this policy. Along with some "research literature" and "federal and state laws" across the US, they also publicly welcomed and endorsed the National Center for Transgender Equality (NCTE), a radical trans advocacy group, as a chief consultant for this policy.

DC's Partnership with NCTE, an Ideological Attack Dog

This group dared, in front of Congress and without challenge to its screed-filled statement, to style themselves as "non-partisan." Some observations about this outfit:

1. Their executive director is Rodrigo Heng-Lehtinen, a trans man. A she/her to me regardless.
2. Per influencewatch.org, NCTE receives most of its funds from these hard-left groups: Evelyn & Walter Haas, Jr. Fund; Klarman Family Foundation; MoveonCivic Action (significant Soros footprint); NEO Philanthropy.
3. The only parental support discussed on NCTE's webpage is advocacy of affirming parents (grown-up child bearers who have abdicated their natural roles as protectors and moral leaders). They show no interest in parents who actually parent.
4. They claim that the 26 trans people murdered in 2020 is an "epidemic." I dug a little into these cases and saw that these people did die through violence. All but two cases are still unresolved, so we cannot label those "murders" because not all violent deaths are murders. Tough to readily determine the facts because it is the multi-gay media reporting it. So I will cover this in depth another time.
5. They want to ban the word "delusion" when discussing a trans or a trans prospect.
6. Not sure if the trans cult is recruiting the children?
7. NCTE's claim that they are "nonpartisan" is hogwash. Look at his Heng's tweets on your own. Case closed. This type of advocacy has made it a reality for some public schools to display this poster: Even Newsweek featured an article condemning this. No such condem-

nations from other mainstream sources, much less from NCTE. Silence is acceptance.

8. Not word one from this sex-change champion partner about the documented high suicide rate of individuals after "surgery."

Ricky Destroys His Temple; Evicts the Holy Ghost with Gusto

Ricky proceeded though all four phases of the gelding process and posted descriptions on social media. The fourth and final phase occurred while we were still in mourning over Barnabus' death. Ricky included this comment on one of his social media postings: That the person accompanying him to the mutilations was "carrying the weight of mother and father in the way only a cool (person) can."

Can things get more demoralizing than this?

Yes. Last May, Ricky went to a convention in Texas for the Black Trans Advocacy Coalition. He posted mostly pictures of himself in front of the motel and ladies' room mirrors. "I'm black and trans, therefore everyone hates me," was no longer just the callow slogan of a profoundly confused young man, it was now the driving groupthink of an organized, moneyed NGO. The more oppressed one is, the more he will feel entitled to attention. I went on their webpage once and that was enough. Nothing edifying. Massive self-lovefest. Salt in the wound.

Conclusion

I hold DC responsible for providing an experimental procedure to a person incapable of giving true consent. The law holds that the mentally incapacitated are not capable of consenting to medical procedures. Even a layman can see that his mental state is severely sullied with narcissism, paranoia and persecutory complex. Because mental health professionals have become hired hands for the trans industry, and the senior professionals have done nothing to stop it, psychologists and psychiatrists are unworthy of trust and we parents must make the best layman's diagnoses we can. That's how I feel about it.

What Next?

We must be ready to fight while remembering that our enemy is strong and pitiless. They have bottomless funds, heavy MSM support, political favor, and hearts smaller than the Grinch's. They play rough and laugh at our misery. Yet despite their plentiful earthly assets, they are utterly powerless to summon God to the aid of their Truth-denying enterprise. It is our exclusive recourse to the favors of Grace that is our greatest weapon. Let us deploy our love of Truth and boldly seek justice for these masterminds who have defiled the innocence, sobriety and modesty of our children.

How to do it? First, take care of ourselves so we will be fit to rescue others. Not unlike what they tell you about using oxygen masks on airplanes. Seek counselling, but beware of to whom you go. Most of my care is under the VA, but that institution is so committed to the mental health of the LGBT+, etc that I see more rainbow flags than Old Glory inside the hospitals. VA phycologists are professionally conflicted.

Now, to the fight. Do not allow people to advance false arguments in favor of trans butchering. Write columns. Avoid businesses that display rainbow flags.

What about more active measures? I do not know yet because I am still working through grief. But I have ideas that I will share when I develop them more. Think: Class Actions.

Hopes and Dreams

Each bedtime comes with a trepidation of dreams. Since 2006, I dream frequently about Ricky without the dysphorian affliction. These days, he appears to me, in his early 30s, as the young man he was meant to be. Tall, a little reticent but cheerful. Happy to be back, free from the cult's stench-filled pit and ready to properly enter the maturing process to manhood. In the faint background, Joshua is leaping for joy that his big brother has returned and is taking him outside to play. When I start thinking that this is too good to be really happening, I wake up. In my profound ignorance and unworthiness, I do not know if this is a sign from God, or a taunt from the Prince of Darkness. So I cry some more.

I keep this painting in the guest room I hope he will visit:

The trans cult has appointed itself the sole authority, judge, jury and executioner, to pronounce good parent or bad parent. The only evidence it considers is whether the parent agrees with a child's delusional denial of his birth sex. All the good we have done as parents counts for nothing. The sacrifices, caretaking, discipline, tough love, gifts of time, attending school events and sports practices, training, support, working through the tough times—count for nothing. In fact, the stereotypical deadbeat dad or parent who abandoned, abused, or severely neglected the child is received with open arms and praise from the cult as long, as he accepted the child's delusion as real.

But it will all crumble under them and we will win provided we try hard enough and God assists us. I pray to the Sacred Heat of Jesus, the Immaculate Heart of Mary and those Saints who specialize in hopeless causes, Jude and Rita.

Sand Turtles Cry Out for Justice

My Lord, give me any challenge, any painful, fatal torture required to win my son's salvation, even if he does not return to us. Bring Ricky back. To You. To us. Forever. Gotta go for a walk on Your beach now. Maybe I will see this sand turtle that Ricky made on the beach when he was ten years old:

> Federal and state laws prohibit disturbance of sand turtles. These include prohibitions against "mutilation ... molestation ... and harassment" of these creatures or their eggs.
>
> I pray that this nation's rulers and princes will start to value human life as much as they do sand turtles.
>
> Until then, I cry unto You. Amen.

17

I'll Love You Forever

When my children were young, I would read to them Robert Munsch's book *Love You Forever*. The first page of the book shows a picture of a young mom rocking her baby and singing a song to him as he falls asleep. As the child grows up, the mom continues rocking her child as she sings the song of her lifelong love and devotion to him.

As a young Mom, I looked forward to my children growing older and being able to continue having a loving and affectionate relationship with each other. But the middle pages of this story have been ripped apart from us and the song has been silenced. My son is estranged from our family—because he wants us to stop seeing him as our son and instead as our daughter. We know this is but a delusion from a very confused young man. My husband and I, his parents, love him too much to join him in delusional beliefs and actions that are destroying his mind and body. As a result, we now have joined an increasing number of parents who have the unwanted label of being parents of estranged children.

During the last 2 years of navigating this sad world of estrangement, I have found that there is a prejudice against parents of estranged children. The underlying narrative is that, if a child estranges herself or himself from the parents, it is for good reason. The parents must have been abusive or dysfunctional in some manner. I understand that there are some parents who have abused their children because of mental illness, addiction or following a pattern of generational abuse. However, a big blanket is thrown over ALL parents of estranged children and an accusatory finger is pointed at them. I have read and heard that children in loving, nurturing, and stable families never leave home. This is not true and it is particularly egregious to accuse parents of being abusive when their gender confused children cut them off.

In today's culture, there is an epidemic of estrangement and a trend toward labeling others who disagree with you in any way, as "toxic". Children and young adults are told to drop relationships with anyone who disagrees with them, therefore justifying a choice to alienate those "toxic" people. At the top of the list of "toxic" people are parents. Society and progressive culture telling young people to cut their parents off, is just a lazy, easy-way-out, cop-out that only leads to more dysfunction and missing out on the joy of authentic relationships built on honesty and unconditional love—even in the midst of imperfection.

Today, mental health experts, institutions, and society at large are failing to address the reasons for estrangement between gender confused kids and their parents. There are powerful cultural, political and economic forces working to separate children from their parents. From schools, to the main stream media, to social media platforms, to mental health and medical providers to government agencies, there's a strategic plan to break down the family. Breaking down the family is easy. All these agents have to do is indoctrinate the kids in gender ideology, lead and affirm them down a transition path, keep secrets from parents, and tell kids that, if parents disagree with their lifestyle choices, they are toxic and unsafe. Dysfunction and abuse then are defined as "my parent doesn't affirm me as my preferred gender/name/pronouns therefore I'm being abused"…. or "My parent doesn't let me get puberty blockers, testosterone or estrogen, therefore I am unsafe at home". These parents are being called abusive simply for standing up for biological and scientific truth, or standing on their religious convictions. This is happening in thousands of homes today.

Another problem is that the term and concept of abuse has been redefined. When abuse is redefined to cover parents who don't agree with everything their kids do and say, it adulterates the true meaning of abuse. This fragile generation of brainwashed kids are being told exactly that. When people say that "misgendering" or not using the right pronouns and name is abuse, it makes a mockery of the true meaning of abuse and it harms those who are truly suffering at the hands of abusers.

The flip side of redefining abuse is the redefinition of love and acceptance. Gender confused kids see their parents as loving and accepting them only if the parents affirm them in their delusions that they are or that they can become the opposite sex. If parents don't go along with the gender narrative, they are told that parents don't love them and that they are not accepted. The need for parental and familial love and acceptance is so great, that these kids will seek those who will affirm them in their wrong thinking and cling to them for love and support. There are evil people who want to use and abuse these brainwashed kids, who jump in to offer "support". Sadly, well intentioned people—sometimes even family members and friends—gladly step in to fill in the shoes of those "toxic parents" and become so called glitter families. The glitter family further contributes to the estrangement between parents and child, leaving the young person unanchored to his or her roots, stability, and long-term support. The support from these glitter families is shallow and not permanent. When things fall apart for the young person, the glitter "family" disappears and parents are left to deal with the aftermath of brokenness and destruction to which the glitter "family" contributed.

I have profoundly grieved my son's absence but, as his mother, my heart breaks most for him, not for me. What makes me saddest of all is what my son is missing out during this crucial time of emerging adulthood, including the daily love and support of his family, and the family bonding, and the shared togetherness of holidays and special occasions. I know there is a hole in his heart that no amount of "glitter" friends and family can fill for him. As he was raised to know who God is and who he is as a child perfectly and wonderfully created by God, he is missing out on his mind, soul and body being aligned together in truth and material reality. What pain he must live in as he is estranged from his own self!

Even though the middle pages of our story have been ripped off, there is an ending and those pages are still there, providentially written, though I can't see them yet. I continue texting my son regularly even though it's only one way communication. There hasn't been a response from him in over a year. But I know the child we raised and what makes his heart happy, sad and the deep longings within it. I will wait for him to come back. The wait is worth it because I'll love him forever.

18

Estrangement

I wrote about the sudden departure of my daughter before. She left home in the middle of the night without warning. Some unknown person or persons picked her up and drove her to a city about eight hours away. At first, we did not know where but, with some detective work on our part and help from our local police, we were able to locate an address and contact her. She responded through the police that she didn't want any contact with us. We were told she could get a restraining order if we reached out again. They didn't tell us not to do that. They said it was up to us but that they advised us that in these types of cases, the children are coached to say what she said, "I'm doing fine. I am safe. I have a place to stay. I have food to eat. I want you to leave me alone." They advised us that this pattern language meant she was being coached and that next she would be instructed to ask for a restraining order - which would almost certainly have been granted.

We did consider driving to the new address and pleading with her in person to come home. In the end though we decided that was not likely to have any positive impact and would probably result in a restraining order. So, we didn't try to see her.

That decision was based in part on the note she left on her bed the night she departed. It said she was leaving and would not be coming back. There was a lot of anger and hate in her words, not entirely about her new gender identity but mostly. The level of animosity conveyed made us think that going to see her in person would not just be pointless but probably counterproductive. It would even further solidify her animosity towards us.

Mind you, we never had any warning she was ROGD. She presented as a typical female teenager. She had long hair. She wore only dresses and skirts, never pants. She never asked us to call her "he" or "them" except in the note where she wrote that IF she ever came back, we would have to refer to her as he/them or she would never speak to us again. The note also informed us of her new name, a gender-neutral name that is not typically used as a name but rather as an adjective. These were the first indications to us of her non-biological identification. That we were aware of.

In retrospect, there were signs that we missed. Like the flag on her wall that looked like a gay pride flag but was not quite the same. She wore strange rings, particularly one we found out later was a symbol for asexual status. She never dated, boys or girls. She was learning disabled and a bit socially awkward.

Her mother and I have always been very supportive of LGB people and causes. So, the flag we ignored. Didn't ask any question. Stupid of us, I know but we both totally supported LGB causes, so why ask about a slightly odd gay pride flag.

I recall thinking, many years ago, that adding the "T" to LGB seemed odd but if the LGB people wanted to add the "T" who was I to object. I support LGB persons and respect them and want them to have all the human rights that we all deserve. No discrimination. No oppression. So, if they, the experts on their movement, wanted to add the "T" their opinion was all that mattered to me.

Plus, the "T" was just a fraction of 1% of the population. Why worry about that, right?

What happened reminded me of the poem by Pastor Martin Niemoller titled:

FIRST THEY CAME

First they came for the Communists And I did not speak out Because I was not a Communist

Then they came for the Socialists And I did not speak out Because I was not a Socialist

Then they came for the trade unionists And I did not speak out Because I was not a trade unionist

Then they came for the Jews And I did not speak out Because I was not a Jew

Then they came for me And there was no one left to speak out for me.

I never thought to look into what the "T" was all about, much less take any action, because it wasn't going to affect me. Or so I thought. Then THEY CAME FOR MY CHILDREN.

The reason I am writing today is that the note my child left clearly communicated that she assumed that I would not support the notion that she was not female. "True that," as she would say. I would never agree that she was, or anyone was, born in the wrong body.

However, I also could tell she thought that meant that I would reject her for claiming to not be a female. That is entirely incorrect. My other daughter is also both learning disabled and a victim of the gender cult. She is out and proud as a boy. Dresses as a boy, has a boy's haircut. She can actually pass as an effeminate looking boy. The general public typically responds to her as a biological boy.

I didn't disown her. We had some very difficult and heated conversations about this but eventually just agreed to disagree. I'm still paying for college. I truly love having her home for the summer. We spend hours upon hours together talking and watching movies. I'm even helping her learn to play ice hockey. I give her advice on her clothing choices, which are all male. While not agreeing that she will ever be a boy, I'm also not insisting that she agree with me or dress how I want her to. I don't feel compelled to refer to her as "he" or use her new name. She doesn't insist on it. It's just something we agree to disagree about and then the rest of our relationship goes on as before.

We almost never discuss transitioning anymore. It is a non-issue. Unless someone in the general public is abusive to her about it. Then I defend her and advise her how to defend herself. As much as I know in my heart, she will always be a female, I still want her to thrive and have as happy a life as possible with this crazy notion that she can become a boy. Maybe someday she will outgrow this dangerous notation. She is still young with room for growth and change for sure. As far as I know, she hasn't taken any drugs or had any surgery. She says she will eventually. If she does, it won't change my love for her or my support for her. I will always be there for her in the ways a father should be.

Of course, I would do the same for my younger daughter. Feed her.

Cloth her. Make sure she got a college education. Everything. For some reason she thinks that because I still know she is and always will be a biological female, that I won't accept that she doesn't want to be one. That everything I want to give her as a father will be held hostage to her acting like a female. Nothing could be further from the truth.

She acts as if what the cult members tell her is true - that I'm the enemy and she has to cut me out or she is not one of them.

I would never stop giving her what a father should. Not because of some gender confusion thing. But because I love her. How could she not know that?

Parents on Daily Life

19

Tale of Two Losses

I recently became a widow. My husband of 35 years passed away a few months ago after his long-term chronic illness suddenly became acute. He fought this illness with determination for many years. The end seemed to come so quickly and unexpected. In addition to great loss there is still lingering shock. The grief is ever present, and the adjustment to life alone is scary and, at times, comes with intense waves of sadness and emptiness. No one really understands the loss of a spouse until it actually happens to you. I certainly didn't quite get it until it was on my own doorstep.

I am lucky to be very supported and cared about by family, friends and neighbors. This support is immensely appreciated. When friends relate stories of my husband and bring up his unique personality traits, it helps to keep his essence alive in my heart. I have our kids to share memories with. They understand exactly how hard life is now without him, because they remember how great life was with him. In other words, my grief is acknowledged and verified in every way. This makes the memory of my husband more vivid and real to me, and that is soothing. Even those who are in long term marriages who have not faced the death of their spouse seem to get what a difficult life transition it is. It is just understood by our society and for that I am grateful.

In the last several years I have suffered through another quite significant loss. It is the loss a mother feels when her child expresses a desire to have a transgender identity. For me it happened 6 years ago. Quite suddenly, with no warning signs, my autistic and socially awkward son announced he wanted to be considered a woman. After raising my child for over 15 years I had to somehow adjust to saying goodbye to my son and saying hello to my shiny new "daughter", like I was swapping sofas.

I will state right now that I totally understand that this loss is not the same as an actual physical death of a child—a thought so terrible I cannot even fathom it. I am referring to death in a metaphorical sense because the son I had is gone, hidden, and disguised. He has transformed into a caricature of an imagined self. Having your child take on a transgender identity causes a grief that takes up residence in your gut and just festers. This grief doesn't get the sunshine necessary for healing. And it is a grieving that is not at all understood by others. It is never accurately acknowledged. There is no empathetic validation. It is difficult for others to grasp this unique type of mourning.

I bonded thoroughly with my son from the day I learned I was having a boy at 17 weeks gestation. I already had two older children. My third child was born late in life for me at 41. Since I had already experienced the baby and preschool years twice, I was well aware of how fast those years slip by. A bit of midlife wisdom kicked in as well—I was determined to enjoy my 'bonus baby" as much as possible. I wanted to slow down time and just be with my sweet baby boy forever.

As most parents do, I felt intense love and connection with each of my children. My last child was particularly challenging to raise due to his autism spectrum diagnosis, but that difficulty only made us dig in deeper with compassion and understanding. Our bond with him was cemented even more. His dad and I focused on how to help him thrive in a world that often won't get him. We supported him through the heartbreaks and disappointments that are often more common and intense for a child who never really fits in.

Now I am being told by every facet of society that that bond doesn't matter. That I can just say a breezy farewell to that boy I so lovingly bonded with for over 15 years. Don't fret over losing a son. Celebrate your new daughter! I guess that bond we so lovingly worked to establish means nothing once your kid is sucked into the gender whirlwind. We as parents were responsible for every detail of our children's wellbeing for all the growing up years (which, by the way, includes the teen years just as much as the toddler years). But now we are not allowed to have an opinion regarding what is good for him. It is profoundly cruel and maddening—an arbitrary decision made by the greater world of people who don't even know him. I guess that parent/child bond matters. Until it doesn't.

Some friends and family have attempted to be supportive throughout this time, but most have with qualifiers. Many have sympathy, but reiterate that I have no control over what my son does. While this is true, these sorts of "supportive" statements just make my grief and loss harder pills to swallow. My pain at the loss of my son is always lurking just below the surface, like a heavy burden on the tip of my heart and mind all the time. There is a hesitancy to acknowledge that this loss can be almost as intense as a death. I find myself unable to articulate that feeling. And this is only half of the equation. The other side is the bonfire of insults, dismissal, and accusations from the greater world, which is totally obsessed with the gender issue. I cannot escape the topic—it's as if the headline of every paper and every public interaction is specifically design to aggravate my pain. I have been talked down to by teachers, school principals, doctors, mental health providers, politicians, talking heads on TV, and clueless acquaintances. Blaming the victim doesn't even begin to cover this phenomenon of total disregard of parents' loss when their kid is caught up in this ideology.

I have experienced two profound losses in my nuclear family. Grief over losing my husband (and 35-year marriage) will travel along a somewhat linear progression. Over time, I will take some steps forward, and a few backwards, on my road toward acceptance and adjustment. Caring and decent people will support me along the road. Grief over losing my son to the transgender craze will continue to keep me trapped in a vicious circle without escape, with no room to heal and no path forward to alleviate my suffering.

20

I Finally Decided to Tell the Truth

A letter to my daughter,

We have been so afraid of losing our connection with our daughter that we have basically been silent. I have always prided myself in being truthful with my children but, in this day and age, the truth has become a matter of opinion. "What is your truth?" young people have been asked. Like everything we hold sacred in this world, the fact that there is only 'THE truth', has been challenged and vilified.

I finally decided to tell the truth:

Please take your time in reading this. I am writing this to you because I believe it is the best way to communicate to you my feelings and my fears, my regrets, and my love—and, because I can't be silent any longer. I can't rein in my emotions enough to be able to speak with you so I am hoping that you will read this and sit with it, and hear me before you respond. Spoken words can be thrown out so quickly. I want you to really hear me when I tell you how much I truly love you.

You are the first person I think of when I wake up in the morning and as I lay my head down each night. I worry about you constantly. I would do anything and everything I can to protect you. I am afraid, and that has kept me silent. I am afraid for you. I am afraid that you will be like so many other young women that have been charmed by the transgender ideology only to wake up one day and realize it was all a terrible mistake. I feel that I am to blame for this. I wasn't there for you when you needed me the most and for that I am truly sorry. I can't begin to explain to you how desperately I want to go back and change that time, to protect you, to let you know that you are so deserving of more than I was able to give you at the time. I used to get so angry with my own mom when she would tell me that she did the best that she could. I wanted to scream, "No! You did not!" What I have so painfully come to realize is that, yes, she did.

There are swaths of time that I don't remember. I was so lost in a haze of depression and self loathing. And you, unfortunately, paid the price. I wasn't and I couldn't be the mother that you deserved. I did the best that I could though. Was it good enough? NO! It wasn't, but it was all I had.

You were a true miracle when you entered this world! We were so afraid of losing you throughout my pregnancy, but you made it! And you have been a shining light so bright since the day you were born. I've told you before and I will tell you again: There is a goodness in you that people are drawn to. I've seen it happen many times.

You ARE special!

It pains me to think of the self loathing that you have been experiencing. I look back and try to see when it all began. How did my beautiful little girl become so scared and so unsure of herself? How did I let that happen to her? Why didn't I see the signs and nip it in the bud? Where was I when you were struggling? You told me once that, when you hit puberty, you felt so uncomfortable in your body. You questioned why everyone (boys and girls alike), couldn't just continue to look the same? The answer is simple. Because that is what happens when you grow up. You were always going to become a woman, with the incredible gift of being able to carry another human life in your body. It is the most amazing gift, to be able carry a life inside of ourselves, a part of us and a part of the person that we love and have chosen as our partner in life. Because that is what happens when you grow up. You become a woman—with the God given gift of being able to carry another human life in your body.

Unfortunately, you have been led to believe that the uncomfortable feelings of going through puberty means you are transgender and that you were born in the wrong body. First of all, I don't believe that God makes mistakes. Secondly, talk to any grown woman and they will tell you that those terrifying feelings when you change from a little girl into a woman are completely normal. Becoming a woman is scary! Sex is scary! Especially today. Young children are being exposed to pornographic materials that they are unable to understand, let alone wrap their minds around. I know that you've seen this firsthand in the children that you care for every day.

I often ask myself, "What were you exposed to? What did you see that left its mark on you?" I know from talking to other parents, and also hearing from young women who have detransitioned, that what they saw on different websites and on social media platforms scared the hell out of them. Is that what happened to you? Dad and I both failed you. We should have protected you from the internet, but we were naive at best.

Negligent is more like it. I am so truly sorry!

Daddy and I cannot stop you from destroying your body. And that is what it is. Transgender medicine is the destruction of a perfect and healthy body. You WILL become a patient for life if you decide to medically transition. There are so many young women like you who have destroyed their bodies; only to come to regret their decisions once they have removed their perfectly healthy breasts, altered their voices, lost their hair to male pattern baldness, grown an Adam's apple, increased their risk of cancer and heart disease, grown facial hair, and ultimately sterilized themselves.

The transgender cult is destroying families. And yes, it is a cult. And you are a victim of that indoctrination. Parents are vilified if they don't automatically affirm and participate in the lie that their children have been born into the wrong bodies.

But I can't be silent any longer. I love you too much. I have to tell you the truth. I think that you are making a terrible mistake. One that you will come to ultimately regret. I think that you would be so much happier if you could find peace in accepting yourself as you are. A beautiful young woman! You will never be a man. It is physically impossible. You will always be pretending, hiding, living a lie. It will be painful because it is never something you can actually achieve. I believe that if you allowed yourself, opened up yourself, to accepting and loving the beautiful body that God has given you, that you will eventually find peace. You ARE female. You ARE a woman. What is keeping you from truly accepting yourself? I want you to think about that.

I have attached some links that I would like you to share with you.

There are videos and stories from many young women much like yourself. Please take your time and open up your mind to the possibility that you may have been misled. That you are actually perfect just the way you are. Just the way God made you.

I love you!

Mom

It's time we take back the truth!!

21

Relationship as Guru

Our closest relationships are often our greatest teachers. I am finding the truth of that in my marriage now, as my wife and I struggle to stay connected and parent through vastly differing perspectives on the current gender narrative. I often find myself feeling angry and withdrawn because of our widely differing opinions about navigating the gender landscape.

We used to share a similar perspective, my wife and I, several years ago. There was a time when I happily offered up my pronouns (she/her, I am a "cis"-woman married to a "cis"-woman) and wondered what gender another person might be, no matter how feminine or masculine their outer appearance. "You just can't know what anyone's pronouns or genders are these days." I would say with a shrug and a knowing look to my friends and partner who shared my inability to connect to the reality of what was right in front of us.

Fast forward a few years, and I have seen the damage that the current gender cult is wreaking on our children and families. Unfortunately, my wife is still caught in the cult. And now our 8 year old son is playing with they/them pronouns and wanting to use the girls' dressing room to change during dance recitals. Just trying to discuss this seemingly minor (minor in the sense that he is not talking about "being" a girl or "born in the wrong body" or any of the other nightmares that so many parents are contending with) situation leads to triggered blow ups and unproductive arguments.

It all started innocently enough. When our son was maybe two years old, he enjoyed trying on his older sister's dresses. Both my wife and I thought it was cute. He didn't play with dolls, and he wasn't otherwise effeminate. He loved, and still loves, trucks and running and climbing and playing with other boys and plenty of stereotypically "boy" activities.

I fully support any person, adult or child, expressing themselves through their clothing and hair and makeup. Boys wearing dresses? Great. Boyish girls, aka tomboys? Awesome. I was one when I was younger, and still am fairly tomboyish as a grown woman. Adult men or women wanting to take hormones and/or have the many surgeries available to them to live more convincingly as the opposite sex if that's what feels right to them? Go for it!

But there are too many people who would see my son in a dress and say "Oh, you must be a girl. Let's fix that!" and set him on a path that could permanently damage his health, mutilate his sexual organs, sterilize him and prevent him from possibly ever having an orgasm. I could tell teachers, counselors, friends, and other parents to take a hike and keep their ridiculous agendas away from my son. But what do you do when it's your own spouse who may promote these ideas? She hasn't yet, but she is fully captured and it wouldn't surprise me if it does go down that road someday.

These days my son likes to wear dresses, although not all the time and not in public. His sister is fiercely protective of him and his enjoyment of wearing dresses. And already, although I have tried to be completely neutral in the way I talk about gender and pronouns and all the aspects that I disagree with in the current radically leftist progressive gender ideology, they both know that I disagree with it all and avoid the topic with me. My son apparently waits for me to leave the house for work in the morning to wear a dress and begs his other mom not to tell me about it. My daughter is sad that I don't support her little brother in his exploration of his "true self". She's reading books about pride and transgender history that tell her men can be pregnant, and women can have penises. And my wife fully supports and encourages this magical thinking.

A hill I will die on is that only women can be pregnant, transwomen are men (and don't belong in women's or girls' spaces), men have penises and women have vaginas, and to say otherwise is misogynistic and regressive.

In so many other ways my relationship with my children is amazing. I say yes to spending time with them in any way they want. We laugh and play games together and watch movies and sometimes when I look at them I love them so much it takes my breath away.

My relationship with my wife, on the other hand, is strained and tense. She thinks I'm queerphobic, and I think she's promoting a dangerous form of magical thinking that could have severely damaging consequences for our children. We are constantly tiptoeing around the gender elephant in the room. We live in a very small town where my perspective is definitely in the minority, so I have to be careful about what I say so I'm not further ostracized from my community.

I hate what the gender narrative is doing to our families, children and communities. Trying to talk to my children and wife about these highly charged topics is beyond challenging. But I can't and won't let this insane ideology tear my family apart. I have to find a way to bridge the gap. Remembering that my closest relationships can be my greatest teachers and opportunity to learn and grow helps. It's all a work in process, and I fail miserably at seeing the situation as a learning opportunity more than I care to admit. I love my family, and I will do everything in my power to keep us together and stay connected to the ones I love, while staying true to my perspective. Staying together and connected in loving and supportive relationships is perhaps the greatest "F*** you" to the current system trying to tear us apart.

22

You Took My Joy and I Want It Back

I watched my daughter perform with her chorale group last night. She has always had a naturally beautiful voice and loves to sing. She saw me as I was looking for a seat and asked to see the program. She said "Dad's going to be mad—I'm with the tenors".

Her name—as it has been for a year—was a first initial (a reluctant compromise). She whispered "I'm sorry". I hugged her. I told her to have fun and not worry about it, but it was I who spent the entire performance anxiously waiting for my husband to notice her standing with the boys. She was the closest one to the girls because she also sang alto, but she was clearly standing with the boys. He noticed, about halfway through, and asked to see the program.

He spent the rest of the show still and holding his heart. He barely applauded. In the past, he has walked out of similar situations, not to be cruel but as means of self preservation. This was growth in managing his feelings, but it is painful to watch. As I watched our daughter sing, laugh, and light up the stage (as she has since she was four whether it was tapping around in a pink tutu and a top hat or leaping across the room with a group of girls in lemony leotards), I became overwhelmed with emotion.

Gender Ideology has robbed us of the joy we once felt in moments like these. It has replaced excitement and pride with anger, fear, confusion, and helplessness. I am able to put that aside, rise above and enjoy the moment of watching my beautiful daughter singing joyfully.

I am able to rise above the fact that she is the only girl on stage with short hair in a men's button down and dress shoes because I understand why she is doing that. I did that, too. I am able to rise above the use of the initial, despite the months we spent excitedly poring over baby names to find the perfect one. I did that, too. I am able to rise above the well meaning parents calling her the male version of her name because I know that they are unaware of the implications. I did that, too, before I knew better.

My husband cannot rise above any of it. He plunges into a pit of rage and despair and begins plotting his next move to sue the school or move to another country. He becomes bitter and obsessed and is prone to sending emails to the school with a lot of raw feeling but no context and spotty punctuation. Then I have to do damage control and try to justify his slightly accusatory tone and sometimes harsh words. They don't understand. They haven't been living this for almost four years. They see a happy, thriving student who is going off to college in the Fall. They don't see the looming shadow of the Gender Monster waiting in the wings for a moment of opportunity. We see it everywhere, and it's hard to differentiate between what is a sign of things to come and what is simply normal teenage behavior.

So, we are constantly doing risk assessments and analysis of everything she does, quietly questioning the meaning behind the black/red/green/blue nail polish and the significance of a moment where she calls herself "girlfriend" in passing. Is she dating her girlfriend as a girl or a boy? Was that social media post of her wearing red lipstick a sign? She is so clearly feminine and naturally gorgeous that even with baggy clothes, a lowered voice, and a lanky walk, she's not fooling anyone.

Maybe—hopefully—not even herself. She will be eighteen soon. In the meantime, we can only rise above and enjoy these last few months before she goes to college. She has all the information—specifically the effect that testosterone will have on her voice. She has all the information. That is all we can do.

23

The Affirmer at Home

For those of us living the nightmare, a lot of thought goes into trying to understand how the medical community could be doing what they're doing to young people. How does someone who has supposedly dedicated their life to helping and healing others cause such horrific harm—not blindly, or under duress, but with pride and hubris? This question has been dissected, and I suspect the theories are dead on—a combination of the classic god complex; a gross misunderstanding of the difference between championing the rights of homosexuals and those claiming a gender identity; the attraction of being a virtuous hero delivering "life-saving," medical care to The Most Marginalized™ population in all of human history; the ego boost from hearing desperate teenagers express their gratitude; the self-congratulatory relief at stopping yet another suicide; and the personal SJW cred that comes along with all of it (plus the "I believed this was evidence-based, even though I'm supposed to be an 'expert' and should have done the research myself because this is so obviously insane" excuse).

But what about everyone else?

Unfortunately, I have the distinct displeasure of being married to an affirming spouse, which means I have a birds-eye view of the opposition. Every day. Every. Single. Day.

Early on, when our kid first made his big, stupid announcement, and we were equally stupid in our response, we were at least aligned. Both concerned and supportive of the "idea" of a trans kid, but skeptical that we had such a rare bird, given the lack of any childhood expression of gender distress. Ambiguity, maybe, but not distress. Neither of us wanted our kid to rush into medical transition (or our ignorant and naïve impressions of it). Neither felt comfortable with a rush to blockers, which we knew the bare minimum about, until our kid started really falling apart. A year past a serious suicide attempt, hospitalization, and 4 months of intensive outpatient therapy (no trans), we were too frightened and traumatized to face the risk of another suicide attempt, so we consented to the absolutely safe and reversible clock-stopper of puberty blockers and awaited the thoughtful, methodical pondering about the meaning of his gender distress that our depressed, anxious, uncommunicative, oppositional 14-year-old would never do. Who would have guessed.

My husband was relieved. I felt a little ill. Something wasn't right. I knew instinctively that what was being done to our kid was wrong. None of it made sense. I jumped into the rabbit hole that pretty much every non-affirming parent heads down. There should be a big welcome sign: "You're right! And you're not crazy! But you will be!"

I read endlessly, looking for proof or answers or something to make it make sense. My husband binged on trans TikTok. I stalled on injection appointments. My husband went in person to schedule them. I searched endlessly for a non-affirming therapist—not one of the five "approved gender therapists" Kaiser recommended. My husband bought our kid a waist trainer and women's underwear.

I tried. Really, I did. I scheduled calls with the big names, hoping to get clarity on what was happening delivered by an authoritative (but kind!) voice. We'd come away feeling united, but within a few weeks, the division would creep back in between us. Nothing stuck. I sent him article after article, podcast after podcast. He stopped acknowledging them. And then it got worse.

I became the one thing standing in the way of our kid starting hormones. I was suddenly a TERF and a transphobe. I'd magically transformed from a lifelong liberal to an ignorant, hateful, right-wing bigot. Nothing I said changed my husband's belief. He was deep in it, overtaken by whatever this mind virus/cult thing is.

Sure, it's not fun being the subject of scorn in your own home, or being unable to talk about anything that even vaguely suggests that it's not just me and a bunch of rabid MAGA yahoos who have issues with the whole Affirmative Care business, or having to say our son's new girl name a thousand times in conversations with my husband to avoid saying "he" or "him" and getting "The Scowl," or worse feeling compelled to say "she" and feeling like I'm in Crazytown, or knowing that the person I have committed to, for better or worse, isn't capable of basic critical thinking skills, at least not about this. But there is an upside, which in simplest terms is, "Know thine enemy."

We don't really talk about gender (although once every month or two we fight about it), and while I think my husband is about 70% sure hormones would be a mistake for our kid, he still believes in the "TruTrans" mythology and the social justice narrative that goes with it. I get no shortage of "white privilege" commentary and goading about whatever dumb, gross thing Marjorie Taylor Green has done, my husband checking to see if I will take this as a personal slight. All of this makes him the ideal subject for my effort to understand the affirming mind. I'm pretty sure my husband would be put off if I asked him to participate in my own private focus group, where I could pepper him with questions like, "Is there anything anyone could say or show you that would change your viewpoint on whether it is ever appropriate to medically transition anyone other than a mentally stable, mature adult and only as a last resort?" Or, "What is a woman?" But I understand what motivates and influences him and can extrapolate to the standard issue trans believer.

1. Believers need to be seen as good people. They may not trust that their own thoughts are good, so they must adhere to the prevailing social mores. Going against the cultural grain would put them at risk of being bad people because they trust the opinions of others over their own. To believe that the aligned masses are at best wrong, and at worst responsible for terrible harm, would be too destabilizing.

2. Believers put tremendous trust in "experts," having somehow avoided comprehending the realities of medical care gone bad, and the benefit of sowing and maintaining division for those who want power and profit, be they politicians or purveyors of mainstream media or your everyday, basic human rights organization.

3. Being Kind and virtuous is, in the minds of believers, what sets them apart from the others. Being Kind means sacrificing for those who are disadvantaged, which would be great if what you were sacrificing didn't always take zero actual effort, truly benefitted the disadvantaged,

and wasn't typically someone else's to begin with (for instance, the sex-based rights of females).

4. Believers uphold the idea that anyone who is in the minority, no matter how influential, is disadvantaged, so any narrative that contradicts this idea must be a nefarious, hateful lie. Anything else is not Being Kind, so believers cannot only not accept the narrative, they can't accept the by-association nefarious, hateful messenger, either.

5. On the flipside, believers must affirm information and actions that support the narrative of the Most Marginalized™ population in all of human history, no matter how absurd, because to challenge or doubt this group is not Being Kind.

6. Believers greatly value the idea of community, often more so than actual participation. Once a believer has established themselves firmly and safely in the believer community, they cannot easily extract themselves. To do so would be to not only admit to a catastrophic level of uncritical thought, but, more importantly, lead to the loss of likely everyone in their social circle. The easier and safer route is to avoid all critical thought whatsoever and to tell everyone that trans kids who've had the misfortune to be born into Republican and/or religious families are almost uniformly being kicked out of their homes for finally (and bravely/stunningly) accepting their authentic selves; that it is good to lie to a child, telling them that they can magically become something they're not and that doing so won't mean a lifetime of them in turn lying to everyone they come into contact with; that removing healthy body parts and introducing damage to an otherwise healthy body is medical care; and that men belong in women's sports and bathrooms.

While these points explain the basic motivations, they don't account for the level of anger and indignation I see around this topic—not just from my husband, but from pretty much all true believers I encounter. The additional layer that drives the torches and pitchforks mentality is tribalism. Liberal Democrats cannot on principle agree with anything supported by Republicans. It makes them uncomfortable. Because the media has successfully made this "medical problem" (by which I mean the problem with the medical model, not the gender distress) a political issue, even considering ideas that are characterized as "right wing" feels bad. Finding any common ground with a conservative makes you magically aligned with everything anathema to your core being and, more importantly, to your tribe. This explains the rageful accusations of "Transphobe! Bigot!" on Twitter and the absolute refusal to do more than glance at the title of references provided to back up a point. You may as well have asked them to review the The Protocols of the Elders of Zion. That's how incomprehensible it is that there could be anything even approaching reason from someone who must, despite any evidence, be a member of the inhumane, incoherent, sub-human Right. The risk that they might find reason and truth and points of agreement is too high. Rational, evidence-based debate isn't tolerable, not because they feel so solidly assured in their contention, but because they're afraid of getting dirty by finding common ground.

Even with my ongoing, intensive home research project studying my husband for signs of enlightenment, I haven't developed a method for reaching the believer. And that is truly distressing, because I have faith that eventually, through lawsuits or self-reflection and shame (but mostly lawsuits), the physicians will stop transitioning minors and will become less enthusiastic about transitioning others as well. I have faith that through vocal parent pressure and the understanding that school staff are not qualified to initiate or manage significant psychological interventions, schools will stop socially transitioning students and hiding a child's gender identity from their parents. I have faith that eventually the brutal reality of detransition will force politicians to quietly stop the affirming narrative, hoping that no one will remember (spoiler alert: we will). But I don't have faith that the general affirming public, which unfortunately includes my husband, will let go of their ill-informed reality anytime soon and, until that happens, this will never truly end.

24

Fighting for Our Son's Life . . . and Our Own

14 1/2 years ago, I met a man and fell in love with him. Like so many others, we combined our two divorced families into one. At that time, he brought in his 4 year old son, LJ, and I brought my 3 and 1 1/2 year old sons, Ace and Colt. We never thought in a million years that we would go through what we've been through. How the hell our marriage even survived is a mystery to us both. We weren't bent, we were broken. We've been broken many times and mended just as many.

Although LJ is technically my step-son, he became my son. His biological mom has been in and out of his life, when it's convenient for her, since he was two. When she would come back into his life, she would wreak havoc on his mental and emotional health. Ace and Colt had a similar relationship with their biological dad—however they experienced physical abuse as well, and Ace was sexually abused. It's a long story, but we didn't know about the physical abuse for years and only recently learned about the sexual abuse Ace endured.

It's important to note that LJ was diagnosed with Social Communication Disorder (SCD) when he was 11. If he were to be tested now (and he will be retested soon), he would be considered high functioning autistic. In addition, he has always been smaller than the other kids. He was born blue (not breathing) and had physical issues up until his toddler years that we think stunted his growth for a while. It is also important to note that Ace was diagnosed as bipolar for a very long time. Nothing ever worked to help his moods. We recently discovered the sexual abuse and now we know that it is actually PTSD. It's also important to note that Colt is gay. We are fully accepting of his preference for men. LJ is now 19, almost 20, Ace is 17, and Colt is 16.

LJ started high school five years ago. He had always had social issues (the SCD), but it was just enough to make him seem a little weird. He was picked on occasionally, but not often. He had a handful of good friends and a girlfriend that he had been with for a year. He had also just completed his first summer job. Even though he lived with the issues from Ace's mood disorder (which were severe), he was happy. He smiled and laughed all the time. He was so damn proud of himself for working all summer and making his own money. He had built up biceps and abs and he LOVED that, though he might be small, now he was mighty! Our sweet little science loving, video game playing, superhero worshipping nerd was growing up. We were proud of him. He was starting high school and becoming a good man.

A series of unfortunate events took place in the time frame of 6 months. LJ's grandfather (my husband's step-dad) passed away. LJ and his grandfather were best friends. He grieved for his grandfather. LJ became different after his grandfather's passing. I think he felt abandoned by his grandfather. I also think he felt alone in his grief because the rest of us did not mourn the way he did.

A few months later, LJ's bio-mom came back into his life. Actually, it was his half-brother that reached out to us and the bio-mom just kind of followed the half-brother's lead. That family had been completely out of touch with LJ for 4 years. We thought he was mature enough to make the decision of whether he wanted to contact his other family. He chose to do so.

Immediately, the oppositional parenting started. His other family would tell him the exact opposite of what we would. It caused a lot of problems. The problem was that LJ knew the things his bio-mom had done, or hadn't done, when he was little. But, he wanted so badly for her to be the mother he wanted that he ignored that. They told him I was to blame for his troubles and he bought into it. It was a terrible situation that began to tear our family limb from limb.

Then, only a few months after that, after a year and a half relationship, LJ's girlfriend broke up with him. He was devastated. She told him that they would remain friends and he believed her. Those of us who have had our hearts broken before know that that almost never happens. Since most of his friends were mutual friends of hers, he really didn't have many people to hang out with anymore.

We tried to help him move on with his life. But, he still didn't laugh nearly as much as he used to and he didn't smile nearly as often. Then, he made some new friends. They accepted him and tried to help him with his break up. We had no idea what was happening socially concerning the Trans community, so we never thought twice about his new friends mostly being LGBTQ.

About a month later, I noticed LJ was wearing a sports bra. It was then that he told us that he wanted to be a girl. We told him that that was not acceptable. We explained to him that real transgenderism is incredibly rare and that you can't just change your gender because you want to. He told us that being a boy was just too hard. We didn't accept this and told him he would not be transitioning.

LJ's sophomore year started. His brother, Ace, was now a freshman in high school. He had been doing amazing with his behavior by this point and we had high hopes for him having a great school year. LJ's friends were secretly taking females clothes to him to change into when he got to school and out of when school was over so we wouldn't know. The school allowed this. The school also started calling LJ by his preferred name and pronouns. The other kids in school didn't say anything to LJ about his dressing like a girl. They knew that that's how you ended up on social media as a transphobe. So, they went after Ace. Ace was teased relentlessly about his older brother dressing like a girl. With his mental issues, this quickly turned into anger and Ace started lashing out. He asked LJ to help and defend him. LJ refused. He called Ace a transphobe for not defending him and abandoned his brother to the bullies.

We noticed that LJ was going to feminist websites, Trans websites, and started talking to random people online and giving them personal information. He even started catfishing men in various places telling them he was a girl and talking to them about very explicit sexual things. After numerous warnings, blocking, and groundings from his phone and laptop, we ended up taking away both permanently. He hated us for it. His friends and other family told him that we were just being controlling and that we didn't really know him. He turned against us. He completely demolished his relationship with me. He was so mean and hurtful that I couldn't look at him without getting angry and hurt. He constantly lied to his dad (who took over the bulk of his parenting at that point) and refused to do what he was told.

Then, the pandemic happened. This was what broke LJ. He couldn't go to school and didn't get to see his other family much because they were afraid of getting sick. He was stuck at home with the brother and parents he hated. He was only able to talk to his friends on our home phone and it had to be in our presence so we knew he wasn't talking to some random person about sexually explicit things. He was spiraling into depression. We tried a couple different therapists for him, but they were all gender affirming and made everything so much worse. LJ kept saying that we hated him because we accepted Colt as gay, but not him as a female. We stopped the therapy after that.

Ace asked to be home schooled because he couldn't deal with all the bullying anymore. Colt didn't want to deal with it, as he would have been going into that high school soon, so they both ended up being home schooled. LJ stayed in public school. He was dressing as a female full time at this point. We were so exhausted, hurt, and depressed that we just didn't even refute it anymore. He and I hardly spoke and the majority of the stuff he spoke to my husband about was all lies anyway. And, LJ's depression continued to get worse.

LJ spent the summer after his junior year with his bio-mom. He was 18 years old by that point, so we really couldn't say anything. My husband made LJ promise that he wasn't going to move out and that he would come home and finish his senior year of school. He came back home for two weeks, was even more depressed, and moved in with his half-brother after that. It was a plan that they set in motion over the summer. I've seen my husband cry a handful of times in 14 1/2 years. That night, I held him as he sobbed for our son and cried with him. We had failed. And we were lost.

LJ moved in with his half-brother. He did finish out his senior year, but because he had to work to try and supplement bills, his grades plummeted and he ruined his chances of going to a prestigious four year college. He was able to start estrogen with only one online visit to a therapist. Before LJ finished his senior year, his brother told him that he was moving and that LJ would have to find his own place. LJ had no real life experience at this point. That other family that said they understood him and wanted to be there for him abandoned him, yet again, and he had nowhere to go.

LJ ended up moving in with his grandmother (my Mother-in-law) after high school. After 6 months of living with his grandmother, and her even calling him by his preferred name and pronouns, she deemed that he was just too depressed for her to handle and told him he needed to move home.

While LJ was gone, my husband and I started trying to put our family back together. Unfortunately, Ace couldn't overcome his trauma, broke the law, and wound up in jail. He is still there. Colt is in therapy for the trauma he has been through and is starting to do much better. My husband and I are still in therapy. We still have work to do, but we are getting there. Thanks to our working on healing ourselves, we were able to make a plan for LJ to come home. And, he did come home.

We compromised with him. We call him by his initials, LJ, but will not use female pronouns and do our best to avoid pronoun use altogether. He is required to go to therapy once a week (that we pay for) and it is a therapist that specializes in trauma that is not gender affirming. He happily goes every week. He will also be starting at the community college in the fall. We bought him a car (in my name, not his until he gets a grip on his depression).

He still presents as a female. He knows that we don't agree with his transitioning and that we will never support it. But, he was also able to sit down and listen to our reasons. His depression is slowly getting better. I've seen my son smile and laugh a lot since he has been home.

So, why did I tell you this long story? So you might be able to learn. So someone might see this and recognize something in their life and try to fix it. What I've told you is only a very small fraction of everything that happened. If I told you all of it, you'd be on chapter 84 of my book by now. But, people need to know. People need to hear what parents are going through. And, not just parents, but the siblings and other family members.

My son wants to transition because he is afraid of dealing with his trauma. He has abandonment issues, difficulty fitting in (the SCD/autism), and has witnessed sexual assault (long story) and that caused him to hate sex and male body parts. This stuff is difficult for children to work through. They think it's easier to just change who they are and leave the past in the past. What they don't understand is that the past never goes away and it will catch up with you.

Even though we are in a better place, we are still watching our son destroy himself. He is fighting his body's natural processes, so he is always sick. He always has a stomachache, headache, or has no appetite. He battles depressive episodes. He is so skinny that he looks malnourished (probably is). It scares me. But, we've just got to keep trying.

And, to those who read this that are on the other side of this transgender movement, those who promote it, those who affirm it: how dare you! How dare you make parents watch helplessly as you take our children from us and then tell us we are horrible people. How dare you say that you know my child better than I do. The child that I raised. How dare you come in and tell my child at one of the most impressionable ages of their lives that I don't know him. YOU don't know him. No one loves my child as much as I do. Because of people like you, we ended up fighting for our son's life and fighting for our own. So take your transgender bullshit and shove it.

25

Malevolent Benevolence

My breath still catches and my stomach still lurches as I remember the betrayal.

It's 9 AM Eastern time, 7 AM for my daughter at college out west. It's not an unusual time for her to call, as, like me, she is an early riser. Yet, my maternal radar sounds internally as I see the caller ID.

"Hi, Sweetie!!!" I say in the impossibly upbeat voice that I've cultivated over the years to drown out the silently trumpeting ROGD elephant in the room.

"Are you planning on suing my school?" She asks without preamble in a voice opposite mine—cold, monotone, and seething.

"What?" I gasp.

"Someone told me that you are planning on suing my school."

"I don't understand…That makes no sense…What???" But I'm starting to comprehend.

"I heard that you've been talking about me in book club and want to sue my school's health center."

There it is. My mind is reeling, but somehow I stay composed enough to answer:

"Yes, I do talk about you in book club. We are a group of mothers who discuss books, of course, but even more, we share our love for, pride in, and, most importantly, our worries about our children. I have explained to the group of women whom I thought I could trust to hear me, understand me, and protect my confidence, what I have learned about gender ideology and what I fear you might do to yourself, and how easy it is on college campuses and at Planned Parenthood to get testosterone. But I have never indicated or even thought that I might sue your school. You know me, I am not litigious, and I believe you haven't even been prescribed anything by them, so how does this make sense?"

That is almost verbatim what I said. I was able to respond like that because for the last six years, I have been constantly on guard for any discussion about, disagreement over, and crisis around my daughter's (ROGD) trans identity.

Her anger deflates, as I think she believes me and deep down knows that all I want is for her to be okay. I manage to learn a bit about the distressing game of telephone that began in book club. A member's best friend is the mother of one of my daughter's good friends who, like most of her generation, is a staunch LGBTQI+++++ "supporter" (which I put in quotation marks not to be snarky, but to highlight how not questioning someone's sudden transgender identity and desperation for body modification might be the opposite of supportive). This fellow reader could not "sit" with what I was saying and felt that my daughter needed to be protected, so she told her friend who told my daughter's friend who told my daughter. Who then called me.

These mothers could not "sit" with my worry that my child might take testosterone and damage her body. They could not "sit" with my worry that my child would amputate her two healthy breasts from which throughout a prolonged period of childhood she pretended to nurse dozens of her beloved cat stuffed animals. (Wait, maybe she's a furry? Should I get a litter box for her dorm room? How the &^%* can I actually have any humor left at all?).

In ensuing conversations I had with both of these women, I stayed calm and tried to convey that I knew they were coming from a place of caring, but that they actually really could not comprehend (and I told them I was happy for them because it meant that they do not have a loved one caught in this generation's answer to self hatred, uncertainty, and fear of growing up; see "Anorexia") what has happened to my daughter. "But," they both exclaimed, "You had an Obama sticker on your car!" "But," they both gushed, "Your daughter is one of the most confident, happy, strong kids we know!" I tried to describe the tangle of self harm wounds she hid under long sleeves, the former plunge into self starvation, the countless nights I spent hours helping her fall asleep as she sobbed uncontrollably, often unable to put anything into words, but sometimes able to whisper, "I'll never look like you, Mommy, or Violet or Emma (very tall, thin friends from her all girls middle school).

No moment of pause occurred for these two warrior women braced to combat my transphobia and child abuse. "So, do you believe anyone is actually trans?" "So, what about being gay?" I tried to explain how homophobic and misogynistic the surge in trans identity in today's youth is, referencing the LGB Alliance's work, the concept of "transing away the gay," how my daughter is passionately in love with another young woman, and that it breaks my heart that they project to the world a heterosexual relationship.

I told them that I felt deeply hurt by the breach of the sanctity of personal conversations in book club and by their resistance to my painful and clear knowledge of what has happened to my own child. But more importantly, I beseeched them to understand that I fear for all the young women, and growing numbers of boys, too, who are being led down harmful paths by well-meaning but misguided and ill-informed "support and affirmation," which I now call Malevolent Benevolence. I shared some more resources (select Gender: A Wider Lens episodes, the "Dysphoric: Fleeing Womanhood Like a House on Fire" documentary, the books by Shrier, Joyce, Stock, and Selin-Davis) which one of them said she probably wouldn't have the time to delve into but didn't really need to since she would never change her mind about supporting "what people know to be true of themselves."

My voice hoarse and my heart broken, I told them both that I was not angry about their betrayal. I told them that I understood they thought they were right and noble and supportive. I told them that if they ever reflect on anything I shared and have a moment when the ideological house of cards starts to fall and reveals the actual harm that the People Behind the Curtain - the activists, surgeons, endocrinologists, captured therapists, pediatricians, teachers, and, most directly, the Glitter Moms like them - are actually doing, I would be ready and willing to resume the conversation.

26

The Gender Party

"The party told you to reject the evidence of your eyes and ears. It was their final, most essential command."-George Orwell 1984

So, you aren't a member of the gender party. At least you don't think you are. You haven't really considered it. You've had no time. Your days were spent working and raising your family. You weren't even sure it was a real party and it had never meant anything to you any way. After all, you consider yourself liberal, at the very least moderate, and don't want to harm the most vulnerable members of society. If you have ever thought about gender ideology, you might have said, "What's the big deal? It isn't harming anyone. Adults should be free to live as they please." You're a big tent person and proud of it.

Then the most shocking, unbelievable thing happens. Out of the blue, your child announces that they aren't their biological sex any longer. They are now magically, 100% the other sex. And they assure you that there is nothing, absolutely nothing, you will ever be able to do to change their mind. And should you try, your child will remove you from their life.

This is when you discover, although you aren't a member, the gender party has a hold on many facets your life—schools, the medical profession, the mental health community, the mainstream media. Worse yet, if you do not pledge fealty, you may lose your child, your job and your friends and family. Welcome to the party.

You will soon discover that the gender party regards your child, whatever their age, as a fully formed adult who know what they want for themselves and will never waiver in this belief. This wouldn't be so bad if it was just an idea, a belief with no consequences. But the gender party demands that your children be medicalized and then perhaps, move on to surgery. Sometimes immediately. Not after a year of waiting or months of therapy, but right now - the minute your child has decided they are "trapped in the wrong body". The only real thing now is their belief.

The gender party controls everyone and everything. They don't need to provide any evidence that what they do is good. There is no debate. It is a fact because the party deems it so. Everyone must believe this. The gender party is a force for good, lifesaving even. And woe to those who ask for a shred of evidence or express a hint of doubt. The gender party will try to ruin you and take away the one thing you are trying to protect, your child.

Now that your child is in the gender party- a fresh, wide-eyed recruit- you learn that the people who you thought knew you and your child best are card carrying, dues paying members of the gender party. They don't understand your doubts. Because if your child says they are another sex-they are! That's how this works.

You will learn that those who succeed in escaping the gender party need to act early and sometimes take radical action. But, sigh, you have other children and a job and so many things that make it impossible to change your entire life and move some place (where?!) that the gender party hasn't taken hold. If your child is already of legal age, you have almost no leverage. And you realize that if you dare to question your adult child's new identity (an identity that may have been formed in just a few months by goggling their questions and talking to strangers online), you may be cut off. The gender party tells all its members that anyone who doesn't believe absolutely in the gender religion must be exiled cut out of your child's life. This seems cultish to you, but you say nothing to avoid charges of heresy.

People you thought would have your back -maybe your mother or your brother, that amazing co-worker, your best friend - are now questioning you. They talk to each other and agree that your child must be affirmed. And that surely you will come to see the gender party knows best. You can understand that some of them are fearful of retaliation by the gender party. They cannot take the chance and stand by your side, but you remain horrified by the betrayal. You have nowhere to turn with your anger and fear. You are alone.

And then a "helpful" person sends a text or email accusing you of being a bigot, a TERF, a transphobe, a bad parent. Or, the ultimate insult, they imply that you would rather have a dead kid than a trans kid. In their eyes, you are a monster. There is no chance to explain that your child might be gay or on the autism spectrum or suffer from severe anxiety or trauma. None of which have anything to do with becoming the other sex. None of these matters. The gender party has the answer for every mental anguish and social problem that ever existed. Not just *the* answer but the *only* answer.

You thought you knew your kid. You were there for everything, every tear, every problem over the years. But apparently, you knew nothing. Their special inner feeling, their new identity, which they confirm by searching the internet and is further affirmed in chat rooms and video game, is now all that matters. Teachers who know them for one semester or a few months of school, along with thirty other kids, know your child best. They withhold your child's new name and identity because your child must be protected from you at all costs. You have changed from being the one person who put your child's welfare and happiness above all else to becoming your child's greatest enemy.

The doctors and therapists, you soon learn, are the most fervent believers in the gender party. They have no questions for you, or your child save one—how do you identify? However your child responds at this moment is the only truth, no matter the consequences of the medical treatments which they happily prescribe on the first visit. Your kid will give "informed consent", a kid that doesn't ever think of themselves at age 30 or 40 and what it might be to live for decades pretending to be the opposite sex. And, of course, they are not considering that they may want children someday. Children aren't thinking of having children. But the gender party can make sure they never do.

But what about biology you ask. Must we relearn everything you were ever taught about biology and history? Clownfish are the answer. Intersex people are cited to prove that you can change sex. But you know that your child isn't a clownfish and is not intersex.

You learn that your child was "assigned" a sex at birth. The nurses and doctors just decided for reasons unknown and possibly nefarious, what gender your child was. The DNA tests and ultrasounds are wrong as well, as science no longer exists. You learn there are 47 genders and that genders can change all the time. Sex is dead. It has no meaning and is just used as an excuse to discriminate against trans people and all the other-gendered people.

You soon discover that yes, even the Holocaust was the source of suffering for no, not the Jewish people, but primarily transgender people. And of course, you are probably a Nazi yourself if you think differently.

Historical figures, mostly women it seems, are also now being reclaimed with their rightful trans identity. Joan of Arc, Louisa May Alcott were not feminist heroes but transmen.

Transwomen are literally women you learn. That's it. A fact. Women now have penises. Women are now committing rape and murder at higher rates than ever recorded throughout history.

Transwomen are also miraculously better at sports than natal women for reasons no one can discern. When competing against women, now known as uterus havers, transwomen win all the competitions and titles. Any "cis" women objecting to this are just sore losers. "Cis" is the new label you must go by if you don't despise the body you were born with and want to alter it. You are told this is a great privilege to be "cis" and that transwomen suffer much more than any cis woman ever could or ever will, no matter what has happened to you as a "cis" woman.

You go underground. You join groups that vet members. Here you can speak freely because all members know what you are going through and share your horror of the gender party.

You are looking for evidence to stop the gender party from destroying your precious child. But the gender party won't consider anything that might contradict its dogmas. Remember the party slogan—"no debate". The gender party has your child, and seemingly, all of society in its grip. You hang on, hoping someday to save your child and end the gender party forever.

Parents with Wisdom

27

This Will Make Me a Better Parent

My daughter was always a good kid. Thoughtful, quiet, and artistic, she attended a public Montessori school. She had a close group of girl-friends, and an outspoken disdain for boys, who she found to be annoying and gross. Her favorite game was stuffed animals, all of whom were female, all with complex personalities and backstories. She had trouble paying attention in school, but got good grades anyway. She liked wearing dresses, but could not tolerate stiff fabric or scratchy seams. Art and music came easily to her, and she always participated in children's choirs and school orchestras.

As for me, I was a progressive mom who purposefully avoided pushing traditional gender roles on my child. I didn't know her sex until she was born. I didn't care—I only wanted a healthy baby. I bought her comfortable, fairly gender-neutral clothes, and I adamantly avoided anything related to Barbie. I had grown up immersed in the unrealistic feminine beauty standards of the 80s, and I wanted my child to have the best chance possible of feeling whole and complete in her natural female body, however she chose to express it. As she grew up, I let her choose her clothes and hairstyles, as well as the toys she played with. I considered myself progressive, feminist, open-minded, and very much an LGBT+ ally. Her friends thought I was a pretty fun mom.

My child was 13 when she told me she thought she was trans. She had already been experimenting with male names and pronouns with her friends and therapist, who had advised her not to tell me until she was ready to fully come out of the trans closet. She was among the last of her small group of biologically female friends to socially transition. It was mid-pandemic, and she spent most of her time with her best friend, who had, unbeknownst to me, shown her hours upon end of transgender entertainment on YouTube and TikTok.

By 8th grade, here's what her friends (and their TikTok feeds) were saying about me:

"Your mom is transphobic". "She doesn't want a son. She wants a daughter." "She won't let you be who you are." "MY mom is so progressive, she buys my binders from a BIPOC trans company." "Your mom doesn't really know you."

And even worse, a succession of therapists:

"You may not know your child as well as you think you do." "Your son just needs your support." "Your child doesn't share your values." "Your child is at risk of suicide if you don't affirm." "You just need some education on having a transgender child."

So much for being the fun mom.

This child. I had nursed her, read to her, fed her healthfully, sang her to sleep, held her when she cried, played with her. I taught her to read, to count, to make brownies, to brush her own teeth, and to be kind to animals and elders. I had read parenting books and joined library play groups, studied her learning styles and tailored her education to them. My Christmas gift was always her favorite, because I knew exactly what toy she wanted the most. When she was little and woke up feeling sick, I had already woken moments in advance knowing something was wrong.

And now, expert strangers were telling me I didn't really know her.

I affirmed her change in gender identity, at first. I thought it was an antipatriarchal movement, a rebellious play on artificial standards of attractiveness, a principled game of pronouns, clothing and hairstyles. I was an out-of-the-box, feminist Gen X-er. I was cool with that.

But I quickly learned this wasn't about self-empowerment. It was about self -rejection. Self-loathing. Self-erasure.

Her friends considered natural breasts disgusting, so binding became a rite of passage. The whole body became a thing of shame, covered by thick, baggy clothes that would betray no feminine curves. A swimsuit was unthinkable, even to swim in the ocean, which we traveled thousands of miles to visit. The new trans-boi posture was rounded forward, with the attitude of a sad thug, black COVID mask firmly in place under a black beanie, so only the eyes were visible. Their given names— many chosen with great care and meaning by thoughtful parents - were proclaimed "dead" and replaced with the names of fandom and cartoon characters.

My daughter's best friend (now an ftm trans child with two gender affirming parents) started calling her mother by her first name, and demanded the removal of all childhood photos from their home—to escape her past as a girl. Soon thereafter, she was admitted to a treatment program for suicidal ideation. My daughter started cutting her forearms, and her demeanor became dark and secretive. Her beautiful art became morbid and even cruel.

I drew the line at breast binding and said no. I could not rationalize the compression of a child's developing breast tissue and rib cage. It made no medical sense to encourage a practice that would restrict the respiratory, circulatory, and lymphatic systems during a crucial physical development stage.

And, of course, the experts told me I was wrong. They said if I didn't buy her a proper binder, she would use duct tape and ace bandages, which would be even worse. They said she would harm herself more. They said she would be at risk of suicide.

I cried for days. I meditated, I prayed, I consulted wise friends who knew my child well. I told her dad everything I knew, and spoke with her stepmom, who works as a child therapist. Everyone who ACTUAL-LY knew my child confirmed what I knew all along—this didn't make any sense. And being trans wasn't making her better. It was making her worse.

I still wanted my child to have the best chance possible of feeling whole and complete in her natural female body, however she chose to express it. If gender exploration necessitated my complicity in her self hatred, I wouldn't participate.

So I stopped listening to the experts and took back my authority as my child's first and primary parent.

I set new boundaries. I profoundly restricted online access, took long breaks from overzealous trans friends, checked daily to make sure she wasn't binding. Her dad, stepmom, and my partner all concurred, and she was pretty mad at all of us for awhile.

So perhaps even more importantly, I added a lot of things that I realized were missing during the pandemic. I facilitated friendships with healthier teens, and had frank conversations with their parents to ensure we were all on the same page. I enrolled her in a music performance program and aerial silks classes. Over the summer, she went to camp and volunteered at a nature center. We took interesting trips, went to live music shows, and watched diverse movies about all kinds of people. We planted raspberries and went camping and brewed herbal moon tea to ease her menstrual cramps. I wanted to show her that the world was much bigger than her friend group.

It's now been a year since she first announced her new identity. My work seems to have paid off. She has developed an identity outside of trans—she's an aerialist, a musician, a good writer, an artist, a traveler, and she believes in a spiritual side to life. Consistent aerial silks practice has made her physically strong and flexible, and she likes what her body can do and how it looks. She's phased out of the ultra-baggy clothes, and regularly shows her arms and collarbones. Sometimes she wears dresses or braids her hair. She doesn't appear to have engaged in self-harm in months, and her art is brighter and even humorous. She stands taller, laughs easily, and speaks confidently with adults. She has new friends with similarly unique interests. She's still quirky, artistic, and alternative in her style. She may be bisexual, and that's fine by me.

I really do want my daughter to be her authentic self, and I know that she has to find that path on her own eventually. I will always support her in all her ups and downs. I'll even love and support her if she decides, as an adult, to identify as a boy. But until she is actually an adult, I'm still the parent. I am a mature, educated, mentally healthy adult woman with many life experiences and learning under my belt. Many of my interactions with the mental health community undermined my legitimate questions, my knowledge of my child, the wisdom I've gained over nearly 48 years on planet Earth. I didn't go to psychology school, but I do know many things. And I do, actually, know my kid. I'm reclaiming that. I'm a much better parent for it.

28

Sam's Story

As a female scientist, I have never been into princesses. So when I had my first baby girl, there was no way she was going to be dressed in pink or brainwashed by commercial movies of pretty big-eyed girls being saved by dashing young princes. Instead, my baby Samantha dressed in a mix of "boys" and "girls" clothes. In terms of toys, she initially had her train phase, followed by her super hero phase, and then her Lego phase.

At the age of 2.5, after her little brother was born, Samantha started pushing back when I tried to put dresses on her. She also started to rebel at the idea of ballet classes and her friends were mostly boys. I started to wonder if my anti-princess sentiment was really a good idea but my pediatrician wasn't worried.

By the age of 4.5, Samantha began expressing frustration with all things gender-segregated. Why was it that all her favorite super heroes were boys? Why is it that her super heroes are only on boys clothes? Why do they divide the kids at school into boys versus girls teams and then the boys always win? Why do the boys get to pee standing up but the girls can't?

Given that Samantha already wore boy's clothes, and had relatively short hair, people were starting to mistake Samantha for a boy, which she enjoyed. So Samantha had an idea: how about she could change her name to a boy-sounding name? She chose "Sam."

At this point, I started to worry. It was 2016 and the transgender topic was starting to get more attention in the news. I did a bit of online research and talked to a family friend who was a child psychologist. This was the first time that I heard the words "gender dysphoria." She encouraged me not to worry because 80% of children with gender dysphoria grow out of it by puberty.

I asked my pediatrician what she thought and she recommended a local counseling practice that specialized in LGBTQ support for children and young adults. I felt like I had hit the jackpot! I had actually found experts that could help Sam! We started by joining group sessions (led by a trans man) where I was able to meet other parents with children just like mine. I found comfort knowing I wasn't alone. At the same time, I started searching YouTube and found some helpful documentaries such as "Gender Revolution" by renowned journalist, Katie Couric. I believed that there was a whole world of transgender men and women out there that I was just beginning to learn about. I felt bad for the transgender kids who were persecuted for wanting to go into bathrooms or join sports teams for their gender.

We met with our counselor, David, who was very good with 5-year-old Sam. She played games with him while they chatted about Sam's gender woes. David asked Sam, "If there was one thing in the world you could have what would it be?" Sam replied, "I would want a penis."

After a few months, David encouraged me to "socially transition" Sam since many people already thought Sam was a boy anyway, and Sam wanted to be a boy. The discrepancy between Sam's boy-like presentation and her use of she/her pronouns was creating anxiety for her. David said transitioning Sam to using he/him pronouns would lessen her anxiety and that I was the only one holding Sam back. In every other aspect of life, Sam had already socially transitioned and pronouns would be the final step. I did feel pressure at this point but I figured that my counselor knew better—so we started using he/him pronouns for Sam.

Our school was extremely accommodating throughout this process. We live in a fairly rural area so our school staff isn't very experienced on this front though they are very loving. Before Sam started kindergarten, I let the school nurse know that Sam had gender dysphoria. The nurse and the principal were extremely kind and asked me what I needed in order to accommodate Sam at school. Because this topic was so challenging for me, I often found myself breaking down crying. Imagine: my first conversation with my daughter's principal and I'm uncontrollably sobbing! How embarrassing! The problem was: the school wanted to know what I needed for Sam but I was still so confused and figuring it all out ... I was the one that needed to know what Sam needed, not the other way around. Either way, I did my best to let our principal know. I suggested that if possible, it would be great if Sam could have access to a gender-neutral bathroom. Since Sam looked like a boy but used the girls bathroom, older girls would make comments when Sam went into the bathroom. One of the girls even was peeking at little kindergarten Sam through the cracks in the bathroom stall! This only aggravated poor little Sam's sense of gender. She certainly wasn't fitting in with the girls in the bathroom!

Teachers were very accommodating with respect to transitioning to he/him pronouns for Sam. Once I was on board with the idea, I now became an advocate for Sam's male pronouns every time she was misgendered at school. To support Sam, I looked for children's books about trans kids such as "I am Jazz" or "Red: A Crayon's Story." Sam also joined the Boy Scouts who had recently began to allow girls. Sam loved it! Perhaps the hardest step for me was when I shaved Sam's hair off into a full boy's buzz cut. I cried so hard but I did it because I loved Sam so much and wanted to support her. I even bought Sam a she-wee so she could pee standing up like the boys. I also looked into children's packers so Sam could have her own little bulge in her pants ... yes they have them!!! In some ways, all this affirmation brought Sam and me closer together.

However, through all this affirming support, I couldn't stop thinking about where this was all heading. How does this social transition unwind itself assuming that puberty reverses 80% of these kids' gender dysphoria? I tried asking this question and David said, "we will just follow Sam's lead since she knows herself." This answer didn't give me comfort though, since I also started to learn about puberty blockers. If puberty reverses gender dysphoria but kids take puberty blockers, have we just interfered with this process? I tried asking David, but I got the same answer about how the kids know their true selves. I also tried asking this question on Facebook and I got chastised. I thought it was a very logical question so I was disheartened by the emotional responses.

How can I possibly let a young child make a decision to block puberty and potentially sterilize themselves without clear answers?

Seeking out additional experts, I found a local medical doctor that specialized in transgender medicine. I again felt like I had potentially opened the door to finally find the answers I was looking for. The doctor sat with me, my husband, and Sam, looked Sam straight in the eye and asked, "Do you want to be a boy?" Sam immediately replies, "Yes." The doctor asked "Do you want breasts like your mother or a beard like your father?" Sam said "a beard like my father." The doctor replies, "No big deal, we will just give Sam puberty blockers in a few years ... It is totally reversible."

This was the last straw for me. Why do all these so-called-experts only have one answer? Where are the stories of the 80% that reverse their GD?

I immediately stopped having Sam attend our gender-affirming counseling and I went back to internet digging. I started researching the science of puberty so that I could get my own answers to the 80% statistic. I was obsessed. Yes, I was still running a household and holding a job, but I would find myself staying up late after the kids were in bed googling down gender rabbit holes.

That is when I found a counselor in Texas named Sasha Ayad who questioned the whole idea of transitioning children, and my world opened up. I was able to have a phone consultation with her and I realized for the first time that the reason I wasn't getting my answers was because these so-called experts didn't have answers! They were literally experimenting with our children. Unfortunately, Sasha was too overwhelmed with patients to take us on but we remained in touch so that she could share pointers. Plus her practice at the time was exclusively focused on rapid-onset gender dysphoria in teen girls versus my little 6 year old.

So I went back to my online gender rabbit holes. I joined Twitter and started following people around the world that questioned puberty blockers. I found podcasts that I began to listen to nonstop while doing laundry, cooking, driving, exercising ... I was obsessed. My child was in danger and I had to fix it before she was permanently sterilized. I had trouble sleeping. I was thinking, breathing, and talking about gender questions non-stop. It was fully consuming me.

I found the Benjamin Boyce "Boyce of Reason" podcast series extremely helpful. It was the first time I had heard such comprehensive coverage of the many angles of gender dysphoria. My challenge was that most of the coverage was related to post-pubescent teens instead of young children. But then one of the episodes was about Stella O'Malley who is a psychotherapist in Ireland who had gender dysphoria as a child and grew out of it as a teenager … bingo!!!!

I immediately contacted Stella and she was available to speak with me. Unlike others I spoke to, Stella didn't take Sam's wishes at face value but wanted to understand the underlying drivers of Sam's desire to be a boy. Yes, the world is unfair to girls in many ways and our competitive Sam likes to be on the winning team. It's not fair that boys can pee standing up. It can feel wrong that boys are often stronger, faster, or more aggressive. But liking Legos, super heroes, and trains doesn't make you a boy. For the first time, Stella helped us dig into these underlying factors in order to assess where Sam's true self really was. Sam knew she was a girl … she just wasn't happy about it. This is not a transgender child.

Truly supporting Sam long term became about helping Sam feel okay about her true self—not hiding behind a shaved head, boys' clothes, and false pronouns. But we had some work to do to get there. We silently started letting Sam's hair grow out and we covertly tried to find the most feminine-looking clothes Sam could tolerate. As I explored this issue, I realized that this wasn't being sneaky, this was like giving a child their vegetables—they may not like them but they need them!

I must acknowledge that my family had been wonderful throughout this whole process. Though I'm sure they were worried, they never interfered … they even started calling Sam he/him. At this point, it had been almost 2 years since we had socially transitioned Sam. We now had neighbors and friends that only knew Sam as a little boy. So our 7 year-old Sam carried around extra anxiety associated with her gender secret. She knew she was a girl but didn't want people to know. I was worried about this so we needed a plan to unwind this social transition.

We decided that the best approach was to essentially break the cycle cold turkey in two steps. The first step was to have a conversation with each person in Sam's life that knew her as a boy and tell them that Sam is indeed a girl and we will now be using she/her pronouns. Not surprisingly, all our friends and neighbors were extremely loving and kind and said they love Sam no matter what her gender was. The second step was to have a conversation with Sam that was very matter-of-fact. "Sam, we think that living with this secret that you are a girl is not healthy for you so we are going to start using she/her pronouns. Everyone knows you are a girl and they still love you just the same."

And guess what? Sam was extremely relieved! We never saw her so happy. She didn't really vocalize her sense of relief but we saw it. She no longer was paranoid about being found out as a fake boy. It certainly helped that we embarked on this effort during COVID when we had less contact with others that could potentially comment on Sam's gender status.

It took approximately 2 years for Sam to start to become comfortable living as a girl again. She continued to use the boys' bathrooms until she wasn't comfortable anymore. She still wears boys' clothes but her hair is shoulder length. Every once in a while, we catch a kid at school calling her "he" but we make sure to find a private way to update them.

One of the biggest vegetables I made Sam swallow was joining our local girls' soccer team. I figured it was the best way for Sam to meet non-girly girls, since all her friends were still boys. When Sam found out the team I signed her up for was a girls' team she revolted. So I bribed her with an iPad in exchange for trying it out for one season. It turns out Sam was the best on her team! She started to feel pride in that. She was then scouted for another local soccer team and felt even more proud. She was even invited to sleepovers at her teammates houses and went! Some of the other girls are even envious that Sam gets to wear boy clothes when they aren't allowed by their parents.

Sam is now in her second year of soccer and loves it! She is calling herself a girl and is using girls' bathrooms. She no longer growls when we refer to her as a big sister or our cool daughter. Sam has even met other trans people and asks us "why would they do that?" It almost feels like she has forgotten her previous self. We don't make a big deal out of any of it because we know she is still trying to figure it all out. She has started puberty though so I can now tell you that she is one of that 80% that I couldn't get answers about.

I am so extremely thankful that Sasha and Stella helped open my eyes when they did. I was obsessed and lost sleep because I almost lost my daughter to so-called gender experts. I feel horrible thinking about the other families that are part of the gender affirming counseling practice that I left. Will those kids be sterilized when they didn't have to be? Why wasn't that part of the story in Katie Couric's documentary?

29

The Too, Too Solid Flesh

"Oh that this too too solid flesh would melt, thaw and resolve itself into a dew."

Perhaps we should reintroduce Hamlet to a new generation, for who else from classical literature captures the struggles of what it means to be a young adult. He is grappling with the sins and failings of the adults in his life; he is struggling with his relationship with the opposite sex; he is struggling with the world of phantoms, and spirit, and death.

When I was 12 years old I was hospitalized for anorexia nervosa. I was told at the time it was a neurosis, which is not as bad as a psychosis, which sounded very scary to a child. I was, however, helpless to stop starving myself. I was obsessed with calories. I had managed to reduce my intake to 90 calories a day: a tomato; a piece of bread; a slice of American cheese. I had always been a pudgy child. I loved food and was not picky. I had also been an active child. I would spend hours outside, climbing trees, running with sticks, and building forts. I also loved to read and was completely enamored of tales of adventure: Robin Hood, King Arthur, and The Lord of the Rings. Puberty arrived like the Angel of Death coming to the homes of the ancient Egyptians in Exodus. I did not recognize it and I felt I had no recourse to its cloak. All I felt was doom. I was about 10 years old.

I looked around me and saw that none of my classmates had been struck down by this cruel angel. Something had taken over my body and I felt unfree. I did not want to run or play anymore—I did not know how to play anymore. My body became rounder, and my breasts grew. I was disgusted and this was made excruciating worse by the fact that everyone seemed to notice the changes going on in my body. Kids at school would call me fat, cousins without filters would point it out to me, and lecherous relatives would ogle. I felt everyone's eyes on me. I disappeared into books and into my own mind. This was 1977. We had no internet, no social media—my favorite show on television was Starsky and Hutch and I had no interest in being like Farrah Fawcett (or Jacqueline Smith, or Kate Jackson.) Get my drift? I was not ready for this.

Looking back on this time in my life, I would say this was a precocious puberty. Generally a child has a reprieve between the "9 Year Change" and puberty. Around 9 a child will have a shift in their consciousness, where they begin to sense themselves as separate from the world around them. They may begin to see the adults in their lives as having flaws, they may wrestle with death for the first time, they may become like mini-teenagers, pushing their parents away with one hand and clinging to them with the other. Once the child passes through this bit of rough sea, they emerge with a developing sense of self and are cognitively ready to take on more complex things. They begin to have more personality and interests which might possibly be separate from those of their family. They are on the road to becoming an individual. They may face a Rubicon and, like Caesar, will have to take a step away from what is known towards a place of unknown variables. It's exciting, and a little bit scary.

Puberty would naturally come later after the child has gained some solid ground following this change in consciousness. For myself, the two seem to have run right into each other, causing me to freeze. I tried to hide everything that was happening to me. I told no one about my menarche (no "Maiden" ceremony for me. This was the 70s in the Midwest anyway, so that hadn't been imported yet.) I made my own pads and managed to keep that on the down-low till anorexia stopped my period. As for my breasts, I wanted them gone. If I had spoken this to anyone in 1976, which I wouldn't have, I would have heard, "I understand your feelings. Puberty is hard, but in time it will be easier." Someone might have taken that opportunity to say to me, "The human body is a wonderful thing. Someday you might even be a mother and you could breastfeed your children." (I think you could still say that in 1976.)

Since puberty blockers, hormones, and surgery were not even in my stratosphere, I took things into my own hands and dieted. Dieting turned into severe starvation, because what I saw in the mirror was not what was in the mirror. I look at pictures of myself from that time and it is sickening. My poor parents. I was a skeleton with downy fluff on my arms, but I thought I still needed to eat only 90 calories a day. Because there was no social media (just the same old 30 kids in my home room class, my teacher and a smattering of cousins—oh, and my family), I had very little "encouragement" for what I was doing to myself. I distanced myself from my friends and was on a trajectory to disappear. My parents turned to professionals and I was swept up into a Children's Psych ward for 5 months until our insurance ran out.

My relationship with my body and being a woman did not necessarily improve, but my way of dealing with it did. I could not keep up the 90 calories any longer, so I switched to bulimia. I also discovered drugs and alcohol as a way to feel more comfortable in my body (or maybe it was to not feel my body.) Now it was the 80s and gender non-conformity was starting to become more of a presence in fashion and popular culture. This was the age of the John Hughes film, which painted a picture of adolescents as wild and sexually active. I have wondered if this was a grown man projecting his fantasies onto my generation. Of course the Sexual Revolution (thanks Boomers) had handed my generation a blank check and we had filled it in and cashed it and thrown a big kegger party. Now the Millennials and Gen Zers are left with the mess.

After 20 years in Moria fighting the Balrog of body dysmorphia and all that goes with that, Goodness, Truth, and Beauty did win. I cannot say I was triumphant, but I was healed. As with many addictions, I had to fall to a place where I had run out of ways to hide, pass, lie, or distract. No matter what I did, I was still there and was the common denominator. Down in the dirt I met someone who had suffered as I had and they reached out their hand and offered me a path out, if I was willing to keep to the map. I joined OA and after 30 meetings in 30 days the struggle with food that had gripped me for 20 years vanished.

The next thing that happened also was a miracle: I became pregnant and that journey brought me to peace with being a woman. I saw the beauty of my sex and the beauty of birth and motherhood. I experienced its goodness. As many of you know, the school of parenting transforms you. It teaches you how to love in a way nothing else can. It took me out of myself. It put things in perspective and helped me to grow and be brave.

Funny how life is though. That little one who taught me to love (and he was the most demanding of all my little teachers) is now suffering in very similar ways to how I suffered. He has closed me out and goes by another name now. I feel I am fighting that Balrog again in pitch black darkness on a spiral staircase. I continue to reach out in letters, but get no response. What is most destructive about this contagion of transgenderism is that it keeps young people locked in a narcissistic-like knot, making it difficult or impossible to become more selfless, which is one noble characteristic of maturity ("adulting"). It is a wonderful characteristic that has become malign in recent decades.

Back to poor Hamlet: what makes Hamlet such a tragic character is that despite his murder spree, he is sensitive to the injustices and failings of the older generation. Our children too are sensitive to the injustices of life, even though their interpretations may be lacking foresight and nuance. They see where we, the adults in their lives, have failed them and have been less than noble or brave. Keep in mind that Hamlet also observed, "What a piece of work is man, How noble in reason, how infinite in faculty, In form and moving how express and admirable, In action how like an angel, In apprehension how like a god, The beauty of the world, the paragon of animals…"

When you look at the sunset, its **beauty** makes you feel peaceful and inspired through the experience. You come to appreciate it as **good** because it gives benefit to your psyche and to the whole world. Finally, how can you deny its **truth**? We have to fight for these and for our children and grandchildren.

30

Close Enough to Open My Eyes

My daughter is at prom. I'm happy about it, mostly, but it's been a long journey here. Not as difficult as others, but our story is similar. However, I'm optimistic, but not confident, that it's actually over.

Like so many others, the challenges in our relationship started during COVID. We live in a very, VERY progressive state, and the COVID restrictions were very real here, and had a huge and still yet to be measured impact on our youth. Prior to the shutdowns, I had a bright, vibrant, outgoing and energetic daughter. Now, she's the opposite. She's finding her way back, but it's slow, and so many things are now impacting getting her back to the girl she used to be.

It started maybe 6 months after the COVID shutdowns. Schools were closed for so long here, so my daughter ended her junior high school years, and started her high school career virtually. There were no other options. Shortly after her freshman year started, she shared with me that she was bisexual. I was surprised, a little, but not really, given her overall lack of interest in any relationships to that point. She was 14 when she made the announcement to me. I asked some questions, but took it for what it was, not a big deal, really.

Sometime after that, she determined she was lesbian, and also shared this with me, also. Again, I asked a lot of questions. I was curious, really, how she decided, how she knew, why it changed from bisexual to lesbian. As weeks went on, conversations drifted toward the trans topic. My general feelings about it, simple things. At some point, I started to read more into the questions, and became concerned.

I'll note here, that we did poorly in dealing with COVID restrictions. I became very lenient in letting my daughter use her computer and phone. I checked on things, but I wanted her to be able to maintain contact with her friends. It wasn't until after school began, that I realized she'd made new friends (from school), online. Kids I didn't know. And me, left wondering, how does a teenager befriend people online, at their school or not? How do you learn to trust them and develop a close relationship? I still don't know, but it happened. So, two new friends entered her life, via online classes, and became part of her life once they returned in person at the end of her freshman year.

Noticing significant changes in her attitude and general level of happiness, I did something I should have done more frequently. I checked her phone messages. She was sharing with a friend that she was "feeling dysphoric" again. I asked what it meant. I made her explain it in full detail. "I just don't feel like a girl." Well, that's too bad, because you are one. Not my original response, but I tried to talk her through it, to some extent, and this was before I found all the other online resources, and stories of these sudden changes in teenage girls. Because yes, it was sudden. This girl of mine has always been exposed to "boy" and "girl" things, but has ALWAYS opted for the sparkles, the pinks, make-up, the typical "girly" things. Yes, she also played in the dirt and played with monster trucks.

She still trusted me then. She'd share (or let it slip) that her female friend, Brynlee, liked to go by "Sam", and use they/them pronouns. Her male friend, Gavin, liked to go by "Kris" and also uses they/them pronouns. By this point, I realized she was in it. Though she hadn't come out and said it, I knew she was following the same path, and these new friends had to have had a big part in it. Eventually, I'd snooped enough, found enough, that I learned her alternate name. It wasn't bad, but was also chosen to "appease" me, because it is a shortened version of her name that she doesn't like. She asked me to start using it. I said no. Partly, because to this point, I'd been on my own in knowing all of this. Her dad (yes, we're married), has had no idea this was going on. I still had no knowledge of how to handle this, but I just couldn't use another name for her, because her dad didn't even know she was lesbian, let alone that she thought she wasn't a girl, and wanted to go by a new name and they/

them. I said we could only discuss this once she started sharing some of this stuff with her dad.

She took her time, but managed to tell him she was lesbian. It didn't go well. He's much more traditional than I even realized, and he's struggled with the losses he didn't know he'd have (such as the potential for no biological grandchildren). They've been at odds, but I'm glad he's talking to her about how things impact her life, and the people she's around reflect on her, and different things like that. She's not always receptive, but I do think she's listening. I hope she's listening.

She never managed to tell him anything other than that. By this point, I'd also dug in heavily to researching the real goings on with trans, or prior to trans, the "they/them" that seems to lead that way. I started arguing with her. This was war, I was determined to win. I had a hard time controlling my emotions sometimes, because the reality of the situation was so heartbreaking. How could my beautiful daughter believe she wasn't a girl? That she's wasn't female? It hurt me as a woman, for all the things I've worked for and fought for, for her not to see that she was capable of the same things, as a young woman, that she really believed that men have it easier, that it would be easier to be one, despite seeing the examples of strong, confident, successful women in her own life.

I don't think I handled the conversations well, ever. But I did not budge from my position that she is a female, and she cannot change it. She can change her clothes (more on that shortly), she can change her hair (I struggle with this one), but she'll always be female. This is what I've stuck to for the last 18 months. We had some good conversations about how it's wrong to allow males in female prisons, and males in women's competitive sports (many discussions around Will "Lia"m Thomas).

Throughout that time, other things also came up. She would "black out" and come to and say she didn't or remember things (I think she was aiming to mimic DID). She acted like she had a sudden tic (she did pretty poorly). I found notes about her sadness, and indications that she may have been considering the end of her life. We talked SO much. I talked at her, she talked at me. We talked circles. It was so messy. It's still messy. I've lost so much sleep. She says she doesn't sleep well. I'm grateful for one of her friends, who stands her ground, doesn't put up with the nonsense, and also lets me know what's going on, or confirms things I'm seeing or the way my daughter is acting or feeling. This friend has stuck by my daughter, in the best way possible.

She also doesn't get along with her new friends, and has no problem letting her know she wants nothing to do with them, and why. I'm very glad she's in our life.

My daughter never changed her clothing style much through this, she's always worn leggings and a hooded sweatshirt. She quit wearing makeup. She wanted a binder, but she didn't get one. She wore tight sports bras. At home, she still wore short-shorts to sleep or lounge around the house. And she cut her hair short(ish), as short as I'd let her. When we went clothes shopping for school it was a nightmare. She didn't know what she wanted, she couldn't choose. I don't think she really knew.

I also put significant restrictions on her phone. When she could use it, what it could be used for, and I insisted on knowing who she was texting. I also required that all her computer time be in a common area. I know she's still communicating through some apps with people, but it's limited, because she knows we're there watching. It's not a perfect system, but unfortunately, COVID made so much school work move online (even while back in the classroom), that it's difficult to do assignment or turn them in if you aren't in front of a screen (which I really dislike).

Where are we now? She's returning to me, but it's not over. She wore a beautiful dress for Homecoming earlier this year (with all the glitter). She still wants short hair. When I take her shopping, she wants crop tops and cute girl clothes. She even wants some dresses. She still wears bikinis. She's seemingly more accepting of her feminine body and feminine features. She doesn't try to hide them. She's requested more appropriately fitting bras, including non-sports bras.

But, she's also still hanging out with the friends who I believe started her down this path. There are many rumors about her and these friends at school. It breaks my heart that she is subjecting herself to this, when she could do so much better. My "lesbian" daughter is apparently dating "Kris" now. I haven't asked her how she's still a lesbian if she's dating a boy. She's also dated "Sam", too. Whenever she does speak about either of them (which isn't often), and uses they/them, I will correct her. I will reinforce the gendered pronouns of the correct sex of these friends. I also use their birth names.

I think we're still pretty close with our relationship. We've had ups and downs, but it feels stronger as time passes. She reaches out to her dad, I think she knows she needs us, and our love for her. Or she has me really fooled. But, she's always been a little immature, and I think she does realize she still needs her family, the people she KNOWS care about her, her well-being, and her future. I wish she'd let go of these friends, I wish she could see the full truth, and be willing to say it to them. We have support from others, quiet support, teachers I trust who see what I see, and know how we feel, and aren't affirming, but see the toll this movement is taking on the teenagers of the world. They see what COVID did to our youth.

I love my daughter. She has made me visit a world of information I never thought I'd have to dig into. We could have it so much worse, and I'm grateful that things seem to be ok where they are, and not headed further down any path toward trans, but hopefully headed down a path of truth and reality. I'm watchful and cautious, for my own daughter, and hope all our children can also find truth and reality like us parents that have dealt with any of this to some degree know.

Tonight she's at prom. She looks beautiful, with a lovely dress, great hair, and make-up she did all on her own. She left with friends. I'm 99% sure she's meeting her "boyfriend" there. I'll have to be okay with it for now, for our relationship, and for my mental health. I have to trust she knows her parent's love is stronger than all of this. And we'll be here to catch her when she finally, fully, opens her eyes.

31

One Family's Story

As I sit here writing to you, our 18-year-old daughter is packing all her things. She says that she will never speak to us again. How did we get to this unfathomable place, to this tragic end for our family?

My daughter, raised in relative privilege, was always a gifted child. She also struggled socially growing up. She had one best friend all through primary school. In middle school, she finally built a nice friend group of girls. However, at this time, I, her mother, went through a significant depression and was unable to work or meet her needs emotionally. We also moved twice during this time. I believe this had a significant impact upon her stability.

My daughter started high school with high hopes. She seemed to thrive—she was academically successful her ninth grade year, winning an award for her participation in speech and debate. However, she withdrew as she entered her sophomore year—locking herself in her room, obsessed with her phone. We grew alarmed at her mounting depression. We found a therapist, and she was diagnosed with major depression and referred to the UC Davis Mind Institute, where she was diagnosed with anxiety, ADHD and Depression. She also suffered from binge eating disorder. She was seen at this time as having conflict with us, her parents, and as gender questioning.

Because of her worsening depression, we got her into an Intensive Outpatient program that included a therapist, a group of adolescents her age and a psychiatrist. She appeared to be getting better. But then,

COVID hit. Once again she withdrew into an online world, immersing herself in Discord, Anime and who knows what other websites. She told me she had found out what was really going on with her on the internet.

She started not wanting to go to school as well as hanging out with a boy who was transgender. I believe this was through a group at school for LGBT allies. Then, in 6th grade, after we watched Dear Evan Hansen, she came out to me as a lesbian and I was fully supportive. Later, in high school, when she announced a trans identity, I tried to be supportive as well, thinking it was the best thing to do.. We tried to be supportive, using her preferred name and pronouns. We even paid for a breast reduction because she was so large chested. I feel so responsible for not educating myself as to what was going on along the way. She was so angry and combative and downright hateful to me, her mother during this time, and I was trying my best under the circumstances.

My daughter eventually went off to college and, after about six months, she announced she was going to start taking testosterone as her therapist had written a letter for her to do so. (The therapist never spoke with us about this, or her gender questioning.) About one month later, she announced she was getting a double mastectomy. We were alarmed at this development, and tried to slow things down. While continuing to pay for her college tuition, room and board, we took her off our insurance, stopped her every other week Zoom therapy, took back our car and stopped paying for her phone. We were beside ourselves with shock and worry, and hoped that our actions would help her to see what adult responsibilities really are. Within a week, however, she managed to get her phone paid for and get health insurance. She will likely be able to continue with her "treatment" on Medi-cal. There was plenty of "help" available for her to destroy her body and separate her from her family.

I fully expect to get a call one day about her de-transitioning. Who knows what kind of emotional shape she will be in at that time? But no matter how she is, or what she's done, we love her and always will. We will pick up the pieces, help her and hope for the best. Our daughter has agreed to twice weekly family therapy sessions and we are grateful for this chance to keep the lines of communication open. However, for now, we have no choice but to let her make these life-changing mistakes, and hope that she knows in the back of her mind that we love her unconditionally and that we will be here for her, waiting, no matter what.

32

My Sweet Baby Boy

It's funny how no one seems to be able to recognize that we all change as our brains fully develop. In my early twenties, I decided I would be okay not having children, but as I reached my late twenties, my priorities shifted. Although I was not able to get pregnant traditionally, I was very fortunate to be blessed with a baby boy. I have never felt such immediate love at any time in my life. I knew I would do everything I could to protect my child from the world and to help him live a happy life. My son changed my life in ways I never thought possible.

My son was never the typical athletic boy. He was interested in how things worked, how plants grew and anything science based. He worried about the world and what would happen if people kept throwing trash away. He was clumsy and awkward (we didn't find out until much later that this was related to a genetic condition that I was diagnosed with and passed on to him).

My son loved to make blueprints for machines he was going to invent. He loved to learn languages and would do so when we travelled by speaking to people that didn't speak English. He was well behaved, with wonderful manners that evoked praise from friends and strangers alike. He had this amazing imagination and I would nurture this with him. We used to build forts and pretend. We would make things out of household items. We did puppet shows and performed for family members.

My sweet, caring, sensitive, funny, intelligent and charismatic little boy went off to junior kindergarten at the age of 3. Shortly after starting school, I received a call saying that my son was hugging other children too much. Despite the school's reprimand, my son continued to be kind and caring to strangers, adults, teenagers, and children his own age. Everyone would remark about how special he was and would really listen to him.

After the hugging incident, my husband wanted to take him out of school and home school him. I wish I could go back in time and do exactly that because, in the end, my caring, loving and sensitive son was relentlessly bullied at school, and the school did nothing to stop it. This school system used "Progressive Discipline" as a misguided way of addressing bullying and it was entirely ineffective. Although I stood up for my son on numerous occasions as he was bullied by other students, the school never really stepped in. My son experienced so much bullying, that he developed anxiety and depression. We sought counseling and programs to assist him. We met with school staff and worked on ways to help him but ultimately none of these efforts were successful.

I'm sure that someone will try to say that there were signs that my son would become trans-identified, based on what I have said so far. Those people would be wrong. You cannot know my son from your short interactions with my son or your observations from afar. I have some very amazing memories of my son up until the gender ideology took over. But once it did, he became a stranger.

Gender ideology is the biggest bully of them all. I have had to deal with a lot of difficult things in my life, but I never imagined fighting this fight. I'm sure that there are other parents that can relate to this feeling. When my son told me he was transgender, very suddenly just over a year and a half ago, it came out of nowhere. He's now on a fast track to sterilization, mutilation and never being able to have a sexual experience. The risks of taking hormones are absolutely frightening, but our government will cover these expenses without question. When I tried to reach out to the gender clinic treating him, I was told that, if I contacted them again, they would contact the police. The first message sent to me went to my junk folder. When I reached out a second time, expressing my concern that our family medical history had not been shared with them, I was met with the same response. How is this medical care? My son could die of a serious heart condition that he was unaware of when he shared his limited knowledge of our family medical history.

I think what no one is talking about is what this is doing to families, specifically mothers. I can tell you that I have contemplated ending my own life, and the various options to choose from (for example I wouldn't slit my wrists because it would hurt too much, but taking pills seems like a sensible way and the least messy for whoever finds me).

I will not follow through because I care too much about those around me. I would not want to hurt my family. I would not want to leave my husband and son. Who would help them through this nightmare we are living right now? You get the point I'm making though—this situation is truly as painful as it gets for me. I am completely shattered and often see no point in living.

I will keep going and fighting as much as I can. If I give up, who's going to save my son from this? I go through most days feeling absolutely defeated. I feel useless and judged in my ability to parent my own child. I know in my heart that my son is not transgender. There is a very good possibility that he is on the autism spectrum.

My circle of friends has grown smaller. I do have some people who seem to be supportive, but I fear that they do not understand how serious this is. Their children are not immune to the gender ideology being taught in schools. Those who choose to ignore me or judge me are not the people I want in my life. I'm sure there are many more people out there who feel this is complete madness and would like to speak out about it. They are afraid of the repercussions, of losing their jobs, of being targeted, of being labeled transphobic or bigoted.

As my son digs his heels in and dives head first into the shallow water filled with rocks, I continue to fight to stop this experimentation on children—and I continue to feel a loneliness I never thought possible. I will try to keep a relationship going with the stranger that used to be my son. I will cling to the hope that he doesn't experience lifelong medical problems as a result of taking a medication I was advised against taking due to complications of cancer and blood clots (HRT during menopause).

To the people that say he's an adult at 18, I ask you two questions: When in the history of medicine has anyone been able to self diagnose? Why are we allowing children and youth to make irreversible life decisions before their brain has fully developed? A friend of mine said, "We have become so open-minded, our brains have fallen out." I sure hope the medical field sees the damage being done before it's too late for our children.

33

The Long Game

For parents of gender confused kids it's a long game, full of ups and downs. A game of waiting for minds to change.

My son has changed his mind a lot throughout his short life—as all kids and teens. As a toddler he loved red, then green, then yellow and then, finally, went back to red. As a senior in high school he dreamed of going to college for music, then animation, then film, then visual effects, then illustration, then back to music, all in a span of less than six months.

Why would trans be any different?

Last summer after breaking up with his girlfriend, my son changed a lot. He had identified for some time as trans. After the break up, he told me he knew he was male and was my son. He said he no longer identified as a lesbian. He also said that, in my words, he was a straight male. (Although he held on to the girl name, which always made me suspicious).

Right before turning 18 this Spring, he told us that he was trans (again) and would be moving out after graduation to transition. He said his living space was all set. He was going to take a gap year to transition. At 18, he took us off all of his shared devices. He closed the bank account he shared with me and opened a new one.

After graduation, he changed his mind again. He did not move out and said he had no plans to leave. Instead, he now planned to take a gap year and live at home. There was no arranged place for him to go, as he had told us. He stopped talking about hormones. He fixed up his room, and set up a recording studio in our home. He was happier than I had seen him in a long time. He was excited to spend the summer going out with friends every night.

Summer did not go as he planned though, and he turned dark again. His friends were moving away and off to college, so they were not eager to spend the summer going out with him. He was paralyzed and gripped by anxiety, and couldn't look for a job, get his college applications together, or create a portfolio. He stopped talking to us and began to avoid us when possible.

Then, suddenly, he moved out, letting us know by text. We have no idea where he is—but we've heard he's safe.

I think my son's trans identity is about power and control—about having *something* in his life that he can control. But life is full of uncertainty, and there is often very little you can control. That's one of the lessons you learn as you experience life as an adult. He hasn't had that chance. You don't need to pick your college major before you go, although you might have some thoughts about what you'd like to try. You don't need to commit to a favorite color and then never go back.

Life is about the choices you make and don't make—identity is not a fixed state. Trans is not control over yourself, and parents are not enemies or prison wardens in your journey to adulthood.

I don't know what comes next for my family, because trans identity is a long game, with many rolls of the dice, and right now, I don't get a turn. Instead I will wait for my son to play a few more rounds and hope that he leaves his mind open to the growth and change that he needs to experience, and we will be here when he figures it out.

34

For the Parent of an Adult ROGD "Child"

Much of what I read and see about gender dysphoria and transgender issues concerns younger children, mainly pre-teen and teens. I'm older (61), and so is my daughter (23). I've been in this a long time (coming on four years since she medicalized). In some ways I'm envious of the "younger" parents, and/or parents of the young. They have some control over the drugs their child takes, name changes, and if surgery is on the table. Don't get me wrong—I understand that dealing with a child who is under the delusion he/she can change sexes is maddening at any age—but experiencing this with an adult child is a slightly different challenge.

Adult children don't need their parents' permission to move forward with any procedures. They can easily obtain hormones at Planned Parenthood. If they can afford it, they can proceed to surgery whenever they want. They can legally change their names. All this is possible from age 18.

So, finding myself in an impotent position, but still terrified of what gender ideology is doing to my daughter's brain and what testosterone is doing to her health, here's what I tell myself. Perhaps these mantras may help you, fellow older parent:

This is a fad and fads end. Someday it may be deeply uncool to be trans.

Most people leave cults. According to Pat Ryan, cult mediation specialist, 90% of people who affiliate with these groups leave them on their own. Gender ideology has cult-like features and attractions. I don't think Pat Ryan would classify gender as a cult but it sure is a powerful belief system

Some of this is normal. These trans-identified adult children are doing an age-appropriate thing—separating from their parents, and developing as an individual—they are just doing this in an inappropriate and harmful way.

Detransitioning is not a panacea. As much as you wish they would detransition, all your problems will not go away if/when they do. I find myself indulging in that fantasy sometimes, telling myself "If she would just desist, life would be perfect". It won't be. I have to remind myself of that. Other problems will arise because…that's life.

Adversity begets wisdom. Many of the detransitioner stories I've read are filled with regret, and some with anger and shame. But those who have been through transition and detransition seem to have also developed a better knowledge of themselves. Having been through this experience, they emerge less beholden to the opinion of others, with a willingness to share their personal history in the service of others. Maybe my daughter will gain wisdom from this experience.

Expense of transitioning can be prohibitive. The older they are, the closer they are to getting off your insurance. It is especially galling to me that my insurance is covering the costs of cross sex hormones and all the associated medical expenses, and those costs are massive. I have entertained the idea of dropping her from my insurance, but I know that may result in estrangement and prevent her from seeing a mental health profession, which I have hoped (in vain, to date) will help her address the underlying issues driving the trans-identity.

Biology is working in two ways. Although they are adults, the pre-frontal cortex is not fully developed in people under 25. Perhaps when they reach that age, they will be better able to accomplish executive brain functions and see gender ideology for what it is. The other way biology is helping me deal with this is that my daughter is not a man. It's as simple as that.

Services for detransitioners. The longer they wait to detransition, the more detransition services will exist to help them. Yeah, I'm reaching on that one but every little bit helps assuage my anxiety. Genspect (genspect.org/beyond/) and detrans voices (www.detransvoices.org/) come to mind.

Momento Mori—Remember that you will die. Try to meditate on it briefly each day. Is obsessing about your child's spectacularly bad decision how you want to spend your precious time? Because...

You can't do much about it anyway. You have little influence with an adult child. And trying to use your influence or reason them out of their trans-identity will often cause resentment, possibly estrangement. I haven't attempted to share an article related to gender with my daughter in years.

At this age, how much would you normally be involved in their lives? If/when they detransition, they will probably move away from you—hopefully with a good education, a fulfilling job, a nice place to live and a loving partner. If that all works, you'll see less of them anyway.

Try to envision a happy future. The less you obsess about this now, the less you will resent them if /when they desist for how much you obsessed about this.

They are alive. No, I don't buy the "better a live son than a dead daughter" emotional blackmail. But I know people whose children have died. That has not happened to us. That's worth remembering. Daily.

These are the thoughts that work for me. Sometimes. I hope they can help you, fellow older parent.

35

When Two Worlds Collide: Part 1 —A World Turned Upside Down

Two years ago my world turned upside down.

Readers of PITT might assume this was the day my young adult daughter announced a transgender identity. But that nuclear bomb was actually detonated in our house six months later. No, I'm talking about when after a week of unexplained high fevers, two drive through COVID tests, a trip to our pediatrician to rule out strep, flu, and mono, and a trip to our local hospital for labs my teenage son was diagnosed with high-risk leukemia.

Looking back there were signs that my son was sick. He was coming home from school and taking a nap. He couldn't seem to stay warm. While other boys in his school weightlifting class were adding weight to the bar and bulking up he was benching less and less and losing weight.

I had randomly read an article in a magazine about a child with cancer whose mom initially became concerned when she noticed how pale her daughter's lips and face were. I noticed that about my son too but dismissed it. I think in my gut I knew something was seriously wrong but didn't want to accept it. So when our pediatrician showed up at our house the evening my son's labs were due back, my husband and I knew immediately this couldn't be good. Our doctor gently broke the news to my husband and me, then to our son, and finally to the rest of our kids. He stayed with us for about an hour while we all cried and he answered our questions the best he could. Then he told us our local children's hospital was waiting for us and we needed to go right then.

The next few days are a blur. My son was very sick by that point and within hours of arrival had IVs in both arms giving him blood transfusions, platelets, saline, antibiotics, and medication.

Over the next week and half in the hospital he had additional blood, bone marrow, and genetic testing to confirm the diagnosis, banked sperm, had surgery to place a port, and began chemotherapy. In terms of childhood cancer we got the best of the worst. Childhood leukemia has a good prognosis and my son is receiving excellent care. But the treatment is a grind.

Over the last two years we've stayed almost 40 nights in the hospital and made weekly trips to the oncology clinic at the hospital for treatment. My son has had 12 different kinds of chemotherapy given many, many times, sometimes stacked two or three at an appointment. His hair has fallen out and grown back twice. He'll be in active treatment for about 3 years total.

Boys actually get an extra year of treatment because leukemia can metastasize to the testicles. Hmm, funny how biology matters. Then he'll be followed for an additional two years until he's finally declared in remission.

With my daughter, there was no inkling. No gut feeling that something was wrong. Like so many parents describe, her announcement came out of the blue. We were completely blindsided and had no idea how to react. We told her we loved her and would try to get her some help.

Her announcement was more of a shock to me than my son's diagnosis. If my son hadn't needed me so desperately I might have crawled into bed and never gotten out. I used the excuse of my son to hide out in my house. I had no idea what to say to family and friends about my daughter.

Initially we affirmed her in her belief and made some attempt to use her chosen name and alternate pronouns. I searched online for information, any kind of lifeline that would tell me what to do. With my son, his treatment was difficult but his oncologist and medical team told us exactly what to do and we did it.

The only information I could find online about my daughter was that if we didn't go along with what she wanted we weren't loving parents, she might run away, or worst of all kill herself. I was wracked with anxiety for both my son and my daughter. I could barely eat and lost weight.

At one of my son's appointments a nurse we hadn't seen for awhile said, "Wow, you've lost weight. You look great." Little did she know. "Thanks." I said. "It's stress and anxiety." She realized her gaffe and apologized. But it was true. I could barely function.

I stayed awake at night worrying and crying. I stopped returning phone calls and texts. Finally, a good friend became so concerned about me she came to my house to check on me. I confided in her about my daughter. I repeated what my daughter had told me. "She doesn't want this. She didn't ask for this, but it's innate and can't be changed. Her brain doesn't match her body. She was somehow born in the wrong body." My friend listened to everything I said, then very compassionately questioned what I was saying. She told me she was confused by the idea that my daughter was born in the wrong body. "It doesn't make sense," she said. "How could someone be born in the wrong body? We are our bodies." She told me that she, herself had a history of anorexia- that she had used restricting food as a way to feel like she had a sense of control. She thought this sounded like a similar maladaptive coping mechanism. She told me she had a friend who was a therapist and she would ask her about it.

My friend forwarded me the text response from the therapist and it changed everything. I vividly remember reading, "Many clinicians do believe in affirming a transgender identity, but there are a few therapists in an online group I'm in who are questioning whether this is the only approach." I felt an inkling of hope for the first time in months. The therapist sent a link for *Gender: A Wider Lens Podcast*. I binge listened to every episode that had been released (there weren't that many at the time) and each new episode as it came out.

My hope deepened. I realized there was another way to frame what was happening to our daughter. I searched for and found other resources. We walked back our affirmation. I happened to overhear the therapist we had found for my daughter telling her in an online session that "If your mom would just realize that you are an adult and can make your own decisions…" and "If your mom would just support you in your true identity"… "you would feel better." We ended the relationship with that therapist and were fortunate to find one that is exploratory.

Using strategies gleaned from Sasha and Stella, fellow PITT parents, an open-minded Facebook group, articles, books, podcasts, etc. we have managed to begin to extricate our daughter from her transgender identity. She rode the fence of nonbinary for awhile and just recently during a conversation when she asked me if "I actually knew any trans people" and I told her, "Well, I know you" she said quietly, "Well, I was trans but I'm not anymore." I haven't dared to push it much farther but am holding my breath and the line of reality for her as she slowly awakens.

Honestly, I'm not as relieved as I thought I would be to hear those words come out of her mouth. Other parents have expressed the same sentiment. I think it's because I know she is still very vulnerable. At any moment she might slip back into the identity. And I realize there are issues that made her vulnerable to being pulled into a transgender identity in the first place that we are going to need to address. But just like with my son, I'm incredibly grateful that it seems our scenario is the best of the worst. I know there are many families who haven't had the same outcome.

36

When Two Worlds Collide: Part 2
—A World of Live Daughters and Sons

If PITT readers each had a dollar for every time we've heard the much debunked, emotionally manipulative "live son or dead daughter" myth we'd all be very rich. We hear the "transition or die" trope from the media, schools, the government, misinformed family and friends, and from our own trans-identified kids, who hear it themselves from the same sources as us and from fellow trans-identified peers in real life and on social media. I've heard it from Governor Spencer Cox of Utah. In February 2021 Governor Cox vetoed a bill that proposed to ban 'transgender girls' from participating in girls' K-12 sports stating, "I don't understand what they are going through or why they feel the way they do. But I want them to live… These kids are… they're just trying to stay alive."

A well-known purveyor of this harmful narrative is Diane Ehrensaft, who is the chief psychologist at the UCSF Benioff Hospital Child and Adolescent Gender Clinic. In a widely circulated video of Dr. Ehrensaft giving a conference presentation, she acknowledges that when children are given puberty blockers and cross-sex hormones as part of 'gender affirming' medical intervention, one side effect is infertility, and she wonders if children can really consent to this. She says, "The other issue that's a showstopper now for many parents around giving consent to puberty blockers is the fertility issue. That if a child goes straight from puberty blockers directly to cross sex hormones they, at this point in history, they are pretty much forfeiting their fertility and so they will not have a genetically related child… The question is, can an 11-year-old, 12-year-old at that level of development, be really thinking and know what they want at age 30 around infertility?" Dr. Ehrensaft answers her own question by likening 'gender affirming' medical care to oncological care for children with cancer. "The answer to that is we don't think twice about instituting treatments for cancers for children that will compromise their fertility. We don't say, 'We're not going to give them the treatment for cancer because it's going to compromise their fertility.' For some youth, having the gender affirmation interventions is as life-saving as the oncology services for children who have cancer."

Dr. Ehrensaft is, of course, insinuating that 'gender affirming care' is "life-saving" for children who identify as transgender because, if not affirmed, they might commit suicide. Her colleague, Joel Baum, states this more explicitly. "I'll just add one thing here. When we're working with families, what is the leverage point for that family?…The fact of the matter is at the end of the day, it is their decision and we just hope they're going to make an informed decision. Just make sure you have all the information you need. Which includes, you can either have grandchildren or not have a kid anymore, because they've ended the relationship with you or in some cases because they've chosen a more dangerous path for themselves."

Activists like Diane Ehrensaft peddle, and stooges like Governor Cox buy, the claim that 'gender affirming care' is like chemotherapy for cancer—life-saving and medically necessary. This is infuriating and deeply offensive to me because I am the mother of a trans-identified young adult daughter who thankfully seems to be desisting, and an older teenage son in active treatment for leukemia. Based on my son's risk factors, his oncologist has given him an 85% chance of survival. His treatment is life-saving and medically necessary. Without it he would already be dead. The hard truth is that even with it he might still die. It is hyperbolic and shameful for anyone to conflate chemotherapy with 'gender affirming care', or to hold parents emotionally hostage with the words "transition or die", "live son or dead daughter."

It's true that my daughter has been in great distress. She is a bright, socially awkward, mildly autistic girl with depression and generalized anxiety. But she is not going to die. In fact, how can she not be distressed when she has internalized what she's heard repeatedly—that she one of the most marginalized, most oppressed, and most hated people on the face of the earth? That people are literally trying to erase her existence? That she must undergo extreme medical and surgical procedures and become a lifelong medical patient or she might kill herself? As she walks the road to desistance she told me recently that she believes she can re-learn to love her body, but she is going to have to "unlearn a lot of stuff."

Advocates of 'gender affirming' healthcare cite high suicide rates as evidence that medical and surgical intervention is "life-saving and medically necessary." It goes without saying that every suicide is tragic, but there is no high-quality evidence to suggest that the often quoted overall attempted suicide rate of youth who identify as transgender is 41%. Dr. Laura Edwards-Leeper, who is the Chair of the Child and Adolescent Committee for the World Professional Association for Transgender Health, has stated, "As far as I know there are no studies that say that if we don't start these kids immediately on hormones when they say they want them that they are going to commit suicide.. So that is misguided… in terms of needing to intervene medically to prevent suicide and doing it quickly. I know of no studies that have shown that." There is also no evidence that medical transition decreases suicidality. In fact, one study showed that post transition adults were 4.9 times more likely to have made a suicide attempt and 19.1 times more likely to have died from suicide than the general population. No one is born in the wrong body. Our sex is written into the DNA of every cell of our body. People cannot change sex. It's a serious thing to insinuate to someone that their healthy body is somehow wrong and might require extreme, irreversible cosmetic interventions to relieve mental distress. There is no right or wrong way to be a boy or a girl, a man or a woman.

Let me spell out for Diane Ehrensaft a few of the many reasons why it's inaccurate to conflate cancer treatment and 'gender affirming care.' First, chemotherapy is given only after a confirmed diagnosis of cancer. We could not have brought our son to the hospital, declared he had cancer, and demanded chemotherapy. Demanding medication based on a self-diagnosis is something only my trans-identified daughter could have done—because that only happens in gender clinics.

Second, pediatric cancer treatment is evidence-based. My son's treatment plan was mapped out from the moment of his diagnosis based on exact protocols obtained over decades of research. It's literally on a spreadsheet his medical team calls "the road map". His hospital is part of a consortium of children's hospitals that share data to further improve treatment and outcomes. 'Gender affirming care' is called the Wild West of healthcare for a reason. After a systematic review of the literature the countries of Finland, Sweden, the UK, and France, and the state of Florida have found the evidence for 'gender affirming' care to be of such low quality that they have abandoned the affirmative model of care. Even the much touted "gold standard" Dutch Protocol is now being discredited due to serious methodological flaws.

Third, outcomes for childhood cancers are well known, published, and updated. Post treatment my son will be followed for many years to assess his outcome. Outcomes for patients of 'gender affirming care' are mostly unknown. Clinics and providers rarely keep data and patients aren't followed long enough to get reliable outcome information. Studies show that the average time to regret a gender transition is 8-10 years, but most patients are given follow up for much shorter times, if at all.

Finally, kids with cancer are given harsh, life-altering treatments because there is no other choice. Cancer treatment is truly life or death. 'Gender affirming care' however is iatrogenic, meaning that the treatment actually contributes to the condition. Eleven longitudinal studies have shown that, if just left alone, approximately 80% of dysphoric kids will simply outgrow the distress they feel and become comfortable with their bodies.

My family is very fortunate that childhood leukemia has a good prognosis, but the treatment is a grind. My son has faced his treatment with grace, good humor, and as much optimism as he can muster. One clinic day though my son just wasn't having it. He was exhausted, nauseated, and facing a long day of treatment. When his nurse came in to get him ready for chemo he was sitting hunched over on the bed, hoodie pulled over his head, eyes closed, earbuds in. She asked him if he had done anything fun that week and he just rolled his eyes. Nurses work with these kids every day for their job but they don't live the reality. It's hard to do anything fun when you feel like crap.

After a few one-word responses from my son to her questions she asked him point blank "Are you having suicidal thoughts?" We felt ambushed by the question and I immediately jumped into the conversation.

"Are you kidding me? Why would you ask him that?" She explained that per hospital protocol she has to ask that question monthly. " Fine," I said. "We get it. But please put the question in context." My daughter announced her 'transgender' identity to us with the help of an adult my daughter felt she could trust. We all sat on the couch in our living room while this man called our daughter by the new name she had chosen and warned us of her "high suicide risk." As shocked as I was I still remember thinking, "Why are you talking about suicide in front of her? She's sitting right here!?!" I understand that one way to prevent suicide is to ask about it directly. I'm not discounting that. But why didn't my son's nurse say, "Look, I know things are really hard right now but it will get better. We're here for you and are going to take very good care of you." Why hasn't anyone except PITT parents and allies thought to say these same words to trans-identified kids? "Life is hard sometimes but you can get through this." There are many detransitioners who have expressed that they wish someone had said these words to them.

Experts agree that suicide contagion is a risk. That's why the media has strict guidelines in how they report suicide. It's incomprehensible why all that goes out the window with 'trans kids.' Sociologist Michael Biggs highlighted this in a recent podcast interview. He stated that the "live daughter better than a dead son" rhetoric has been around for a long time, and that it is true that a large number of young people who identify as transgender claim that they've thought about or attempted suicide. Suicide and self-harm can be a real concern but, he explains, "...when you make suicidality a central part of the [trans] identity, that actually that sort of enhances the likelihood of making claims about suicide. Because 'to be trans' in some ways means 'to be suicidal' because 'society is rejecting you' or 'your parents are rejecting you'. So it's very important to actually know how many deaths result." Data he obtained with a freedom of information request from the NHS in the UK showed 4 suicides out of 15,000 transgender identified individuals. That's not 41%. I wonder if Utah Governor Cox would still think boys should be allowed to play in girls' sports if he understood it's really not a life-or-death situation.

PITT readers, we have to get this suicide myth stopped in its tracks. We must take back control of the narrative. Speak up and speak out whenever and wherever you can. Call out this emotional blackmail for what it is. Challenge your kid, your medical providers, your legislators, your schools, your friends, and your family. Debunk this untrue, harmful myth wherever it's being perpetuated. "Transition or die" is one of the flimsiest reasons among a host of incredibly flimsy reasons for the chemical castration and genital mutilation of kids. Calling the suicide myth out for the harmful nonsense it is will help to bring an end to this horrible era of medical experimentation on kids. Proclaim the truth! We have live daughters and sons!!

37

When Two Worlds Collide: Part 3
—The Collision

I am the mother of both an older teenage son and a young adult daughter. My son was diagnosed with leukemia two years ago and is still in active treatment. My daughter announced a transgender identity six months after my son's diagnosis. Thankfully she seems to be desisting. Having one child with cancer and one with gender confusion has given me next level anxiety. There have been many days when I can barely get out of bed and function, and may not have except for how much care my son needs. To say that these past two years have been the hardest of my life might be the understatement of the century. In order to survive these ordeals I've had to compartmentalize my separate roles as a cancer mom and ROGD mom.

During the day you'll find me doing whatever I can to help my son—keeping him comfortable, making any food that sounds appetizing to him, administering medication, doing endless laundry because he sweats out chemo that makes his clothes and sheets stink, and being with him at the hospital for treatment.

Late at night you'll find me scouring websites and substacks for information, reading the latest PITT article for support, and crafting endless dialogues in my head that might plant just the right seed to help bring my daughter on this tenuous journey back to reality. I have real life and online cancer mom friends, and real life and online ROGD mom friends and have to be careful to keep straight who is who so I don't inadvertently say the wrong thing to the wrong friend. Most days I'm walking a very thin line of sanity. Occasionally my two worlds have unexpectedly collided. This has very nearly pushed me over the edge into a complete meltdown.

When you're a cancer mom you spend a lot of time at the oncology clinic at the hospital. There are two types of families that come to clinic—those whose kids have hair and those whose kids are bald. Kids with hair are either at the end of treatment or just diagnosed. It's easy for a veteran cancer mom to tell the difference. Kids with hair who are at the end of treatment look great! They're through the hardest chemos so their hair has grown back. Their eyes are bright with relief. They've been through hell and back. Clinic feels like a reunion. The parents greet the staff by name and hug other kids and parents who have traveled this journey with them because they have come to feel like family. These families come to clinic in regular street clothes because the kids are going back to school and the parents back to work after a quick check of labs and a visit with their doctor. They travel light. Just a small backpack or purse will do. They won't be in clinic very long that day and don't need much. Other parents look enviously at these families hoping to be them someday. Many families will get to this point, but some will not.

Kids with hair who are newly diagnosed don't look so great. They're in the early days of treatment and their hair hasn't fallen out yet. Their eyes are tearful, full of worry. The parents are scared and a bit shell-shocked, still in the early stages of grief and disbelief that this could be happening to them. They sit huddled and isolated in the waiting room. They don't know anyone at clinic yet and can't imagine how someone could come to this place and smile. They too are in regular clothes and have packed light. But it's because they don't yet know that it takes a lot of stuff to keep a kid comfortable and entertained during long treatment days. Other parents look at these families with compassion. Everyone remembers how the early days felt.

Then there are the bald kids. These are the kids in the thick of it, the hardest most grueling part of treatment. These families have eyes heavy with fatigue. It's a lot of work to care for a very sick child. Parents wander the clinic halls familiarly, helping themselves to snacks, blankets and pillows, and maybe even a toy or game from the cupboard if the kid is up to it. They might visit briefly in the rooms of other families they've met, but keep it short because kids are tired, nauseated, and immuno-compromised. No one wants to risk spreading an infection that could be serious in a kid with no immunity. They're dressed in comfortable clothes. The kid might be wrapped up in a blanket from home. They pack heavy in big backpacks and bags full of whatever they can think to bring to get through the long day—snacks, electronics, chargers, an extra change of clothes. Other parents look at them with concern. They've either been here or will be soon. Sometimes people tell cancer families how brave they are. But really, what's the alternative? It's not bravery. It's just putting one foot in front of the other and hoping you get through it.

I don't have to describe to PITT readers what it's like being an ROGD mom (or dad). They're in the thick of it too. ROGD parents are full of anxiety. They analyze every detail of their child, looking for any signs of movement towards or away from the most serious harm. They do everything they can to support and love their child, to affirm the distress without confirming the identity. To preserve the relationship. They do this even when their child has been groomed by online and real-life influences into making impossible demands, and when they're treated in appalling ways by their child who has been conditioned to believe that their parents are the enemy. These parents hold the line and hold space for their child's true identity. They do all this in the face of blatant opposition from ignorant people who undermine their every effort, because the hubris of ignorant people makes them believe they know what's better for a child than loving parents do.

My son is one of the kids at the clinic with hair. We've made it through the worst of treatment. You're never completely out of the woods when your kid has cancer, but for now things are looking good. Thankfully too, my daughter seems to be desisting. She told me recently that she clung so hard to the belief that she was trans because she wanted it so badly to be true. Otherwise she would have to admit to herself how much time and energy she wasted over many years believing in something that turned out to be nothing more than wishful thinking. She says it's "so embarrassing." And she would have to come to terms with the fact that she has problems in her life without a straightforward solution. We know we're not out of the woods with her yet either. Kids boomerang in and out of 'trans.' But again, for now things look good.

Here's how my two worlds have collided. A few months ago I happened upon a long social media post from an affirming mother. "My son got his 2nd blocker yesterday! YAY!" She then described what an ordeal it was getting the blocker. Numbing cream was applied and numbing medicine injected. When the doctor came in, her son "freaked out." It took over an hour to convince her son to go ahead with the procedure, requiring a child life specialist's intervention for distraction and reassurance, and bribery with money. Her child cried, and she was scared the child wouldn't comply. She said the medicine cost $43,000 and has a limited shelf life, so coming back for sedation wasn't an option. She expressed pride in her son's "bravery for going through with the procedure" even though her son declared how "unfair it was that he has to do this." She said that she can't explain to her friends who don't have a "trans child" how "stressful it all is", and that "being the parent of a trans child is not the same as just being a parent."

I could sympathize with this mother. This is my reality too. Numbing cream, tears, child-life specialists, unfairness, bravery, even bribery to comply with treatment are the experiences of cancer families. But then it dawned on me. This mother was talking about her *daughter*, a girl, who she is referring to as her "son". This child is being cajoled into getting 'treatment' using the same techniques cancer moms have to use when their kids are getting chemotherapy. I say 'cajoled' because this child isn't sick! Her healthy body is being irreversibly damaged by so-called treatment. Reading the post I began to shake and cry. I felt like I might throw up. This mom wants to be a 'cancer mom.' She wants a medical team to take care of her 'sick' child. She wants to be 'brave' in the face of adversity she didn't ask for. She wants to be me! Well, she can have it! Hard treatment days, fear of an unknown outcome, taking care of a very sick child, being a parent with hollow eyes that has to steel yourself to make your child go through the unimaginable. Hearing your child beg you to not make them do this. She can have it all!

Reading about this child's manufactured medical crisis felt almost beyond comprehension. But parents don't manufacture a medical crisis alone. It requires clinicians who believe they're doing the life-saving work of oncologists. The hubris of clinicians who provide 'gender affirming' care is jaw dropping. The arrogance and lack of clinical curiosity is something to behold. It's known that tragically one of the patients in the original Dutch study died from a post-surgical infection. Describing this medical atrocity and the questionable data used to justify it UK sociologist Dr. Michael Biggs stated, "There was much less of the empirical evidence. In fact…when you read the article carefully, a lot of the results, the 'good results'… they didn't give the questionnaire to all the kids or the kids didn't fill out the questionnaire. So some of the results might rest on 32 kids. So the 70 [kids in the study] goes down to 55, but actually they've got data on maybe 32 kids which is a relatively small number to base a massive medical procedure on. And then they kill one of the 70 of the kids! That's actually a big deal and would close down any other treatment if you had that kind of fatality rate among healthy kids. I mean these are not kids with leukemia or cancer. These are kids who are healthy Dutch teenagers. And they killed one of the 70 of them!" Some time ago my son and I were checking into the hospital for treatment. At the reception desk I noticed a posted list of department phone numbers. I scanned down the list and was sickened, but I guess not surprised to see that the children's hospital where my son has gotten such excellent care has a "Transgender Medicine" department. I'm horrified to know that the hospital that is saving my son's life is also harming children. But hopefully not for long.

Early this year the state of Utah made headlines as the first state this year to pass a law banning 'gender affirming' surgical procedures on minors and placing a moratorium on puberty-blockers and cross-sex hormones. Some states have already done this, others are set to follow suit. To many this seems like the obvious right thing to do. But of course, that's not how it's being framed in the media. Somehow banning the chemical castration and genital mutilation of kids is deemed "controversial." The bill has gotten a lot of press. The sponsor of the bill is Senator Michael Kennedy, a family practice doctor. Based on his comments to the press he seems to have a very clear understanding of the issue. In interviews he's explained that European countries and the state of Florida have halted medical and surgical procedures for minors after they've done a systematic review of the literature and found that there's no evidence to support them. It's such a relief to hear him saying things that are true.

I knew there would be push back against the bill from activist organizations but I've been stunned to see the passionate pleas from parents who seem truly convinced that their children need these extreme interventions. During a legislative hearing one local father recounted his daughter saying "'if she cannot be who she knows she is, then there is no point in her continuing to live.'" He went on, "I guarantee you that if she did not have access to these life changing opportunities, she would not be with us today." My heart breaks for these parents. I can only imagine what it must feel like to be in a legislative hearing where testimony is given that there is no evidence to support the extreme, irreversible medical and surgical interventions your child has had. I can understand why parents double down. The cognitive dissonance of these parents must be overwhelming. You'd have to double down. The only other alternative would be to admit that your child has been irreparably harmed by interventions you were promised would help. It's unimaginable. No wonder these parents feel like this is a personal attack.

Realizing you might have harmed your child when you were trying to help would be almost too much to bear. Helen Joyce explained this in a recent podcast interview. "The specific people who are going to be most angry are those who have made irrevocable choices on the basis that the rest of us would go along with those choices. Most of all the parents who transitioned their own children, because if you transition your own child you are in effect making a promise to that child that the whole world is going to step in line for the entire rest of that child's life, and now there's people like me saying, actually that's not going to happen. You can tell your boy that he's your daughter if you like but he's not going to be able to play in women's sports, and I'm going to fight tooth and nail to get him out of women's changing rooms as well. Those people are all in. They've bet the house. They bet their lives on an ideology that we're now fighting back against. They're going to fight to the death on this."

The response from activist organizations is exactly what you'd expect. Lots of talk of "marginalized" and "vulnerable" kids for whom this care is "life-saving" and "medically necessary." The ACLU of Utah and the National Center for Lesbian Rights have already said they will be filing a lawsuit. "We're putting together a challenge as quickly as we can," says Shannon Minter, the NCLR's legal director. "If a child cannot get treatment they will be harmed, they will become sicker, they'll become worse, they will suffer very serious consequences…even life-threatening consequences." Once again my worlds collide. Is Shannon Minter talking about chemotherapy being withheld from kids with cancer? No! She's advocating for a 15-year-old girl to be able to amputate her healthy breasts! British legal commentator Dennis Kavanaugh has foreseen this moment. He's described the eventual "fall of the gender creed" in three stages: "The flight of the cowards. The howl of the zealots. The prosecution of the monsters." It seems we're witnessing the howl of the zealots. The statement from the NCLR is so hyperbolic as to be almost comical. It's really next level and doesn't make for good optics. It's almost as extreme as aggressive men shouting down women for simply talking about their sex-based rights. It's enough for even the most casual observer to say, "Hang on now. What's actually going on here."

ROGD parents and affirming parents are not enemies on opposing sides of a battle. We both want what is best for our kids. With legislation removing medical and surgical treatments as an option for kids I encourage ROGD parents to reach out to affirming parents whenever we have the opportunity. Offer them a golden bridge. Model and invite them to explore other ways to support and show love to their child. I know this can be hard when so many of us feel the need to remain anonymous for the sake of our children. Senator Kennedy said he crafted his bill as a "firm and responsible but also compassionate response to this very complicated circumstance." He wants to "partner with honest, professional people to try and do justice to this community" and make sure "our children are cared for in the safest most effective fashion." This is what PITT parents have been asking for all along. Compassionate, evidence-based care. Senator Kennedy, as parents with inconvenient truths about trans we couldn't agree more.

Parents on Schools and Universities

38

Post Pandemic Public School Propaganda

Parents re-entering the Public Schools Post-Pandemic, long after the students were welcomed back, should prepare to be bombarded with a heavy dose of "Trans" Propaganda. After a two-year COVID hiatus from scarcely stepping foot inside our local high school I, along with many other small town Canadian parents, was recently readmitted for parent teacher interviews.

Greeting students and visitors alike was a "safe space" sign decorated with the "progress flag" on a door just beside the front entrance, a *virtuous* signal begging for the entry of any student who has taken their place under the "trans umbrella". Within its periphery were at least three other signs and flags all bellowing the same message of *inclusivity*, one that couldn't be missed by any set of open eyes.

As my daughter who claims to be my son, my actual son, and I zig-zagged from one teacher to the next, the number of "trans" representative flags, banners and signs on doors and walls, windows and whiteboards, slid into the category of complete overkill. What I didn't see, however, was one prominent piece of paper or plastic that silently bolstered the embrace of any other categorizable group of individuals. The visual environment in which my kids, and some of yours, are regularly sequestered to receive their government-directed education had been filled floor to ceiling with "trans" propaganda.

The brick and mortar of the high school was not the only aspect in which not so subtle *progressive* change had occurred since my last visit.

Well aware that staff members had been participating in a campaign, willingly or not, to preserve or propel my daughter's "social transition" to a pseudo male student, seemingly without my knowledge and definitely without my permission, I had come prepared for potentially awkward exchanges. My exasperating expectation was not left unmet.

I spoke with a grade eleven English teacher, who had crafted a space for incoming parents to sit directly across from a very large "trans" flag, which also served as her outspoken *allied* backdrop. Though the discussion was meant to revolve around my son's progress in her class, she spent an unwarranted amount of her time side-eying my indoctrinated daughter and gravitating toward topics like "inclusivity in the classroom". She seemed to have a very clear message that she didn't want to miss the opportunity to candidly convey. A spontaneous chant of "trans rights are human rights" or "trans women are women" would have only slightly intensified the point she seemed so adamant to make.

In a much less gauche meet-and-greet, the first of my daughter's teachers on our roster used no name and no pronouns while referring to her throughout our entire exchange. The friendly visual arts teacher managed to stay on task and talk about assignments, lesson plans and my captured kid's level of participation in both. He artfully praised her talent and skill without a "he" or a "she" reference and I wondered if he did so out of a commitment to reality or to "protecting the trans child" from a potentially bigoted parent. Since I can't recall a slathering of propagandized art projects or conspicuous sloganeering within his classroom I'm going to allow my optimism to prevail.

At another stop on our *woke* walkabout, a grade 10 math teacher, who actually gave the impression of truly trying to be kind and inclusive, fumbled around with my daughter's "new name" but again, at no time referred to her as "he" or "him". She is an example of a well-meaning but misguided adult, guilty of helping to solidify my child's adopted "gender identity" on a daily basis. In this particular parlay, however, she just appeared foolish, probably even to my kids, through her floundering display of obliged "affirmation". I've told my daughter many times that just because the adults around her are using her made up name and calling her a boy, it doesn't mean they actually believe that she is one. Knowing my highly intelligent and incredibly perceptive teenager, coupled with the telling look we shared upon reentering the TQ+ laced hallway at the end of the interview, I don't believe that any of this was lost on her.

Promisingly, the awkwardness that sat like a stone between another of my daughter's teachers and myself seemed to be sprinkled with subtle codes of common sense camaraderie. In the presence of my two teens, this teacher seemed to be cautiously skirting around the woke witchcraft that had cast an unwanted spell on his entire vocation. I wondered where our conversation might have gone had *Big Brother* not been watching.

This seemingly un-captured and covertly concerned teacher laid heavy emphasis on his plans to instill a sense of discernment in his students while they sift through the world wide web for entrepreneurial materials in an upcoming portion of his course. He emphasized the once valued adage that you can't believe everything you read on the internet, to which I emphasized my concurrence. Whether or not wishful thinking played a part in my interpretation of our conversation, I found a now rare sense of relief with this particular professor of grade ten business.

It's incredible how much can be said with just a few real words and phrases that happen to naturally counter the nonsensical narratives that have candy coated much of the language our children are exposed to each day. And it's frightening that, in small town Canada, a mother of an obviously troubled teenager and her conceivably concerned teacher are being strong-armed by a government-backed ideology into conversing as if sitting in front of a Telescreen.

I completed the teacher tour with my two teens, the undeniable overload of "trans" propaganda peppering the hallways and classrooms, the guidance office and cafeteria, knowing that not all of these professionals have bought into this salacious social sickness. I wondered if my kids, both of whom are receiving an ongoing education in critical thinking and common sense at home, were able to pick up on the little hints of anti-*wokeness* with the business teacher or on the hesitancy for any of my daughter's teachers to actually call her a boy.

My country has solidified their allyship with the "transgender agenda" and it has turned our public schools into its living advertisements. I couldn't have been the only parent present who picked up on the TQ+ littered lobby to library landscape that seemed to pop up out of nowhere post-Pandemic.

Those of us who haven't pledged our allegiance to the "progress" flag have been deterred from entering our kids' increasingly private public schools—but I encourage those still standing on the other side of the suggested blockade to go in and see the splatter of TRA sign-blasting for themselves.

When we left *the youth indoctrination center* that evening I had note-to-self to find an excuse to contact the business teacher and assess the possibility of deeper dialogue tucked in my back pocket, and a pit in my stomach over the zealous onslaught of "trans" propaganda within its walls.

39

The Precipice

My child stands on the precipice. He's been perched there more or less for the past three years but, in a month, most of the last remaining guardrails will be taken down. At 17, a year earlier than expected, my son leaves for college.

Once a sign that you've raised your child right, setting him on a path toward a (somewhat) more certain success, the idea of sending your vulnerable, indoctrinated kid to college is now the stuff of nightmares. Perfectly happy children leave, full of excitement and promise, only to return having rejected their bodies and their entire childhood. Or they don't return at all. University health plans across the country blindly support the self-destruction of their students, providing drugs that introduce illness, and setting them on a path to the surgical removal and mutilation of functioning, healthy body parts. Who could have dreamed up such a dystopian horror show? What parent could have anticipated this heinous level of betrayal from an institution entrusted with your precious child's well-being?

Instead of enjoying the excitement of your child's hopeful future, feeling the pride of seeing him or her launched carefully toward adulthood, parents approach college with fear and trepidation. "Don't send your child to college," they warn. "Encourage them to take a gap year so you have an extra year of control. So they have another 12 months of neurodevelopment." Maybe common sense and acceptance of our physical realities will start to sink in. Maybe critical thinking skills will shake loose from their adolescent shackles. Maybe they'll learn to love themselves as the perfect, authentic beings they are, the way we so clearly see them. Maybe they'll wake from their internet-induced, ideological sleep. Maybe if we can hold on, if they wait just one more year, the world will shift back on its axis and stop working so hard to destroy them.

My son started high school during the COVID lockdown in Northern California, less than a year past a suicide attempt for which the only explanations were loneliness, self-hatred and an inability to fit in. He had a history of being bullied. He was the gentle kid in a school with a diverse student body, with its deeply troubled cohort, its "restorative justice" practices, it's Gay-Straight Alliance and its enthusiastic blue-haired advocates. The first year was a worthless disaster. He barely went to his online classes. His second year was hell. A solid year of daily truancy reports, calls from administrators that he was walking out of classes, laying down in the road, wandering off the closed campus, unstable. He was raging, furious that I wouldn't consent to hormones. But somehow, despite a level of emotional turmoil and upheaval I could never have anticipated, he went from failing most of his classes to eeking out a few Bs and Cs, and then to a smattering of As. The few friends he had were two years older, graduating, so he decided there was nothing at the school for him any longer. He set his mind to graduating a year early and the school was only too eager to accommodate.

His third, and last, year was almost uneventful by comparison - a blur of generalized anxiety and relief, and still regular truancy reports. He owned that school. They played by his rules. And then it was somehow suddenly over. Without bothering to take the SAT, he'd been accepted at a university in the middle of nowhere, 2,400 miles away. He skipped graduation, allowing no celebration.

Given the choice between another year in the Bay Area - with no real friends (despite becoming surprisingly social and well-liked), enabling teachers, in a school district that is introducing gender to elementary school children, in a liberal community so tolerant that my signs supporting Detransition Awareness Day were twice torn down, in a state determined to rip the seams of childhood and family - college in the middle of nowhere seemed like a safer bet. He'll be in a program that keeps its students engaged and busy, and he already has friends there (a small group of gaming buddies he's known for years), somewhat mixed up, but finding their way. And by some miracle, he unwittingly picked a school that doesn't facilitate sex-reassignment, in a state that is on its way to passing legislation banning these treatments for minors.

Maybe altogether it's enough to buy me that extra year I lost, but there is no breathing easy. No sigh of relief. I know all too well the range of options available to my wayward child, dark paths I've seen my friends' precious children take. He's talked about estrangement, "going no-contact"—the words of vile, disturbed activists—on and off for years now. Teen rebellion or ultimate plan? Flip a coin. And even though the school won't participate in his self-harm, the next state over is eager to help, dotted with poisoned Planned Parenthoods and their lax, dangerous practices. Anything could happen. Having a child lost to this hideous cult teaches you to accept uncertainty. Beats it into you with a brick.

I love him so deeply and I'm so incredibly proud of him. Yes, the school made it too easy for him to graduate, but he set goals and he attained them, largely on his own, through pure determination, despite himself and his worst impulses. He could find tremendous success at college. He could be launching into an adulthood I didn't know was even possible for him a year ago, couldn't allow myself the luxury of considering. Or he could implode. Dissolve. Disappear.

I lay awake at 3 am, or I've never even made it to peaceful sleep, thinking about what the world is prepared to do to him, to his perfect, healthy, beautiful body. Unimaginable horrors that I can't shut off. The torture of a beloved child. The torture of a loving parent. This world has gone bad. Become unbelievably cruel. But I have to hold onto my hope for him, if not for the world, that he'll find his way while he's 2,400 miles away. And find his way back.

40

Please Don't

I am a teacher and my daughter goes to school in my district. Two and a half years ago, right before the pandemic, my daughter, then 13 years old, told me she thought she was trans. She said she had studied me for a long time before deciding she could trust me with this information and then swore me to secrecy. I didn't overreact, and worked to radiate my unconditional love but, meanwhile, part of me sank into dread.

Instinctively, I knew I was in for the long haul, that conversations would be guarded and I was now playing a game of chess. Over the next few months, our few gender conversations led me to say "you are being lied to on the internet", "we don't make decisions based on our feelings" and that "what you and your friends are into is dangerous". Each of these statements was met with the slamming of doors. I said no to her request for hormones and surgery with the practical "we can't afford it and not on my insurance" while, behind the scenes, I searched for information and help. I got lost in the rabbit holes on the internet before I could sort out the truth and find the "adults" in the room. It was overwhelming. I read and listened to so many great stories from around the world in the last 2+ years, at least two a day. I couldn't believe what I was reading. It seemed like there was an enormous group of adults indoctrinating the children, while at same time taking advantage of other adults who are just trying to be kind. To these indoctrinating adults I say: Please don't.

I am a Christian, and my faith is an important facet of my life. At the time of her pronouncement, my child had already been seeing a Chris-

188

tian psychologist for years for other problems (which I now realize are related), including anxiety, depression, and ADHD. I started seeing a Christian therapist myself shortly after her trans announcement. At that time I didn't realize how rare it was to find the right people who wouldn't bully us into affirmation only, and how lucky I was to find help. For the sake of other parents who were not as lucky as me, to these affirming therapists I say: Please don't.

I am a teacher and an adult. Part of that means taking responsibility for my influence over a group of people, especially teenagers. I am acutely aware of the power dynamic involved in an adult/teen conversation—something that many of my well-meaning liberal colleagues haven't realized yet. If I can't preach Jesus in my classroom, why can you preach pronouns? Because you want to show students unconditional acceptance? That is exactly what Jesus is all about. Because of their safety? It is not safe to lie to children. To these teachers taking advantage of their positions to preach their gender religion in the name of kindness I say: Please don't.

I stay curious and ask questions for the sake of keeping the lanes of communication open with my daughter. I say "something is going on in the world because growing numbers don't lie". I bought Abigail Shrier's book and directed my daughter to *Pique Resilience Project*. My daughter showed me a YouTube video where trans man Sam Collins said the book was transphobic. My daughter said there is a part of her that knows she will always be female, and I told her parts of trans man Upperhand Mars' story, who believes biological sex matters. To those who resort to cries of "transphobe" rather than engage in cogent debate I say: Please don't.

I told my daughter: You have a great brain and you will figure this out. I told her she is so much more than gender. She told me that when her friends call her "Max" at school, she feels like her true authentic self. Hmm, where have I heard that before? I make sure she spends time around people who still call her her real name, including all of our family. Then there are two of her friend's moms who use male pronouns for their child and mine. To those other moms that think you are being helpful by using the male names I say: Please don't.

At the beginning of the school year, I asked my daughter, "Please don't ask adults to use he/him pronouns with you". I avoid it in my own classroom. My school pronouns are you/me because everything else means I am talking *about* you, not *to* you. I had a meeting with her teachers to ask that they please not use male pronouns with my daughter and I explained why—opposite sex pronoun usage is a powerful psychosocial intervention for children that teachers are not licensed to give. I only got pushback from two teachers, including a millennial-age science teacher who believes that people can be born in the wrong body. It is easy to love my trans students in class and just avoid pronouns. I avoid them at home and it is easy to love my kid. Children tend to believe the adults in their life that they admire, including their teachers. When these respected adults tell my daughter, "yes, you are a boy" this is very harmful. To those teachers that think they are being kind by asking for preferred pronouns I say: Please don't.

I want to speak with my school board before gender ideology comes to our district full force. I am afraid of being targeted, bringing trouble to my district and then possibly getting fired. Most importantly, I am afraid of damaging the relationship I now have with my daughter. It is a true blessing from God and I wonder if we would have gotten here any other way. While I pray that my own daughter comes around, there has to be something I *can* do, on a bigger scale. I want to get information to the parents of my child's friend group—at the very least they should know about Genspect and PITT, who are speaking up for the parents who are not going along with gender ideology. I know God will use me at the right time to speak out but for now I am just building my story and waiting to help.

For everyone in this fight, when you get discouraged and tired, look at how far it has come since Susan Evans raised the alarm, Keira Bell bravely took a legal stand—Tavistock the British clinic that permanently harmed so many children, has been deemed no longer safe and will be shuttered. Eventually, the US will have to follow Sweden, Finland, Belgium and the UK in their dramatic dialing back of medical interventions for children's identities. To all those parents who are hanging on by a thread, ready to give up I say: Please don't.

41

When You Fear Communicating with Your Child's Educators

My daughter has an IEP and has a new case manager this school year. I responded to an email from the case manager to check in and provide some info. Knowing they had recently met, I also asked what name and pronouns my daughter used when introducing herself. The case manager responded and said my daughter used a different name (I know what it is but am not going to use it here) and he/him pronouns, and then said she would be using that name and pronouns in her communications with me "if that was ok."

In trying to decide how to respond, I was struck by how fearful and completely devoid of confidence I felt in responding. I am very knowledgeable of my daughter and her needs and have never before felt this way in communicating with her educators.

If in my response I say "No, please use her legal name and pronouns" it feels like a pretty safe assumption that I will be negatively judged, which could impact how we work together on the things my daughter actually needs support for, related to her "other health disability" (ADHD), and in her level of trust in my input and feedback. Could the non-mental-health-professional case manager also use my statement to lead into conversations about her gender and "lack of affirmation" by her parents?

If I respond more thoroughly, attempting to explain that I detest and reject the way gender theory has infiltrated my daughter's life and sense of herself, that she has found a celebrated, trendy way to avoid dealing with her lack of self esteem, self-consciousness and social difficulties, and that "affirming" her different name and pronouns is not helping her in any way, but actually harming her, what would this non-mental-health-professional case manager do then? Is she so deeply entrenched that she would equate this to abuse or neglect of some kind, and report me to Child Protective Services? If I respond in this most honest way, I am actually, literally terrified of that happening.

If I respond with a lie, saying it's okay for the case manager to use a name that isn't my daughter's and pronouns that are wrong, will all of my future communications with this case worker just remind me of how angry I am that we are in such a hopeless battle?

Regardless of my response, her polite yet cursory question is actually meaningless—as is my response, however carefully strategized and considered. No matter what path I choose, after hours of agonizing, the case manager will continue to use the name that isn't my daughter's when seeing or meeting with her—as will the rest of her school. The schools have overstepped, by a mile, and pretending to seek my input is patronizing and infantilizing.

It doesn't matter that I haven't approved their involvement in a psychosocial intervention like social transition. They don't want or need my input or my approval. I've been completely pushed aside and marginalized and they are in a position of power. I have no choice but to fear, and no way to fight back that doesn't drive a wedge between me and my daughter.

42

What Happens When Schools Follow the Parents' Lead?

On January 22, the New York Times published "When Students Change Gender Identity, and Parents Don't Know," at last acknowledging that secret gender transitions were happening in schools. It featured a 16-year-old teen with autism whose parent discovered the teen had socially transitioned at school. At the time of publication, the Bradford teen continued to persist in a transgender identification. The article dared to report what many parents of ROGD kids have known: our kids often have psychological issues, and many of us skeptical parents are liberals. It even alluded to the danger of schools socially transitioning distressed youth. It did not, however, delve into whether schools who facilitate secret gender transitions actually cause the identify to persist longer or how in the world school staff are qualified to implement such a powerful intervention.

So what happens when loving parents challenge a school's unquestioning, one-size-fits-all approach to affirming transgender youth, and the school agrees to follow the parents' approach?

Over a year ago, I called an administrator at my teenage son's school. With my spouse by my side I explained we had read messages from a teacher referring to my son by another name. I stated that we loved our son more than anything, and we were concerned that he wasn't able developmentally to understand the consequences of social transition. I

193

detailed my concerns that my son was diagnosed with severe depression, and that he was seeing two medical professionals, neither who recommended social transition. He was struggling with his mental health and by far not in the best position to make a life changing decision. I pointed out that our school guidelines for trans students are "non-regulatory." My last argument, in desperation: my son leaves the house without combing his hair. He is not a girl, but a depressed young man.

The day after my call, I received a voicemail from the administrator. She was in the process of speaking to all my son's teachers. He would be addressed as James again in school. It was the day before Thanksgiving. I had joined a support group for parents skeptical of their child's sudden trans identification less than a month before. So I still didn't realize how fortunate our family was that the school realized they were out of their league and acted on our concerns.

At the time, we had greatly reduced our son's internet usage, and later, sprinkled in doubts and concerns we had regarding his sudden trans identity. As a parent, I have never faced a greater challenge or more immensely stressful time period with so little support.

A month after the administrator's phone call, my son started to show signs of desistance. A sudden shocking statement: "trans isn't real." A shorter haircut. No more Gender Sexuality Alliance (GSA) Meetings. The "friends" from GSA vanished. As the months went by my son's sweet, sensitive personality returned. Walking on the beach, he grabbed my hand and held it. Twice. Eventually, he stopped shaving his body hair.

I followed up with the school, asking for a meeting to discuss what had transpired. Several administrators and counselors listened while I explained that facilitating a social transition on distressed youth without family involvement was reckless. I fought to remain composed as I explained how the school, not considering the whole child, overrode our approach and created turmoil in our home. As we wrapped up, the administrator in charge of the counselors asked me a question.

"What is social transition?"

She didn't know.

Then another bumbling statement from a counselor: "but the suicide rate...we need to listen to our students...."

A month after the meeting, outside a school 30 minutes away, an acquaintance's fully affirmed trans-identified teen took his life. According to his mother it was due to his long struggle with mental illness.

In more rational times educators would not need be versed in transgenderism. But the reality is that, under guidance developed by activists, the two people in charge of my son's decision to socially transition at school were my severely depressed child, and the school counselor. I can't imagine that schools would want this burden, the constant worry of if we were doing the best for our child, and the lifelong repercussions if we didn't.

The school superintendent, in a phone call response to a letter outlining my concerns, acknowledged the lack of expertise and that "what happened with my son should never have happened."

While I'm grateful that my son's high school eventually followed the lead of my son's real experts, his parents, my son's time as a high school trans girl was not "reversible." As his depression lessened he was able to grasp what occurred: while mentally ill he was indoctrinated, he dressed in women's clothing, and was referred to as Anabel by school staff. That reality would strike suddenly, such as when our family visited an ice cream shop for a treat. My son's upbeat demeanor tanked as he remembered that the last time he visited the shop, he was with his trans friends, and he was a trans girl. These episodes were scary. I had worried about losing my son to suicide while he was trans-identified. This concern intensified as he navigated living in a conservative community as a desisted teen.

With their rush to affirm trans identities and follow flawed new guidelines, schools haven't considered the deep embarrassment faced by a teen boy who insisted that he was a trans girl, pushed childhood friends away, and then realized he was wrong. Many of us made regretful decisions as teens. Returning to school as a desisted teen, minus friends, is next-level embarrassment. Schools, who claim to be moving teens towards being independent, critical thinkers, are not asking "what if we get this wrong?" My family has experienced what happens when they get it wrong.

Some would wonder why we didn't move. My experience in living with a desisting teen is similar to that of having an alcoholic relative. We lived waiting, expecting a relapse. In short, the stress of watching a child move down a path towards more harm, while having to battle interfering adults, left us parents with nothing left in the tank. My brain was not firing on all cylinders, even many months later. I thought of the trans medical and school scandal from the time I woke up to the time I went to sleep. Several times, my body reacted with hives, swelling my face. Possibly due to stress, I went into menopause 5 years earlier than my mother had. I distinctly remember feeling, as my son started showing signs of desistance, that should he slip back into the trans identity, I had no more fight left. So we watched quietly each month he struggled through and concentrated on repairing our family.

The family pictures hanging in our house are all "preannouncement;" the recent years are just too painful of a period to reflect back on. I avoid speaking of gender, allowing my son to move on. My son now says he is "one of the lucky ones." He did not continue on the pathway. While true, I have spent some late nights with him while in tears, he discussed how difficult returning to school as himself has been. I wonder what the other students think was going on with me, he tells me. He states he cannot wait to finish high school and start new. He has more than a year to go. His high school experience is not reversible.

In allowing an ill teenager to diagnose himself, the school certainly stoked the fire, making walking back the trans identity more of an ordeal. My strong son is proving that he refuses to be collateral damage to school policies enacted without consideration to adolescent development by activists focusing solely on what they believe would have been best for them.

The current school policies for trans identifying students that do not require parental involvement may actually harm more students than they help, but there are no numbers, just the feelings of activists. Desisters and detransitioners, of course, are not invited to work on committees developing guidance for trans identifying students in schools. Imagine what Helena Kerschner or Chloe Cole would have to say. Or my own 16-year-old son.

Left unanswered by the New York Times article is the question: how many students would have grown comfortable with their developing bodies had the schools not rushed to intervene? We don't know. We don't know if the Bradford's teen would have desisted if not affirmed by the school. And yet the schools rush ahead, a runaway train off the rails.

I can share one statistic on what may happen when a school is willing to listen to parents: after roughly 2 years of identifying as transgender, and having briefly socially transitioned, my son has been living again as a young man for over a year.

There is no justification for secretly transitioning students in schools. It is not a "wrenching decision" as reported by the New York Times. Teens typically turn towards a more permissive parent, pushing for independence, while not yet able to foresee consequences. It's time for parents to reclaim their authority from schools, before more harm is done.

43

How Schools Can Better Support Gender Non-Conforming Kids

As kids head back to school all across the country, debates rage on as to how teachers and schools can best support gender non-conforming kids. These arguments often pit teachers against parents in a fight that sees students as the most common casualty. As the parent of a gender-distressed kid, I have felt betrayed by school officials in the past; at the same time, I have great respect and empathy for teachers and guidance counselors. I do not think deepening the divide between families and educators is the way to solve this problem, rather, here is my three step plan for creating a more supportive environment for ALL students.

Step One

Stop conflating "gender non-conforming" and "transgender." As Dr. Erica Anderson recently pointed out on *The Megyn Kelly Show*, these two descriptors are not the same thing. "Gender non-conforming" simply means a person who does not adhere to the societal stereotypes of his or her sex. Almost everyone I know is gender non-conforming in some way. I know boys who wear their hair long and girls who wear it short; boys who hate sports and girls who love them; boys who excel in art and poetry and girls who climb trees and snatch frogs out of river banks. None of these kids are transgender. The term "transgender" currently has many different meanings—for the purposes of this piece, I use "transgender" to refer to a person that has taken social and/or medical steps to live as the opposite sex.

To say that all gender non-conforming children are transgender, is to say that anyone who doesn't act or present themselves in a way stereotypical of their sex, should be grouped with the opposite sex. How have we landed here? Don't we want men to help in the kitchen and women to have a voice in the boardroom? Saying that "gender non-conforming" people are literally the opposite sex is completely regressive and not what we should be teaching our children. In the classic John Hughes film *Some Kind of Wonderful*, there is a brilliant scene where Watts (a gender non-conforming girl played by Mary Stuart Masterson) says to another character: "This is 1987. Didn't you know a girl can be whatever she wants to be?" Thirty-five years later, I am left wondering, *what happened to that message?*

Step Two

Stop asking for "preferred pronouns." I understand teachers have been led to believe that this question is necessary and kind. But who is being helped by this ritual? And who is being harmed?

Students are typically registered for school with their name and sex. I recently registered both of my kids for school and provided this information. Therefore, any teacher who understands how pronouns work, would already know what pronouns should be used when referring to each of their students. If a student is in the process of transitioning (socially and/or medically) with the support of their family, therapist and doctor, the parents can (and should) make that information clear to the school. These families can then work with school administrators to determine what needs to be shared with teachers and how best to support the student in question, in coordination with the family. (Social and medical transitions are serious interventions and should be carried out with psychological support that the school, alone, cannot provide.) Since this information will have been communicated to teachers and school personnel in advance, transgender students don't need to regularly announce their pronouns to rooms of people, drawing more attention to what might be an awkward and vulnerable time for them. Therefore, transgender students are more likely to be harmed by pronoun rituals.

Next, let's consider the gender non-conforming kids. A girl who, until recently, would have been considered a "tomboy," does not want to stand up and state her pronouns, just to have people openly wonder if she'd rather be referred to as "he/him." (Same goes true in reverse for effeminate boys.) This is an unfortunate situation that is occurring more and more, where well-meaning *adults* who are hung up on stereotypes, try to "be kind" by placing alternate pronouns on a gender non-conforming kid. If the student is registered as female, refer to her as such. Yes, even if she has short hair and wears "boyish" clothes. This is a dynamic that author and journalist Lisa Selin Davis has written and spoken about extensively, I encourage readers to check out her Substack, *Broadview*. As Lisa states in one of her many nuanced pieces: "Though many feel the current gender revolution makes room for organically gender nonconforming kids, I'd argue it actually pathologizes them. Telling a stereotypically boyish girl that she can be or is a boy doesn't manifest a liminal space for her to occupy. Telling a feminine boy that his mannerisms and tendencies make him a girl, or affirming his fantasy that he is one, tells him he's doing boy wrong, that there's not room for him in the category he naturally, biologically belongs to. I think this not only creates more shame, but can lead to very serious medical interventions." Since most gay adults report being extremely gender non-conforming as kids, we are talking about creating an environment where pre-gay kids are led to believe that they were actually "born in the wrong body." Gender non-conforming kids and gay teens are, therefore, more likely to be harmed by pronoun rituals.

How might this pronoun exercise affect neurodivergent kids? For a kid who is prone to obsessive thinking, intrusive thoughts and/or hyper fixating, this constant request for "preferred pronouns" can lead to obsessing over identity in unnecessary and unhealthy ways. Maybe they never thought about it before because it was always just a given, an immutable fact that they didn't need to ruminate on. (For some, it may have previously been the ONLY thing they didn't need to analyze to death.) But, once a slew of teachers keeps asking this question, a neurodivergent child may become fixated on trying to find the answer. Unsure, they will likely turn to the internet for advice. They may pose a question into the cyber void, *"How do I know what gender I am?"* More often than not, the internet will respond *"If you are asking this question, then you are trans."* The child then announces they are trans and becomes showered with praise and affirmation, something they have been longing for. This solidifies an identity that was the product of obsessive thinking, rather than actual gender dysphoria. Ritchie, aka Tullip, a detransitioned man, writes about how his OCD led him to believe he was transgender, only to pursue a medical path that he later deeply regretted. He writes: "The definition of Gender Dysphoria is deeply appealing to someone in distress, it's an invitation to abandon all your other obsessions and ruminations, in place of Gender, but the only difference between this and every other obsession I had, is this was being affirmed socially, legally and medically." Seen through this lens, it feels less like we are supporting gender distressed kids, and *more* like we are creating them by asking for preferred pronouns.

What about the teens who are politically active, or, at least, sensitive to things happening in the world around them? Here, I'm going to focus specifically on girls. Imagine a girl who is exposed to world and cultural news either through her family watching it on TV, social justice activism in her community, or stories she picks up online. Imagine this girl hearing that "cis" people are oppressors. Does she want to stand up and say that she *prefers* the pronouns she/her? Isn't that saying that she *prefers* to be "cis"? In other words *prefers* to be an oppressor? Is it fair to make her claim that mantle? Or perhaps this girl has seen stories of the #MeToo movement, and how women are vulnerable to sexual harassment and abuse, or not taken seriously at work, or objectified in society. Maybe she reads about the girls in Afghanistan being denied education by the Taliban, or the horrors of sex trafficking that primarily affects young women and girls. Can she hear these stories and then stand up and say she *prefers* to be a girl? By saying she *prefers* to be a girl, is she acquiescing to this treatment? Is it fair to pose this as a preference, knowing the implications? A girl who doesn't want to be an oppressor or a victim is not helped by the question of preferred pronouns.

And what of the budding feminist? What questions swirl in her mind when she hears the newest Supreme Court justice unable to define the word "woman"? Maybe, in search of answers she reads Andrea Long Chu's book *Females* commonly lifted up by liberal feminists. There she reads that Chu "transitioned for gossip and compliments... for Daisy

Dukes, bikini tops, and all the dresses, and, mygod, for the breasts." Is that what one is choosing when they say they "prefer" to be a girl? Or is it more of a fantasy as Julia Serano (author of *Whipping Girl*) has stated? "I would imagine myself being sold into sex slavery and having strange men take advantage me. It's called forced feminization… it's about turning the humiliation you feel into pleasure…" Julia Serano was born male, but *prefers* she/her pronouns. Is this what we are asking our girls to endorse when we ask for their preferred pronouns? What about a girl who doesn't want to be a fantasy in a man's head, one who prefers cargo shorts to Daisy Dukes, is uncomfortable with her growing breasts, and could never turn humiliation into pleasure? As Louise Perry writes in a review of Andrea Long Chu's book *Females*: "When a porn-obsessed writer can be lauded as a feminist prophet for describing the 'barest essentials' of 'femaleness' as 'an open mouth, an expectant asshole, blank, blank eyes' we should wonder how on earth we got to this point." So, where do our would-be feminist daughters turn when looking for a better example of "she"? To Joan of Arc? Not so fast.

Our fiesty daughters, who were raised on stories of fierce women who broke boundaries (and often paid a heavy price for it) such as Joan of Arc, are caught in a mindbend, as well, now that we are seeing those women being rewritten as non-binary, with "they/them" pronouns. Joan of Arc, and Queen Elizabeth I, have been posthumously transed along with other great women of history. How do our daughters process this mixed message? How does this impact *their* "preferred pronouns." As Victoria Smith wrote: "The transing of women who cannot speak for themselves—either dead or fictional—is not a break with patriarchal norms. It is an extension of them. It tells women and girls not just that there were too few women of significance to matter; it suggests that to be significant is not to be female at all." Clearly, the concept of preferred pronouns is not helpful to girls trying to become "women of significance," themselves.

Perhaps those harmed the most by the pronoun obsession, are desistors and detransitioners. (Desistors are people who socially transitioned before reverting to their birth sex, while detransitioners are people who medically transitioned, with hormones and/or surgery, before reverting to their birth sex.) Desistors and detransitioners generally go through an incredibly difficult period of time while sorting out their identity. They may not know how to honestly answer the "preferred" pronoun question. They already risk being shunned by friends. They risk being accused of "faking it." They often feel ashamed or embarrassed for believing they were trans. There is no "D" in LGBT, and the flags, and celebrations, and "inclusiveness" seem to go in only one direction—toward transition. Chloe Cole, a young girl who transitioned *and* detransitioned all while in high school has been speaking out. Her story was recently shared on the substack Common Sense. "Detransitioning senior year was tough: She was dressing like a girl again, but still had 'rough' features and a deep voice from all the testosterone. 'I got looks from people, and other students would talk smack behind my back,' Chloe said. Her friends abandoned her. Another friend told her that 'the gay side of my school hated me' because she detransitioned." Desistors and detransitioners need space and understanding, recurring pronoun circles are harmful to their process.

So once again, I ask: *when you ask your students for their preferred pronouns, who is benefitting from the ritual?* Not transgender kids, not gender non-conforming kids, not neurodivergent kids, not girls who are socially and politically aware, not young would-be feminists, and certainly not desistors or detransitioners.

Step Three

Stop making parents the enemy.

With a huge rise in kids and teens identifying as transgender at school, the question that keeps being asked is: *Should teachers "out" students to their parents?* Over and over I hear the refrain that "schools should not 'out' kids to their parents, because the parents might not be accepting, therefore the student would be unsafe at home." I would argue that this answer, and actually this question, misses the point entirely. It's not really a matter of "outing" kids, but rather a question of how can we best support kids in distress? In nearly every situation, the best support comes from schools and parents working together, not through creating cloaks of secrecy.

If a student approaches a teacher and says: "I would like you to call me by a new name and different pronouns," the teacher should respond: "I need a letter from your parents making that request." Seeking parental permission is required for field trips, after school programs, and sports participation—why not something as life altering as social transition? I have only heard two arguments for why teachers should immediately honor this type of request from students (without parental consent), and both of these arguments are rife with contradictions.

The first argument is that teachers must support this change in identity, no questions asked, because gender-dysphoric teens are at an increased risk of suicide. This narrative has been proven to be exaggerated, misinterpreted and misrepresented, as the Society for Evidence-Based Gender Medicine (SEGM) has pointed out on its website. An additional study, titled "Not Social Transition Status, but Peer Relations and Family Functioning Predict Psychological Functioning in a German Clinical Sample of Children with Gender Dysphoria," stated, "claims that gender affirmation through transitioning socially is beneficial for children with GD [gender dysphoria] could not be supported from the present results. Instead, the study highlights the importance of individual social support provided by peers and family, independent of exploring additional possibilities of gender transition during counseling." If the best evidence for improving mental health is keeping kids connected to their families—then telling distressed kids that they cannot trust their parents, and should keep secrets from them, is a dangerous idea. Additionally, if you truly believe that being gender distressed makes a child more likely to be suicidal, you are obligated to tell the child's parents. School officials who are keeping this information secret from parents are either derelict in their duties to inform parents that their child is at increased risk of suicide, or they don't truly believe the manipulated narrative in the first place.

The other argument you hear for why schools should not alert parents if their child is requesting a change in name and/or pronouns, is that the parents may not be supportive. The word supportive, in this case, is twisted up to mean only one thing: parents willing to socially transition their kid without question. Most of the parents that I know are extremely supportive, willing to go to the ends of the earth for their kids. At the same time, they do not think transition is a cure-all for their kid's distress. Parents typically know their children better than any teacher does. They may know that their teen has co-morbidities such as autism, or ADHD, or disordered eating that is influencing their gender confusion. The parents may know their teen has been subject to peer pressure or bullying or sexual trauma, and their child is seeking respite in a new identity as a maladaptive coping mechanism. Parents often are working hard day and night to help their kids work through their distress. Just because a parent doesn't think gender transition is a good solution for their child, does not mean they are abusive. If you would call a parent in to discuss a dramatic shift in their student's academic performance, you should call a parent in to discuss a drastic shift in their identity. If you have to ask a parent's permission to give a child Advil, you certainly have to ask a parent's permission to initiate a psychosocial intervention, which is what social transition is. As Dr. Stephen Levine, and others, pointed out in a paper titled "Reconsidering Informed Consent for Trans-Identified Children, Adolescents, and Young Adults, social transition is an intervention that requires *explicit informed consent.* They state, "While the causality has not been proven, the possibility of iatrogenesis and the resulting exposure to the risks of future medical and surgical gender dysphoria treatments, qualifies social gender transition for explicit, rather than implied, consent." Working WITH parents, not against them, is the route to better outcomes for *all* students.

I recently had a meeting at my daughter's school. As I sat in the office, I noticed a poster beside me that said: *"Feelings aren't facts. Feelings are real but they aren't always reality. Feeling like a failure doesn't make you a failure. Allow feelings to come and go without judging yourself for having them."* Wouldn't it be nice if we could teach kids that message with regard to their bodies? We need more posters that say: *"Feelings aren't facts. Feeling your body is wrong, doesn't make your body wrong. Allow these feelings to come and go without judging yourself."* This is how schools can truly support gender non-conforming kids.

44

To the Administrators of My Son's School

Dear Ms. L. and Ms. J:

I requested a meeting with Ms J. several weeks ago but I think instead I will just ask that you read my email today regarding our son, T.

He has been wanting to identify as transgender for some time and we understand that he is now referred to as Tess and she/her in some of his classes. We were anticipating this and think we understand the rationale for teachers and staff complying with kids' wishes. We think it ostensibly comes from wanting to be kind and of course, so they can just get on with teaching our kids, so I thank you for that.

My husband and I are liberals but we are also firm believers in science. We are both surprised that something that was so strange and rare has become so trendy and not so rare with our kids. T, (we don't call him Tess) seems to be trying to fit in using transgender as a way in.

T was diagnosed as autistic five years ago. He has always struggled to fit in and nearly always gets rejected probably because he just doesn't know the best way to relate to kids his age. He is currently seeing a therapist who focuses on his social skills and autism. T's feelings that he is a girl are treated as secondary but likely related. The idea that he is trying to fit in by saying he is transgender may seem strange but hear me out. People these days get a lot of positive feedback for coming out. "You're so brave!" "Good for you!" "Be your true self!" For a teenager who is isolated, awkward and struggles to connect, this may also make puberty easier to deal with since suddenly all the negative things about puberty can go into the same box. In our case, it seems like T feels that becoming a girl will magically fix all uncomfortable things for him.

I understand that, on the surface, it appears kind to comply with our kids' wishes to be socially transitioned—but it's a lie and it feeds the delusion that we can actually change our sex just by declaring it. No matter what we may wish, we cannot fight biology.

This brings me to what I am hoping to accomplish with my email. First, I would like for all his teachers to read this email. Some are aware of our feelings—specifically the five I met with during parent/teacher conferences. One teacher sent him an encouraging email regarding his trans identification. This was inappropriate. Again, I understand teachers and staff using the preferred name and pronouns to create the best environment to teach. However, we believe that actively encouraging him "in their journey" steps over the line. So, secondly, I would say, just be neutral or maybe ask if an initial such as T might be okay. I understand this may be too awkward for teachers who have already starting calling him Tess, but my request still stands. Thirdly, I would just ask you to try and imagine what parents are going through with this. Social media and peer influence is huge and surely you have noticed a spike in trans identification especially since the pandemic. We really believe there's a lot more to the situation for a lot of these kids other than a sense of mistaken gender.

T has a tough year ahead because he will probably be having jaw surgery in September and unable to attend in person for the first couple of months—an issue we hope to discuss with Ms S. when her availability improves. Unfortunately, this will likely make him feel worse about himself as he is healing.

Thanks for listening.

45

An Open Letter to a School Board Anywhere from a Concerned Parent of a "Gender" Confused Child

I have to say that I am confused.

I never ever in my wildest dreams thought that I would be speaking at a random school district's board meeting to help spread the idea that parents are the real constituents of their child's educational experience. I personally thought this was common knowledge or a commonsense value. Teachers work for the parents, and the administration is democratically elected to facilitate in service of the needs and interests of the parents. Parents are interested in having their children receive an education, and they have entrusted you to fulfill that task.

Your primary task in that endeavor should be that of continued transparent communication. In fact, much of this problem could have been avoided by sharing all aspects of a child's educational experience, including sex education, up front. This would include full log in access to all curriculum materials regardless of copyright rules. Parental access should be part of the negotiated contract with the curriculum publishers. Publishers, school administration, and teachers should have nothing to hide. With technology, it shouldn't be that big of a deal unless you have hired people that don't understand their job.

I also never imagined that this discussion point, parental rights in education, would be politically divisive in any way. I am constantly flabbergasted that all parents, all teachers and all administrators in all schools, whether public or private, would not wholly and completely agree with this simple principle. I never thought I would have to state out loud that I have been a registered Democratic voter my entire adult life in order to prove that I am not some sort of right-wing extremist (whatever that means), merely because I believe in family values and autonomous parental rights. Something odd has happened within our political system that has forced so many of us to be shamed into submission. As an educator myself, I never thought I would witness teachers willing to throw my, as well as their own, parental rights away while asserting that somehow my ability to understand and know my own child could be less than theirs.

I never thought the grownups in charge would be too busy to take the time to understand a massive social phenomenon that is happening amongst young people- young people whose childhood is vastly different than mine and most of yours given the unfettered access to unlimited information. With that access comes the impact of psychological disruptions of development when children are exposed to age-inappropriate content with which this generation is bombarded. Have we all forgotten how socially significant our adolescent and young adult years were? And how easily influenced we were? I know I am not alone in this thought. Imagine being that age now with the exponential rise in the use of technology and social media beyond any of our wildest thoughts. A perfect vehicle for the planting of bad and harmful ideas.

This is a vulnerable age and we have to ground our youth in reality. I never thought schools would be complicit in fueling this new social contagion. The reality is you cannot change your sex, so why are we promoting this as a normal thought experiment. Experimenting with the idea of transgenderism (which is a relatively new concept/term) is not the same as exploring one's sexuality. Frankly, it is a type of psychosexual abuse. "Transgenderism" is about decoupling yourself from your sexed body, which at another time in history would have been classified as body dissociative disorder, which would have warranted a call home to parents. And then parents get to decide which trusted adult, including family, would be equipped to best help their child. This is a task that should never be undertaken without the expressed written consent of parents. In fact, I believe consent rules got changed without full public discourse but that's a conversation for another time.

Wondering if you are gay is vastly different than wondering if you were born in the wrong body. One allows you to completely retain a healthy physical body. The other tries to convince you that you were born "wrong" and need harmful body modifications via drugs and surgeries. Does that seem like a healthy idea? Who benefits most in this scenario? Whistle blowers are speaking out. Why are you not doing your due diligence?

You know back when I was growing up teachers did not share many aspects of their personal lives with their students. We rarely knew what teachers' relationship status was outside of school. They didn't have personal photos hanging around their room. The focus was on educating us and keeping us physically safe. So, I find it quite peculiar that teachers would be discussing or proclaiming their personal sexual interests and proclivities. And likewise, if a student has a conversation with a trusted adult at school that crosses over curriculum topic boundaries and into an area of concern, a caring and ethical teacher's first course of action should be to facilitate a conversation with parents in a timely fashion.

The bottom line is parents know and love their child best, and that should be the presumptive, default position for any school employee. We have always told children that if an adult asks you to keep a secret from your parents, that adult is suspect. So it also stands to reason that any teacher or adult keeping a secret from parents is suspect. Best practice is full transparency.

(Feel free to use/read on a concerned parent's behalf at your local meeting - Permission Granted.)

46

The University Agrees—There Are No Clinical Metrics of Gender-Affirming Care

Our son recently started graduate school. He began hormone therapy during his final year of undergraduate education. Because he began to identify as a lesbian, transgender woman at 20 and showed no sign of gender dysphoria before that, we never had a chance to reflect—or advise him—on his choices. Going through the published medical research on the effects of estrogen made me aware that psychologically, excess estradiol in the serum causes depression among males, and physiologically, there are potentially much more severe side effects, including some impacting the brain and the immunological system. More of that in a minute.

Fast forwarding to the present day, before our son left for graduate school at a university with one of the country's most renowned medical schools. I decided to write to their student health center and share the studies I had found and, more relevantly, the psychological history of our child. What follows is the text of the letter and, after deleting potentially identifying information, the response from a high-ranking official within the health center. They are, for the lack of a better phrase, quite revealing.

First, my letter (I have not disclosed the name of the university and have changed the name of our child here, with apologies to the real Jonathans of the world; furthermore, apologies for the triggering usage of pronouns—I did not want to be dismissed as the "usual, hateful, bigoted transphobe"; rather, I wanted to be considered as the deadly serious parent who would do anything in their power to prevent their child from coming to harm):

Dear Apex University Health Center,

Our child, Jonathan, who is joining the graduate program at Apex University this Fall, identified themself as transgender during their sophomore year in college (2021) and started estrogen therapy in early 2023. Since every one of these interventions is off-label, I have been looking up the peer-reviewed literature on the effect of estrogen and whether there are any risks that our child needs to be aware of as they continue on this path. My findings, which I summarize below, have been alarming. Several endocrinologists—some who publish extensively—have told me they were unaware of the new literature. I have also been in touch with the Endocrine Society, and their response heightened my alarm.

While we respect our child's identification with their gender identity, we felt that they exhibited several psychological symptoms right before identifying as a lesbian, transgender woman (Jonathan was assigned male at birth and did not show any inclinations to identify as female before April 2021), and these co-occurring symptoms were not considered at all before he started on the prescribed medicines. Most tellingly, just before identifying as transgender, Jonathan's romantic advances were rebuffed by the woman of their affection. Subsequently, Jonathan also lost every friend they had, thereby remaining completely alone in their dorm room for the greater part of their last two years of undergraduate education. However, these psychological symptoms were never explored. Jonathan was recommended to start on estradiol and spironolactone immediately, which they did—and their physical and mental health symptoms have deteriorated since. Jonathan is also quite depressed, spending all their time without emerging from their room.

That is not surprising since, when it comes to the recent research on estrogen in natal males, excess estrogen in the serum in natal males has been associated with depression—studies among adult men and adolescent boys show that. Clinical studies (i.e., studies that recruit actual subjects and follow them clinically rather than rely on anonymous, online, non-probability surveys) that *promote* gender medicine fail to show any improvement in psychosocial outcomes among natal males. For example, the New England Journal of Medicine study from early 2023 concluded that hormone therapy is psychologically beneficial for transgender youth. However, in the main text, the study finds no improvement in depression, anxiety symptoms, or life satisfaction among natal male youth (the relevant paragraph is at the bottom of page 244 of the journal issue).

Thus, psychologically, there is ample evidence that excess estrogen is associated with depression among natal males. *Physiologically*, recent research shows that estrogen might have far more deleterious effects. A study showed that 12 months of estrogen treatment among transgender women leads to a decrease in serum BDNF levels. That is significant because a separate study shows that this decrease in serum BDNF level is associated with increased risks of developing MDD (or major depressive disorder). Lower levels of brain BDNF levels have also been associated with neurodegenerative disorders and found in the brains of patients with Alzheimer's, Parkinson's, MS, and Huntington's disease.

A high-quality rodent study shows that estrogen therapy among adult male rats leads to changes in their brains that resemble the changes in the brains of trans women. (There have been several other studies (2 links) among trans women that have shown these changes, but the rodent study indicated the *mechanism* by which these changes occurred in the brain.) Specifically, estrogen seemingly reduced the water content in the astrocytes and thereby disturbed the delicate homeostasis in the brain by increasing the relative concentration of glutamate (the brain's most abundant excitatory neurotransmitter), leading to glutamate excitotoxicity. As the Cleveland Clinic informs us, an increase in glutamate in the brain is associated with higher risks of neurological disorders like Alzheimer's disease, ALS, and many other diseases like multiple sclerosis. The research also showed that estrogen decreased brain cortical thickness and volume (which other studies have linked to patients with schizophrenia and bipolar disorder and lower levels of general intelligence). Furthermore, it was found to reduce cortical white matter integrity (which is related to cognitive instability). There is also empirical evidence of the lowering of cognitive abilities among transgender women that was presented at the EPATH conference in April 2023 (in Killarney, Ireland) - the researchers noted this decline among long-term patients at Amsterdam's famed gender clinic.

Research in the last few years shows that estrogen therapy among trans women has been associated with higher risks of various autoimmune diseases, from multiple sclerosis (recall, too, the association of MS with an increase in glutamate) to rheumatoid arthritis and many others in between. It has been associated with increases in the risks of prostate cancer and breast cancer. It increases risks of cardiovascular diseases (2 links), often by as much as tenfold compared to their cisgender counterparts.

Empirically, we see a much higher incidence of many of these physical and neurological diseases in the transgender population. It is perhaps not a coincidence, therefore, that population cohort studies (2 links) show that trans women, on average, die decades earlier than either cisgender men or women.

When I approached the Endocrine Society with what I had found and pointed out that many of these findings came out after the publication of their guidelines in 2017, I received an email from their Director of Clinical Practice Guidelines that they are currently fast-tracking a revision of those guidelines. She also mentioned that their evidence evaluation criteria have changed since the guidelines were published and that they now use the GRADE criteria for evaluating evidence. This is encouraging, but I have no idea how long it will take for the new guidelines to appear.

I point all of this out because Jonathan has the chance to start afresh and be reevaluated at Apex University's healthcare system. We increasingly see them stumbling with their memory, something that we could not even think of a year earlier—Jonathan used to have a photographic memory ever since they were a child. Having heard so much about Apex's medical school, we have high hopes that Jonathan's evaluation at Apex University's medical system will be more thorough than it has been so far. Let me be clear: We have no doubt about their gender dysphoria or their intense discomfort in their traditional gender role—we worry about that all the time. It is just that we have observed that medicalization has not brought them any balm so far—in fact, just the opposite. While the absence of any upsides (and the possible significant downsides) in the literature—psychological or otherwise—heightens our alarm.

After all, it is not only a lone voice like ours, but even mainstream media like the *Economist* (their April 5 issue with the cover story "The Evidence to Support Medicalized Gender Transitions in Adolescents Is

Worryingly Weak" comes to mind) and storied institutions like the British Medical Association and the systematic reviews of the literature from national medical associations of very transgender-friendly countries like Sweden, Finland, Norway, the UK, and (most recently) Denmark that are raising the alarm on the lack of high-quality evidence of any benefits from hormone therapy. (And these reviews I mention above cover only the evidence of the psychological effects of the hormones—they do not even consider the long-term *physiological* consequences.)

If all the evidence from the past few years is to be believed, there is now quite a body of evidence of genuine harm from administering estrogen to the natal male body (I have not researched the effects of excess testosterone on the natal female body, and so I cannot comment on that.)

As one of the world's leading lights in healthcare to nudge society toward better outcomes through research, Apex University will be well placed to lead the march for evidence-based care in gender-affirming care.

Thank you very much for reviewing the evidence that I have found and considering our child's health as they start their journey at Apex University. Please let me know if you have any questions. I look forward to hearing back from you.

With warmest regards,

XXX

A few days later, I got their response. I **have highlighted the relevant portions of their email** and annotated them within brackets [*all formatting mine*]. As I said, it's quite revealing.

Dear XXX:

Thank you very much for sharing your concerns about your child with us.

… **Apex U's Student Health Center (Apex SHC) is not directly affiliated with Apex Medical School and we do not provide care under the umbrella of the hospital.** [*Is the respondent making sure that the med-*

ical school is not implicated if something goes wrong with our son?] However, we do collaborate closely with our colleagues at the hospital and medical school, including in the management of our students receiving gender affirming care.

…

Gender affirming care is a unique process in medicine in that we are not aiming to treat and eliminate a disease process. [*Ah, an admission that there is no real goal of treatment through this care. Finally! But read on…it gets better.*] **Instead, we are using the tools of medicine to help individuals achieve very personal and sometimes nebulous** [*nebulous? WTF? After all these years of "settled science," all we have is "nebulous?"*] **physical and emotional goals. Success is not based on a clinical metric but usually involves a better quality of life balanced with potential risks including morbidity and mortality.** [*So, finally, an explicit admission—success is not based on any clinical metric. That makes complete sense to us inconvenient parents. After all, how can there be? There never have been any metrics, ever. At. All. All we have are some "nebulous" ideas of "better quality of life"—as decided by the patient right now, with no consideration of what might happen in the future as a result of the free dispensation of off-label medication. And oh, by the way, that "better quality of life" includes morbidity factors and dying much faster.*] We at the Apex SHC make every effort to ensure that our patients are **well-informed** [*in other words, make sure that they have signed the informed consent forms!*] about each decision that they make and **have time to consider these impacts without pressure** [*The irony of the sentence—"have time to consider these impacts without pressure." Wow! really?*]

Should your child decide to engage with us in care, our commitment to them is to **prioritize their safety** [*oh, the irony, once more!*], **the elements of their well-being that we can support** [*the rest—whether caring for them for the rest of their lives or paying for their illnesses and hospitalizations, with a big fuck you to your dwindling retirement funds—is up to you, you bigoted parents!*], and to help them make a **bright future** for themselves.

Very best,

AAA

As I read and re-read the email, all I could think was—Wow! What an amazing letter! AAA has no qualms admitting that there are no clinical goals of treatment when it comes to gender-affirming care. This is really quite convenient if you think about it—if there are no aims, any outcome is fine! No wonder these physicians get all flustered when we inconvenient parents ask them about clinical goals and outcomes.

All that these caring physicians want to achieve are some nebulous (which the dictionary defines as unclear, vague, or indefinite) goals. Oh, and please remember—once again—that those are *personal* goals, so please don't ask about evidence of well-being. (An inconvenient question, though—why should such personal goals be funded by others, whether it is the government or private insurance?)

And what if, as a result of those nebulous goals, the patients go through psychological, emotional, and physical distress for the rest of their lives, as detailed in the medical literature? Really, shame on you, you bigoted parents! Always such a nag! Always the party pooper. Why do you have to ask such inconvenient questions? Haven't these caring physicians already made it clear that these are personal goals and that it really doesn't matter that young children who are distressed might have no idea how to make a rational choice about the future? Who cares if they become hyper-fixated about something, as young children are wont to?

But then again, really, there is no pressure. No pressure at all. These kids are otherwise well-adjusted grown adults who know exactly who they are. Probably from the time they were toddlers. (What? You want evidence? This is getting really tiring. Give it a break, will you?) These are kids who are *not* immersed online, who do *not* gulp down narratives about "gender euphoria." They are stable, rational human beings with a very clear idea of what the future holds.

All these well-meaning saints—these gender-affirming physicians—want is to give these kids a bright future: a future so bright that it will probably include that intense bright light these pitiable young men will see when they die decades earlier than their non-medicalized peers. Who are you parents to stand in their way?

Parents on Social Contagion
and Indoctrination

47

Why Are We Erasing Neurodiversity?

Neurodivergence is a newer term meant to encompass differences once known as Asperger's syndrome and/or autism spectrum disorder. The term is somewhat controversial among advocacy groups and autistic individuals. However, the widespread adoption of the term has accomplished what advocates set out to do—destigmatize what they view as simply another human variation. Neurological differences are now thought of more in terms of immutable qualities, like ethnicity or race; the neurodivergent person is another instance of differences in the rich tapestry of humanity rather than a disability or mental disorder.

There is, though, a risk to this reframing. The ways in which neurodivergent people see and interact with the world can make them feel very different from others, and non-typically presenting relative to stereotypes, especially those relating to social interactions, sex, and gender. And, because of these feelings of difference, neurodivergent people are much more susceptible to gender ideology and its related social contagion than the neurotypical population. This is a fact that is blazingly clear and obvious to parents with trans-identified children, many of whom are neurodivergent or autistic—and we know that neurodivergent or autistic individuals are disproportionately overrepresented in trans-identified populations. Even gender clinics report a significantly high percentage of neurodivergent or autistic clients.

There are a number of reasons put forth to explain why these types of kids are so vulnerable and struggle so much with sex expression and sexuality. For instance, neurodiverse teens may have a more rigid, black and white thinking style that prevents them from seeing commonalities with same sex peers, and the difficulties in showing empathy puts up further roadblocks to developing strong peer relationships.

But lack of empathy does not mean lack of sensitivity—these kids are highly sensitive to rejection and being othered. They live in a world filled with shame and embarrassment from not fitting in and are always trying to figure out why. Isolated from ordinary peer groups, neurodivergent people still long for connection and belonging—thus making them more likely to succumb to social contagions and cults. They are prime targets for gender ideology which, unfortunately in our society, is trumpeted from all directions as a magical solution to loneliness and feeling awkward in your body. The internet and all aspects of entertainment are drowning in it. The very people who should be autism advocates are totally captured by the transgender movement. Civil rights language is incorporated into trans activism and is especially appealing to the strong sense of justice innate to these folks.

On top of the omnipresence of the ideology, the promise of becoming a new person entirely is thrilling—and also especially alluring to the autistic kid who, driven to academic success, seeks strategies to achieve social success as well. Embracing gender ideology gives the ultimate misfit an intrinsic excuse for never quite fitting in. A childhood of awkwardness and shame of rejection can be swept away. Failure as a man can, for the high achievers, be replaced by a shot at success (or partial success) as a woman. And, with trans, there's a built-in excuse if the success is only partial: If I don't master being female there is a good reason. I wasn't born one. Surely others will understand. The black and white thinking of this population creates an all or nothing scenario.

Our society seemingly worships at the altar of diversity, but gender ideology is bent on erasing the actual diversity in our society. How can we promote diversity while at the same time telling those who are different that they need to be fixed—that they need to medically alter their bodies to be whole? Moreover, to accept gender ideology, one has to embrace regressive sex stereotypes of clothing, appearance, interests, and social interactions, and find a way to fit oneself in a proper box based on these caricatures. That philosophy is as anti-diversity as it gets, especially when you consider that there is more than a hint of eugenics in transgender ideology, as the "treatments" themselves are essentially chemical sterilization.

I believe that shoving this marginalized group into transition is discrimination. We should just let them be in the world as they are if we truly respect neurodiverse people and actually value diversity in our society. We should let their minds remain a boundless spectrum of intellect and creativity—and leave their bodies alone because, after all, sex is an immutable characteristic, observed, not assigned as activists would have us believe. When we promote transgender ideology, we are making it clear that, if they want to fit in, they must change their bodies and their very nature. This is erasing neurodiversity. Instead, we should help young people sit in the reality of who they are, and learn to love their immensely valuable selves. Only then we can say we value diversity—natural, real diversity.

48

They Need Space to Grow

My older daughter is autistic and thought she was a trans boy from ages 14 to 16. She's now 19 years old, very feminine and doesn't want medical transition but remains confused on the concepts of trans and gender. She thinks gender can be a mythical creature identity. Five of her friends have been medically transitioned, all autistic girls. They are girls that have long hair, wear dresses and flower blouses. My younger daughter also thought she was trans from ages 14 to 16, primarily because of her discomfort with puberty which caused body dysmorphia.

I love my kids. When I'm sitting in the living room and overhear them talking with each other, I love them. When they run up to me, excited to tell me something that interests them, I love them.

They are innocent teens. They get attached to ideas, concepts, colors, stickers, flags, labels, boxes, identities, and groups just like any other teen (especially autistic teens). I've known them for their entire lives, every stage they've gone through and grown through. I've been with them through all the feelings they've navigated and shared with me. I've always been an open and available mom to them. I've always let them explore and be themselves. I relate to them and understand them.

But, this issue of gender dysphoria and medical transition is a big deal. It's a deep issue. Often teens are dealing with serious concerns that are hard for them to navigate.

It doesn't feel cool to be a girl struggling with puberty and body image and all the complications of feeling appropriate in public after female puberty. Not when all they want is to throw on a t-shirt and run around like they did when they were 11 years old.

But, putting them through a medical transition that has major health impacts while they're navigating puberty means they'll suffer life-long consequences that they won't want at 20-something, 30, 40, or 50 … when they've become comfortable with adulthood. I know my kids. I understand them.

They need space to figure things out without all these people around them, pushing them in an adult direction they don't understand, with celebrations that are so much more fun than the hard work of facing their issues and growing into themselves.

I don't want my daughter to be harmed. I will be the one that sticks by her for her entire life, no matter the pain she faces. All the people making her feel celebrated to go down a harmful path will walk away and not be there for her when things become difficult. They might even turn on her and be hurtful to her, as many have been to me.

I've been living through this for five years with both my daughters and their friends. Many people with no first-hand experience of being a mother to teens right now think they know better and won't listen or un-derstand. They've never even met my kids. This isn't like being gay. Being gay doesn't require medications that are not suited to their natural body health and life altering surgeries with consequences they don't yet fully grasp. How could they? They are kids. They need space to grow.

49

We Lost Our Daughter to a Cult

Our case is typical. An intelligent, young adult daughter, possibly on the high-functioning end of the autism spectrum, involved in social justice issues, suddenly professes a new supernatural belief. We, the parents, scramble to understand, but simply don't accept this new faith as "true." A few months of wary communication follow, then all contact is cut-off.

What the hell just happened?

We lost our daughter to a cult.

We didn't see it coming. Sure, there were always the social issues—she didn't seem to make close friends in high school, and also seemed to lack close friends in college. People seemed to know and like her, though, especially adults. She did well in college, and held a campus job. Later, we found out she did indeed find a new group of accepting, friendly people to hang with. They even had regular meetings on campus. Her new friends really seemed to love her for her authentic self. She finally experienced the thrill of group acceptance. She never mentioned this to us.

She was still doing well as a student. Even though there were some warning signs in retrospect, we thought this was just typical young adult stress and she would learn to handle it. At some point, we can't keep catching them. Kids need to skin their knees, but hopefully not get a concussion.

Then came the pandemic. Looking back, we see what could have been different, but we will never know if the outcome would have changed. Locked down in a room with nothing but an unfiltered internet connection, the new information systems went to work on her.

At first we sought to use facts and figures to convince her. In hindsight, we now realize how foolish this was—when one converts to a new religion, the convert won't engage in an honest debate. We tried to keep open minds. But one bright line we immediately drew—we would never support self-mutilation, which seemed to be a key aspect to this new cult. And that is where she chose the cult over her family.

By now it should be clear we are talking about the transgender cult. And we keep saying "cult"—but is this really a cult? Here are some definitions: en.wikipedia.org/wiki/Cult#Destructive_cults, "A highly manipulative group which exploits and sometimes physically and/or psychologically damages members and recruits." Also, people in cults show "behavioral and personality changes, loss of personal identity, cessation of scholastic activities, estrangement from family, disinterest in society and pronounced mental control and enslavement by cult leaders."

The situation checks all the boxes but one—there are no cult leaders. So this can't be a cult, right? Unlike, say, fundamentalist groups, this campus group didn't have a clear central authority figure. Isn't that the hallmark of a cult?

Technology has recently enabled destructive cults to arise that have no single authority figure. The authority is now "likes" and upvotes. No single person determines what is presented to the cult member as truth, it is the judgement of an anonymous, terminally online and unwell collective. The collective is enabled by social media.

And what are "social media" companies? Facebook, Instagram, Twitter, YouTube, Reddit, and so on. Despite the description, these aren't social media companies. They are mining companies. All of them have vast industrial infrastructures which mine human attention for advertisement revenues. And they optimize for the most effective and efficient mining without regard to any environmental side-effects.

Like real mining companies before regulation, they produce severe environmental damage. They are dumping untreated waste into our information rivers, and polluting the very information air we breathe. Unlike real mining companies, regulations haven't caught up with them. And also unlike real mining companies, the waste is addictive and insidious, like cocaine in soft drinks.

Is it any wonder our kids are getting sick?

This isn't the only new cult people are dealing with—we can get insight from the misery of others. For instance, Mike Rothschild's book *The Storm Is Upon Us* is about the Q-Anon distributed online cult.

From Chapter 13, "… How to help people who want to get out of Q":

"Cultic movements like QAnon substitute good feelings of like-minded strangers and the dopamine hits of hating the things those people hate for the ups and downs of personal relationships. They blast away the possibility of strenuous debate or disagreement with someone you love, preferring to create a world where those who don't feel the same way are the enemy, meant to be either destroyed or cut off from contact."

Seems about right. What does he have to report from the collected wisdom of cult experts? Here is advice from that chapter, paraphrased:

* Family and friends are mostly powerless to help until the person is ready to change.

* Stay in touch if possible, but on your terms. You don't have to pretend to share their new beliefs.

* Try to unplug them from the internet (i.e. get them away from the toxic sludge).

* Understand it won't happen overnight - disengagement is a process

* Do not use outdated terms or concepts (like brainwashing, deprogramming, etc.).

* Do not mock or belittle.

* Do not attempt to debate or debunk.

* Do not give up if it matters to you.

So we wait for the concussion to heal.

A close friend told us recently: this is just getting started. Your time horizon is going to be years.

Unfortunately, he is probably right.

50

Culture of Death

I was moved to tears watching the body cam footage of the police respond to the active shooter at the school in Nashville yesterday. It reminded me of my child's small school and the hallways... how easily this could have happened at any school. I imagined the horror and terror the little children and teachers must have felt while this was happening... the precious children and staff who were brutally massacred in a matter of minutes. How utterly senseless and sad as I watched the cops take down the shooter and to see her body laying there. I had a pit in my stomach as I cried and thought, could that shooter be any of our kids???? I am so grieved.

The TG culture is a culture of death.

Dead name

Dead past

Dead history

Dead family

Dead to anyone who opposes you

Dead self

The slow murder of our loved ones and their families... and people in their wake.

Murder is an act of hate... we can even murder in our heart when we hate someone.

The level of hatred that is being propagated in this ideology is undeniable. The hatred most of us feel not only from our culture, but from our own families and even our own children who have elevated transgender ideology to the highest religion in the land—with absolute allegiance or die attitude. This transgender religion that has created the most narcissistic legalistic Pharisees, who spew hatred if one dares to even show concern, question, disagree, or try to logically debate...

Fact: 42% of those who identify as Transgender have attempted suicide... Even in the most affirming cultures!

Not only does gender ideology fail to provide any solutions for mental health, it creates even more problems. Study after study shows that depression and suicide is HIGHER after transition than before. This is one reason why other countries in Europe and Netherlands are backing away from "affirmation only care". Too bad the US is full steam ahead in the wrong direction. Just look at how news agencies are stumbling to address the shooter by the correct self-identified pronoun rather than opening up a dialog on the mental health struggles that undoubtedly contributed to this week's shooting in Nashville.

Is my daughter on this same tragic path? Are other's daughters?

My daughter was once a loving, sensitive, ray of sunshine and such a cuddle bug. That laughed easily and so full of joy. That was the first to hop in my lap or grab my hand even in public. That after a youth retreat, came home and washed my feet. That was so sensitive and had a bleeding heart for anyone or any animal that was treated unfairly or cruelly. My child that wrote me sweet letters of love and won a necklace for Mother's Day for a poem she wrote about me.

Now as a young adult, going into her 3rd year of "transitioning"... she has slowly, methodically, coldly detached from me. Now, I feel nothing but indifference, resentment, and rejection from her. Once so close to her family that loves her, many of them have felt that as well.

The moment I saw her changing a few years ago, I grew concerned... as she slowly withdrew, sucked into her phone and screens despite my many efforts to pull her away. She slowly grew sullen and withdrawn and depressed, and started to "socially transition" (I had no clue what that all was then), growing out body hair, wearing masculine clothes, wearing men's body products, changing her room, cutting off her hair, binding her breasts, etc.

As I saw this happening before my eyes, I grew very concerned. I tried hard to talk to her, to reach out, to get her counseling, to get her off the screens and into new schools and more healthy peer groups. But then COVID hit, and she had to be "online' for school. What little socialization she had drifted away, and her propagandized online world grew bigger to fill the space. The more I tried, the more she pulled away.

When I was able to address her more undeniable effort to look like a boy, one of the first things I said to her was that I was so concerned that in her efforts to be like a boy, she was denying her femininity and herself. That this was a form of self-loathing and self-hatred. I know now it's part of this culture of death. It is a spirit of suicide that wants to kill and destroy.

Now what I hear from her is:

Don't use my dead name

Don't talk about my "dead" history

Don't talk about my "dead" self

Don't show me pictures of my childhood

Don't talk about the past or share memories

Don't hug me without asking

Don't expect me to say I love you when you tell me you love me.

Death, death, death....

The same spirit of death that convinces kids they are worthless, that their lives don't matter, to self-harm and attempt suicide. The same spirit of death that lies to kids, drives them to addictions, risky behavior, self-harm/mutilation and destruction.

What my daughter was doing to herself was deadly. It was a self-hatred fueled by addictions—to screens and her online world, her peers and this ideology, to transitioning, to affirmation and "acceptance". She insisted on being someone different at all costs, even to the point of self-harm and mutilation that we know is part and parcel of gender ideology and transition—the breast binding that causes physical injury and permanent damage to breasts and back/spine, the "tucking' for boys, the cutting up and mutilation of their perfectly healthy bodies with all these surgeries, the lifelong injections of hormones into their precious bodies... We know that all of this has irreversible long term effects and increases in stroke, cancer, bone loss, heart disease, and much more, including sterilization.

On top of all this, these "treatments" have disastrous effects on mental health. In addition to these gross dosages of hormones, these kids are usually also fed a steady diet of "meds" to help their anxiety and depression (made worse by the "help" of these therapists and doctors) of which have the very side effects of psychosis and suicide! I was just talking to a young woman in her early 20s who had to get off Prozac (taken for depression) because of the sudden spiral into suicide idealization she suddenly found herself in. It scared her so badly and she knew without a doubt the thoughts she was thinking were not hers and nothing she's ever thought before, she quit cold turkey.

I personally know of another young woman who decided to transition and use testosterone. She became incredibly violent and mentally unstable to the point her partner had to obtain a restraining order against her. I know from another friend that her daughter is getting FREE testosterone and "affirmation/transition therapy" from her public university in the south. Since starting this "care" by a "team of professionals" last August (including starting testosterone & changing her "meds") by Christmas, she had a nervous break down… failed her classes, almost lost her scholarship and lost her job. Literally could not get out of bed and had to take to take a semester off from school.

What saddens me and I think about as in the case of this tragic school shooting is that, perhaps like this confused girl, and so many others, beyond mental and emotional illnesses that are NOT being addressed, a whole new brand of psychosis is being sold as the "solution" to their problems by every institution around. I feel that my daughter is traveling down a road of mental illness, anxiety, depression. I pray to God for her and so many others that it doesn't lead to suicidal or homicidal idealization as I feared it may have for this young woman who shot up a school with an intent on dying that day. Lord, have mercy.

51

Mental Illness Equals Social Credit

My daughter was in middle school when she had her first major depressive episode. I knew she was being very quiet—but then she'd always been a quiet child. I knew she had social issues at school—but she did have one good friend, who had now moved away but with whom she was still in touch. And a few new ones. I knew she was worried about her friend, to the point of wondering if the friend was suicidal—but I didn't know she was projecting her own issues on the friend.

I found out over a school break that my daughter was suicidal. She was afraid to talk to me (why, I didn't know then). I of course hugged her, told her we would get her whatever help she needed, for as long as she needed it. We loved her, she never needed to be afraid to tell us anything, we would always listen. That was a long conversation, but I thought it ended well.

So off to our wonderful primary care doctor, who has taken care of all of us. She talked to her a lot, very gently, prescribed an antidepressant, and recommended counseling, which I was already in the process of arranging.

Over the next year, with various medical and counseling appointments, adjustments to meds, and many long talks, she seemed to get better. She came out as bisexual a few months later, then atheist, then lesbian. I did my best to not over-react or reject anything she said. I think I did pretty well at that, however much I felt mounting confusion and concern inside about the shifting identities. I read and read and read some more, and continued to listen, with as little advice as I could stand to give (since it seemed to backfire—but hey, I'm a mom. It's what we do).

And then the pandemic hit. In some ways, it wasn't bad. School had always been a sore spot—well, now she didn't have to "people". Sleeping in was easier with online school, and more time to herself to do her own thing was good. I knew there was a large LGBTQ community at school, and truthfully, the more time she spent around them the more screwy her thinking got.

What I didn't know was that the worst of the bad influences on my daughter were the online communities she had found and latched onto. Particularly Reddit and Tumblr. If you've read Irreversible Damage by Abigail Shrier, my daughter was the classic case of ROGD. By the end of the first year of the pandemic, she was non-binary and made the accompanying requests for a new name, and pronouns. Everything I got from those who cared for her said not to push, not to fight with her, so we went along with that.

It's not been easy. They/them was very difficult to adjust to. I was able to help pick a new name, that we both liked—she didn't realize that I picked it at least half for the feminine-sounding nickname. Her friends thought it was so cute when she went back to school with a mom who went along so far as to already have a fun nickname for her.

Over the last few years, we've had a lot of fights. I swear, the first time I tried to discuss bathroom issues and sports, she rattled off verbatim a list of trans talking points. Ending with accusing me of being a TERF, and screaming, "If you're against one of us, you're against all of us!" Followed by tears and hiding out in her room. More on this later.

There was about a year with no counseling, then another depressive episode sent me looking for a new counselor as the old one had moved away. More meds, changes to meds. A trip to a psychologist for a full workup—and now we have multiple official diagnoses, including ASD, ADHD, a personality disorder, major depressive disorder, and bipolar. And I've seen episodes of all of that—the first time I saw a manic episode that was eye-opening. She has a psychiatrist now, because our family care physician just wasn't up to all of that.

But, apparently all of that, while it's gratifying to be "officially" mentally ill, is not sufficient. You see, there's another dynamic at work with these kids. Mental illness equals social credit. They research it all on-line. The more diagnoses you have, the better. "Oh, I know better than to self-diagnose—but I do have this list of symptoms…" The look on the psychiatrist's face as she rattled off the terminology and symptoms straight out of the DSM, using all of the words correctly, and explaining exactly how it all applied to her was something to see.

Among other things that privately, doctors and counselors have told me that they don't really believe, but it's not worth fighting over, is dissociative identity disorder—what we used to call multiple personality disorder. All I know is that when things get bad, I never know who I'm going to be talking to—a male, a female, a non-binary. A teen, a little child, a robot, an older adult. Or perhaps someone who has selective mutism. My ASL is not up to the task.

She got a binder from someone who mailed it to her. I refused to buy one, so she went around me. I decided not to fight it, other then to bring up that they can cause damage. "I know how to wear it SAFELY, mom. I'm not dumb!" Okay, whatever. I do not have the desire to have a non-stop battle around here. I have to pick what I will and won't try to fight.

There are days when she feels "femme". Supposedly, she likes her curves and being pretty. She still loves to dress up and look cute—and even when she feels "masc", she doesn't pass to anyone with eyes. Little kids, sure. But that sad, sweet, elfin face, even with the short hair, the binder, the lack of makeup and the baggy non-gendered clothes says "girl" more loudly than any camouflage can hide. And I wonder if she realizes that the "masc" days almost always coincide with the depressed days.

And of course, many of her issues are my fault—according to her. Not the whole LGBTQ stuff—that OF COURSE is innate. But all the mental health stuff. I was abusive and neglectful, and she has lingering trauma over all of that. She has recast her entire past in the terms she learned online. You see, it's not what happened, it's how you assign meaning to it. And if you can turn your loved ones into the enemy, then you can cut them and their toxic ideas out of your life, guilt-free.

I will be the first to admit I was anything but perfect—but what kid does get a perfect parent? I have a lot of things I would do differently. At the top of that list is no smart phone or internet access. Second is public school. I would have found a way to home school, after we had taken care of a few financial issues.

I am infinitely thankful that we started the medical and counselling for the depression, and now all of the rest of the underlying issues, not the trans stuff. I have not had to fight with providers over that.

As she is getting a bit older, occasionally there are glimmers of independent thought. We recently had another discussion about bathrooms and sports—and it wasn't pure regurgitation of talking points. There was some nuance in there—we should divide sports by height, weight, hormone levels, and fitness capacity. NOT gender or sex! Horrors! That's got NOTHING to do with it. But given where she started, it's progress, if small. Bathrooms should be male/female/non-gendered. We were able to agree that while we disagree on means, we do agree that we both want everybody safe and happy.

I tried to bring up the side effects and long-term damage of blockers, hormones, and procedures, statistics on detransition, studies—and of course, all of that is a lie by haters. But I put the information out there. I dearly hope she does some research to try to prove me wrong.

I did manage to bring up the new sexual violence support center, Beira's Place, founded by JK Rowling. Of course, I didn't bring up her name at first! But, would it be okay, given there was already an inclusive center—would it be okay if someone started a second, privately funded, assigned female at birth (AFAB—man I can rattle off ALL the terms these days!), center for those who were traumatized by being around any AMAB (assigned male at birth) people. Can we allow them the right to their feelings, and honor their wishes? Yes. Then I brought up the founder. Oh, the fireworks then. "Please tell me any quote that indicates she wants any harm to come to any trans person." Didn't have any. Only the propaganda they've swallowed. I don't even care about JK Rowling. Only that everyone, TERF or not, is judged based on actual evidence, not a screaming match.

Shockingly enough, I was told that while I sometimes sound like a TERF—at least I'm not one of those horrible homicidal ones who want to erase and kill all trans people. I'm one of the good ones—if there can be such a thing.

One thing I started a couple of years ago was to just try to repair our relationship. I stopped talking about LGBTQ stuff, for the most part. At least, I'm not the one who brings it up. I listen, sometimes for much longer than I can take, inside. I'm in counseling myself. I needed it! My counselor has validated many thing—including trying to keep the peace. She's told me that certain things are not worth fighting over, as those are issues my kid has decided that "she would pick that hill to die on."

And I show physical affection. That didn't work very well at first. We had gotten out of the habit, as she grew into an adult-sized body that didn't fit in a lap anymore. But now, almost every night, there's a goodnight hug. We play, a bit—making the dog bark, goofing around. If it doesn't happen, it's because there's a mental health episode going on, or we've had a now fairly rare fight. But she gets over it pretty quickly and, usually by the next night, I can get a hug. That one thing, the hugs, I would have to say has been the biggest help in repairing the relationship.

I am going forward without expectations. We allow each other to have our own opinions. Our own beliefs. I have no idea when or if any further progress towards sanity will happen. Given that she actually likes being mentally ill, can't imagine not being not just neuro-divergent but all the rest of it, I don't think progress towards wellness can happen yet. I'm just going for stability and peace, and hopefully no medicalization of trans. I'd kick her off our insurance first before we'd pay for it. I'd rather pay cash for everything else before I let that happen.

Legal adulthood is right around the corner. And high school graduation. Can't wait to get her out of school and away from the in-person peer support system, and I'm dreading not having any say in her care. My greatest hope is to get her through to a decade out of high school without self-inflicted damage, continue to be there, to love her, and just wait and see. Maybe by then, she will outgrow it. Maybe by then, the truth will be so loud these kids can't continue to play deaf.

52

My Son's Story, and the Breakdown of My Family

My son announced that he was transgender at the age of 19. Today, he is 25.

Like so many others have said about their sons, there were no indications of this his entire years growing up. So, how did this come about?

In retrospect, his last year of high school was not good. He had always struggled socially and did not seem to be maturing at the same rate as his contemporaries. He was on the internet constantly, and obsessed with Anime, cosplay and role-playing in addition to a lot of comic-style pornography.

When he went off to college and took an LGBTQ course to fulfill a graduation requirement. Unbeknownst to his family, at the time he was suffering from major depression and homesickness, being away from home for the first time. He also became involved with a group of girls with significant mental health challenges, suicide attempts, and family traumas. This group began attending meetings at a local Gender Clinic. After ONE 'therapy' session at the Gender Clinic with an intern therapist from the local college (her day job was a postal worker), he was given hormone medication directly from the clinic. Very soon after came his announcement about being transgender, he went on to claim that he was also polyamorous, pansexual and asexual.

My son eventually quit college and moved to another very progressive state. He rarely communicates with family. He has not held a job for nearly six years and lives off of public assistance and the generosity of others—and has mainly virtual relationships. From the little bit of communication we have, he is still on hormones and spends most of his time online with virtually no human-to-human contact. He has admitted that he believes he has a mental illness. Before he left the state, we tried in vain to get him some quality mental health treatment, but as you know, this is a nearly impossible task given the rush to affirm.

That's our story. It has been the heartbreak of my family's life. We strongly support the need to step back from the direction of the WPATH guidelines and the pressure placed on the American Academy of Pediatrics to go along with this madness and malpractice. I cannot imagine having to endure this with a very young minor child!

These children need mental health assessments first and foremost, not harmful, life altering medical intervention that is truly being 'tested' on them.

53

Forks in the Road

Early this morning I lay awake in bed thinking of the forks in the road during my daughter's childhood.

She is nearing 16 and has been trans-identified for over 2 years now, starting with middle school peer group influence, and the customary deep-dive into internet/social media/anime during COVID. While she has shown some signs of desistance recently, she has also told me that she's committed to her daily chest binding and plans to have a double mastectomy at age 18.

I reflect on the decision I made to send her to public school instead of a small parochial school when she was diagnosed with ADHD. Could that fork in the road have propelled her in a different direction? Instead, she was in a public school that placed 5th graders in middle school, where she was exposed to older kids and older kids' ideas.

In 6th grade, we moved her to a smaller private school, but one with a more liberal culture. Already in 6th grade, her peer group was discussing their different sexual orientations and/or gender identities. That year she told me, "It's okay, Mom, I'm a girl". Had I known the continued influence and insidious nature of gender ideology on the internet and in her peer group would lead her to believe otherwise a year later, I would have made different decisions. Was this comment another fork in the road, where I could have somehow taken action to shield my daughter from this ideology?

By the next year my daughter was identifying as "non-binary" with they/them pronouns. Then a few short months later, she was "trans" with he/they pronouns. Today, she has settled on "non-binary", sporting pins proclaiming"He/They".

I go by a shortened version of my daughter's legal name to keep the peace, and I typically just *avoid* using pronouns around her. I have never actually affirmed my neurodivergent, intelligent, and artistic daughter's transgender identity. Like most gender critical parents at some point, I have argued with her against it. This has basically gotten me nowhere. The big lie of gender ideology is something she will have to eventually realize herself.

I continue to support her in all other areas of her life and love her with my whole being. I have told her that I will *always love* and *accept her* no matter what, but that I do not believe in gender ideology. Furthermore, I know it isn't *her truth*. It's like agreeing with an Anorexic who thinks they are "fat"; it is a lie and a delusion, a maladaptive coping mechanism that will ultimately cause more pain, damage, and regret. Kindness and inclusivity have no relevance to gender ideology.

Her mental health has suffered throughout this period of trans identification. The first therapist I brought her to due to her severe depression, low self-esteem, and self-harm behaviors, was instantly affirming: "A lot of these kids commit suicide, otherwise", she told me.

We are approaching another fork in the road. My daughter is going to leave her small private school after this, her sophomore year, and enroll in our public high school to take classes at a local community college. A couple of her friends will still be there, others will have moved on. They are nice friends, although they do affirm her identity. Overall, the school has been a good fit for her. It has been a supportive environment which has made accommodations for her ADHD, and she has received the personal attention that she needs to succeed academically. One might say removing her from this environment is foolish... to just have her *finish* high school there, even though she has proclaimed herself that she ready to move on.

If I don't take this opportunity for a potential trajectory change, what do I do in two years when she graduates, when potentially nothing will have changed regarding her "identity"? Should I then send my daughter off to a 4-year college campus, when she is 18, and of age for medicalization? The first piece of advice I received when I reached out for support as an ROGD parent was to *not* send your child off to a 4-year college campus. Colleges, I was told, act as a "catching mitt" for your gender-confused child. I wholeheartedly believe this and have witnessed it happen to other kids. After all, gender ideology started on college campuses; they are literally ground zero for the gender cult.

So here I am, at another fork in the road, hoping and praying that I am helping my daughter make the best choice for her future. I am trying to guide her on a trajectory where she will have a happy and successful future as an adult. I want her to accept her female body and understand that emotional pain cannot be fixed surgically. I want her to have new experiences that will change her perspective on herself, and on life. I hope she will abandon the lies she has been fed before she makes choices she will regret in the future. I can only hope and pray that I am guiding her on the right course. That I help her choose the right fork, if such a thing even exists. I can't see where this road goes, but I have to keep moving, to act. I must do whatever I can *right now* to save my daughter. I have to try, even if it's just another decision that goes awry—another mistaken fork that keeps me up at night.

54

There Are Two Phases—A Mother's Intuition about Gentle Deprogramming

Note: I'm not a therapist. My parenting experience is limited to children and teens with no significant mental health issues or spectrum disorders.

As a mom of a newly 18 year old son, who has been questioning his gender identity for the last twenty months, I'm no stranger to the ups and downs of this terrifying and depressing journey. My recent hobby, called "Helping My Son Accept Biological Reality," led me both to research and rumination, and lately to an attempt of some kind of personal growth. When I randomly picked up a book at a used bookstore, titled "The Spirit of Happiness: The Monks of New Skete," I was simply attracted to its tattered cover and soothing title. The very first chapter, however, gave me an insight into deprogramming the cult-captured teens which I haven't encountered before.

When we fall in love, start a journey on a spiritual path, sign up for a new exercise program or find ourselves in a cult, our initial experience is of excitement. Our attention is selective, and we notice only the positives. It is common to feel renewed—a new name certainly helps, whether you are a monk or "simply born in the wrong body." This phase lasts about six months, and then the mundane sets in. While a monk who just started his monastic journey might want to continue seeking this initial tingly excitement, he would be advised that this is futile. He is to embrace the mundane, because it is in the ordinary that he is to discover himself and

God. The mundane is never as attractive and shiny, and without a supportive community this is the phase where most do give up.

A teen captured by the trans cult will likely also experience a phase of disappointment, frustration and doubt following the shiny new phase. The phase of pure, joyful belief in the God of Trans does not last forever. Immature and narcissistic influencers will tell them that there is always the next step to achieve in order to rediscover the so quickly passing tingly gender euphoria—paint your nails, stuff your bra, paint your lips, wear a skirt in public…The list goes on.

I believe this is similar to the previously described boomerang effect, when it seems the teen is on his or her way to desistance, only to boomerang and dig deeper into the ideology. However, if we break the gender questioning journey into the phases of doubt and belief, we can develop better communication and gentle deprogramming strategies with our teens.

During the phases of belief, teens are irrational and emotion driven. They are happy, excited, confident. Watching detransitioners or bringing up the side effects is not going to be effective and will likely only alienate them. This is the time to do everything we can to bond with them, without mentioning the elephant in the room. This is the approach that was recommended by Sasha Ayad and Stella O'Malley in their "Gender: A Wider Lens" podcast. They believe that gender dysphoria is not about gender, but is, instead, a socially-sanctioned manifestation of distress. Accordingly, talking to your teen about gender is not productive, and it is better to talk about anything and everything but gender. During the happy first phase, we can build on those positive emotions and spend time with our teens doing happy things, making our relationship stronger.

Invariably, the disillusionment will set in. Compared to a monk whose life is centered around prayer, work and study, and who needs to find answers within himself, our children are only a click away from being reassured that they are still "really trans." The ones on the spectrum or with ruminative OCD tendencies might mindlessly redo the "Am I Trans" quiz. Others will ask their friends and will be love-bombed in their LGBTQ+ communities.

I believe that taking away or limiting the social media is one of the key elements of deprogramming, and attempts should be made relative to the teen's age. However, even when social media is still present, this is the time to be more proactive in engaging their critical thinking skills. This is the time for that podcast, that video, that conversation about the binary of biological sex, that documentary on the "transracial" Rachel Dolezal, on the Opioid epidemic and the big pharma. This is the time to plant those seeds of doubt, prime their critical thinking sills, and throw facts at them.

I doubt that any teens will be immediately grateful for those facts. They are already in a very uncomfortable phase of doubt. No one likes uncertainty. No one likes being told that they are wrong. If you would like to experience how it feels to be challenged about your previously unchallenged core beliefs, I urge you to expose yourself to the other side of the opinion spectrum—it is a viscerally unsettling experience, which helped me understand what my teen is going through when his beliefs are challenged. Depending on his or her personality, your teen might storm out of the room, become emotional or rebellious. She might tell you that she hates you and that you are transphobic. As parents, this is when we go into our own dark place, thinking that our teens are digging deeper and heading for medicalization. However, it is very likely that this level of discomfort is healthy and the lashing out is indicative of the fact that they feel safe with you while they are processing the very unsettling truth and the feelings of doubt.

With the omnipresent grip of the Transgender Cult, I expect teens to cycle through those phases many a time. If they are on the right track, their discomfort when encountering gender critical information should be lessened in each subsequent cycle. Alternatively, their joy at finding their "Authentic Trans Self" during the belief phases should also be reduced. As parents, we should try to look for the bigger behavioral pattern, instead of the focusing on the "signs of desistance" which are invariably followed by our own despair and disappointment. If we learn to recognize these phases, we might be able not only avoid our own emotional rollercoasters, but we also might be able to tailor our deprogramming approaches more strategically and thus more effectively.

55

No Contact

"No contact" is a new phrase pushed by indoctrinators on Facebook and TikTok. The narrative pushes the notion that, if your family does not affirm your trans identity, you must separate from them. There are also sites like The Trevor Project—which was recommended at my son's school, and probably at most schools—that persuade youth to pick chosen family and allies over their own family. People who coach children to separate from their families used to be called predators, but now they are pushed as good LGBTQ allies.

I have, unfortunately, experienced "no contact" firsthand when my son, at 18 decided to go "no contact" with us. I'm trying to understand how this happened. Was it the negative treatment he received because he was the most active boy in his class? Was it shame over the constant teacher notes, or the behavior meetings about why he couldn't keep his hands to himself or stop wrestling the other boys in class. Did he feel singled out? Was it because of the bullying in middle school? Did he seek out an answer online when high school was socially challenging and didn't feel like he fit in? Was the trans identity his way of coping with rejection and loneliness instead of accepting his ADHD or ASD traits?

How do these anti-parent voices penetrate through to our children? There are lots of vectors, it turns out: pornographic books in school libraries, drag queens teaching sex classes—even school assemblies featuring trans women, like at my son's middle school. My son came home asking questions. My husband thought nothing of it at the time. Why would he, it was a school-sponsored event and therefore okay? But this encounter planted an idea in my son's head.

This idea was not in his head as a child. This did not come from some organic innate place, this was true indoctrination, social contagion, or mass hysteria. As a child I could not get him to go into the women's public bathroom with me at a very early age. He fought me about this. He would crawl out of the restroom stall and run into the men's room as early as three. I would have to gather my things and try to run after him, other women would sometimes help me and chase after him. I'd call into the men's room or run in myself to find him happily there. He couldn't wait until he was old enough to go into the men's room by himself. I let him go alone much earlier than other parents.

He embraced being a boy. He loved being the last born male of all male cousins on my husband's side. He loved getting his first shaver and my husband teaching him to shave. He loved the fact that he was going to be very tall. We would measure his height often. He loved being one of the tallest in his class. When the trans cloud struck him, he hated that he kept getting taller and we were no longer permitted to measure him. He loved video games and playing with his male friends. He never had female friends. I never imagined that there would be porn or trans ideas embedded into all these video games. How naive I was. It didn't occur to me that anime would plant the next idea. I thought anime was innocent.

The thought that he never wants to talk to me or see me again has profound effects on my psyche. I tried to give him a magical childhood; maybe I even spoiled him. I now know that a magical childhood, where children do not experience discomfort, makes adolescence more difficult and unfathomable, as explained in Stella O'Malley's new book, *What Your Teen Is Trying to Tell You*. I had a tough childhood because of my father's alcoholism and gambling addiction, and my mother joining a cult-like church that took over her life. There was a divorce, money issues, and a scandal.

I wanted my son to have a great childhood, unlike mine. And he did. We gave him all the things my husband (also from a broken home), and I wished we'd had as children. Plenty of kids were spoiled throughout history, including many I know, but they are not estranged from their families. Even though my parents said no at times, and despite my difficult childhood and their problems, I would never cut my parents out of my life.

I wish I could re-do the moments when trans first hit my household. I rehash everything that happened, but I did the best I could. There is no way to navigate something you were not prepared for. How could anyone be prepared for this? His reasons for saying he was trans made no sense to me and I pushed back. Besides, if I had pretended to go along with his new magical thinking—he would have known I wasn't sincere.

I also said no to him, but this **NO** to transition deemed me abusive, and reinforced the "no contact" idea in my son's head. I'm sure I made mistakes, as all parents do, but there isn't a mistake I made that deserves "no contact."

56

When My Teenager Came Out as Transgender

"I am NOT a girl."

That was the text our 14 year old sent us. This came after an hour of her being locked in the bathroom, crying and telling us to "go away", as my wife and I tried to coax her out and talk to her.

She couldn't even bring herself to say it, she had to text it to us. Not because she was embarrassed, but because she was afraid. Afraid that we would hate her, that we would kick her out of our home. "You won't accept me." "You always say that it's wrong." "You don't want me to be a boy." "You aren't going to let me be who I am." Those are the texts that followed.

My response was one question. "Can I give you a hug?" Not because I wanted to celebrate what she had told us, but because she needed it. My child was scared and hurting, terrified that we hated her, and I needed to give her a hug. Ok, maybe I needed a hug too.

The next day, I tested positive for COVID and had to quarantine myself in a bedroom at home. Being quarantined away from my family during this crucial time was brutal for me. We were heading into a 4 day holiday weekend, and my office was closed, so there was nothing for me to do. My teen had just delivered some earth-shattering news that I did not know how to comprehend. I wasn't sure what I should do, or how I could help my family, but I knew I needed to do something even though I was separated from them. So I researched what "being trans" really meant. I studied. I read the Bible. I prayed.

That was a year ago.

The days, weeks, and months that followed were hard. My daughter began to suffer from deep depression and anxiety. Something as simple and routine as going to a restaurant or church would send her into panic attacks. I have had to restrain her to keep her from grabbing kitchen knives and hurting herself. Four police officers showed up at our house on Father's Day looking for her because she told her friends she was going to kill herself and one of them called the police (thankfully!). She studied the traits and symptoms of Autism and ADHD, and began mimicking them in an effort to convince her therapist that she had them. She began starving herself, to the point of becoming anorexic. At one point her medical doctor, who is very pro-LGBTQ, started discussing having her committed to an in-patient psychiatric facility. We watched her turn away from everything she loved, and everyone that had ever loved her, including us.

I needed to help my daughter, I needed to "fix this". I needed to figure out what was going on, and why, and what I could do about it. We would come to understand that there was more going on here than we initially realized, and this situation was much more complex. This was not necessarily a matter of something my wife and I did or did not do in our daughter's upbringing. There was something deeper going on.

There is a lot of confusion out there.

As the year went on, I began to see more and more people start speaking out about this. Parents. Medical doctors. Even people in the LGBTQ community, many of whom had actually gone through the "transition" process of hormones and surgery and were now "de-transitioning" back to their birth sex and openly speaking out about it. I learned about Rapid Onset Gender Dysphoria, and how psychologists in Britain reported a 4000% increase in cases in less than a decade, with 800 dysphoric children in England being administered puberty blocking drugs in 2018, including some as young as 10 years old. I learned that an estimated almost 18% of 15- to 17-year-old high school girls (predominantly white middle class) now identify as some form of LGBTQ+. I read where in 2020, half the student body at Evergreen State College was identifying as LGBTQ, and in 2021 nearly 1 in 10 students in over a dozen public high schools in Pittsburgh identified as "gender-diverse" (differing from their actual sex). I exchanged emails and had Zoom calls with professors, psychologists, and researchers from all over the world, some of whom referred to this as "the new anorexia." I learned about Affirmation Therapy and Conversion Therapy and the dangers and pitfalls of each one.

And what I learned scared me. Knowing that my daughter willingly wanted to cause herself irreparable damage over something that some are considering a social contagion, and others are calling a cult, was terrifying to me. Everywhere I turned for answers led to more questions, and most everywhere I turned for help seemed to be a dead end. There is so much polarizing hatred and confusion on this topic that it's hard to find the truth.

You are not alone.

If you are going through this now, know that you are not alone. At times it may feel like it, but you are not alone. In fact, there are many, many families going through this every day, but a lot of them are afraid to speak out or don't know where to turn for help. As one therapist I spoke to put it, "Because of the current social climate, parents are either waiving the trans banner and shouting from the rooftops, or they are hiding out of fear."

Whatever your situation, whatever your beliefs, you need to seek the truth. You need to do what is right for your child, and that may not mean just giving in to whatever they've told you. While many people are applauding and championing this transgender movement, there are also those in the medical profession that are speaking out against it, including the former president of the U.S. Professional Association for Transgender Health and president of the World Professional Association for Transgender Health, both of whom are transgender themselves.

There are therapists out there that believe in addressing a child's mental health issues first. There are doctors out there that do not agree with a child's self diagnosis to receive drugs and surgery. You just have to be diligent in finding them.

Our story is not over.

We are still in the middle of this, trying to navigate through it and help our child. My faith in God tells me that we will come through this stronger and in a better place as a family. I also know that I will not hide out of fear any longer. I have an obligation to speak out and help other fathers who are going through this, or may be about to. I have started compiling lists of resources that I will be publishing soon, in hopes that others may be able find these to get some answers.

57

The Frantic Search for an Identity

Since my son's revelation that he can be who he wants to be and learn to love and accept his body as it is (and this will take some time) we have felt enormous relief all round. But this evening's conversation with my 13 year old son was yet another heartbreaker for me—and evidence that the war isn't over for us yet.

My son is transgender identified. I am gently encouraging him to drop the "trans" identification label and trying to explain to him how just the label itself is endorsing a much bigger and potentially dangerous and life damaging concept.

We are amongst the lucky ones. Because he is young, time was on our side and, for whatever reasons—and I couldn't pin point exactly how or when—things changed for my son. He decided he was ready to listen and try to be happy. The road is long and I'm sure we'll encounter many potholes along the way, but we are heading in the right direction at long last and I can finally (almost) sleep again. But the fear is still there, looming over me, that any day now we could wake up back in the nightmare.

My son is so lost without the "Trans" label. This evening he asked me, "but who would I be if I'm not a transgender" to which I replied, "do you need a label to define who you are?". To this he replied, "but it is part of my identity". So I told him: "we can and will figure this out and if you feel you belong in the LGB community they will still accept you with open arms—you do not need the trans label (or any label) for this".

This need for identity and categorization is so toxic. Even though my son may be emerging from the fog, I am still devastated for him, for what he's been through and for the loss he is feeling—and for the other thousands of children still searching frantically for their identities. And my mind still races everyday, looking for more stories, more evidence and information. And the worry and need to change things is still immense; who will this happen to next?

Parents on Heartache and Tragedy

58

Letters We Never Received

Family

Dear L & B,

We did as you requested and read up on trans ideology. We were surprised and horrified to find how little we knew about the harm being done to children and teens in the name of kindness and acceptance. We now understand why you were so upset about S's claim of being trans, and we hope you'll accept our apology for the way we undermined you. We realize going along with S's insistence on being called "he" was a huge mistake and we know we need to walk that back. If we had just taken the time to listen to you, we wouldn't have made such a mess of things, and we're sorry. We hope we can talk together about how we can best help prevent harm to S. We're here for you.

Dad & Stepmom

****

Dear L,

I've been thinking a lot about how things have been going between us since S declared she was trans. I realize that I've caused real damage—to you, to our relationship, and to S. For years I've gone against your express wishes and affirmed S's new identity. I shut down your attempts to talk to me about this. By calling her my grandson, I colluded with your daughter against you, and I encouraged both her self-rejection and delu-sion. That's hard for me to admit, but it's true. Instead of supporting you and your family, I went along with S's fantasies and in doing so, helped push her away from you. I was very wrapped up in being the "good lib-eral grandma." I know now my actions made things worse for everyone and I think you've been in anguish over this for a long time. All your efforts to share information with me resulted in my being defensive and aggressively lecturing you. I'm so sorry I attacked you when all you've been trying to do is keep your daughter safe.

I finally read the books you gave me. I have the idea of letting S know I've been reading and learning, and I hadn't realized how unsafe and risky gender ideology is, and that I made a mistake in how I handled things in our family. I want to support her towards her healthiest self even if that means she's angry at me. I'm so regretful for how I've added to your pain this past year. I hope I can undo some of that.

With love,

Mom

****

Hi L & B,

I'm sending you this card on S's birthday to tell you I saw the way you raised that girl, and I can't imagine a home more filled with love, closeness, creativity, and care. I know she's acting like none of it mat-tered, but I'm here to say: it mattered, it was real, I witnessed it all and it was incredible. Over the years I have been lucky enough to be a part of so many of her birthday parties, and even though she seems brainwashed right now, somewhere inside her she remembers how special and sweet you made all those celebrations, as well as all the other days of the year. Even though it's been a long time now, I haven't forgotten what you're going through with this painful estrangement. I don't buy any of this gender garbage. It's hurting families everywhere, and I hate how much it's hurting you and your daughter/my niece. You were (and are) great parents.

Love,

H, your sister/sister-in-law

****

Dear L,

You haven't shared much with me about what's happened in your family, and I'm guessing that's because you've been hurt by the reactions of others. I respect your privacy, but I want you to know that I've done my own research and have learned a lot about how trans extremism has captured so many impressionable young people, especially girls. I am so sorry that your daughter, my niece, got caught up in this. It's clearly a powerful social contagion.

I've tried to imagine what I might feel if one of our daughters estranged herself from us and wanted to cut off her healthy body parts or put dangerous hormones in her body. I would be devastated, heartbroken, and I doubt I'd be able to get out of bed. You always make such an effort to be cheerful with me on the phone, but I know there must be deep sadness behind that good cheer.

Out of the blue, S texted me yesterday. She made a point of mentioning she had no contact with you and B. I'm unsure if this is a kind of triangulation, or a way to come back to the family, or both, but I am wary. I want you to know I plan to keep the conversation always leading back to you and B, her parents. I will share memories and stories of her childhood, and I will never let a conversation go by without mentioning your name. And I'm certainly never going to agree that girls can magically become boys. I know you'd do the same for me if, God forbid, I ever found myself in the same situation.

I know you are terribly worried about S, and I am too. I never want to make your situation more painful, and I especially don't want any part of helping S down a path of irreversible harm. What can I do to help? Maybe if the whole family could get on the same page, we could have some impact on her thinking? I'm happy to talk to mom or dad about this.

Love you sis,

D

****

Friends

Dear L and B,

We're writing to let you know S came by tonight and had dinner with our family. We know S is living on her own and not speaking to you, and we also know how awful we'd feel if one of our kids cut us off but was spending time at your house. We wanted to let you know right away what went on here.

We love the long friendship between our kids, but our first allegiance is always to you, our dear friends. I spoke to S as I know you would speak to one of my own daughters were the situation reversed. I said she was welcome here, but that I expected her to tend to her most important relationships first- namely, her parents and brother. We told her there was no one who loved or cared for her more than her family. We told her *people who truly love her will always point her in the direction of home.*

I also wanted you to know that K and I only used her real name and pronouns, even though our kids kept "correcting" us. After S left, we had a long talk with our kids about how cults operate, and the importance of not making delusions or estrangements worse. We hope we did right. If not, and there are things we can do to better support you, or S, let us know. We can't imagine how painful this all is.

We love you,

A & K

****

Dear L & B,

It was so great to have you guys visit! We loved seeing you.

M and I talked after you left and realized we owe you both an apology. We really pressured you about going along with your daughter's pronouns and then picked an argument with you about gender. Quickly we realized you were the experts here. We thought we were offering a brilliant solution when obviously you've already tried everything, read everything, thought about this daily for years. Sorry for our arrogance.

We also realized we were insensitive towards you by talking so much about our daughter and how well she's doing, etc. We know you raised your daughter with absolute love and it's so unfair and shocking that now she won't even speak to you. In our happiness to share our lives, I think we both forgot that you are two grieving parents who have lost so much. We should have been more tender with you both.

We now understand this is a cult, and cults can ensnare anyone. Please know it is not lost on us how painful and draining it must be to educate and argue with your friends and family while being so heartbroken and sad. We won't hurt you that way again.

Lots of love,

P & M

****

Teachers

Dear S's parents,

We have been S's teachers for 3 years now and watched her grow and take on many new challenges as she heads towards high school graduation. The 4 of us have always felt lucky to have her in our classes and have only positive things to say about your brilliant, studious, and deep-thinking daughter. It's clear she comes from a loving and supportive home.

Recently, along with many of her classmates, S has declared she is trans and has asked us to keep this a secret from you. We don't believe it is a teacher's role to hold secrets from loving parents, especially not in service of a dangerous social contagion. That is why we told S that we could help her with math, writing, science, and history, but any caring teacher would never try to be her parent, nor keep secrets from parents. We told her she should go directly to her mom and dad, both of whom we know and trust.

The four of us have formed an alliance and we are working with the administration to educate staff and parents about the harms of gender identity. We hope we will not lose our jobs, but we also can't go along with any belief system that so clearly harms both kids and families.

Let us know if we can support you in any way,

S's Math, Science, Language Arts and US History teachers

****

Planned Parenthood

Dear Parents of S,

I am a provider at Planned Parenthood and am writing to alert you that your daughter visited our clinic seeking cross sex hormones as part of our Gender Questioning Care Program. After an extensive medical history, including seeking records from all her medical and mental health providers, it is our professional opinion that S does not meet the criteria for being a part of our program, much less for a prescription of testosterone, which is what she was seeking.

As you know, S has a history of struggling with both an eating disorder and cutting, both of which have gone woefully unaddressed by her therapists and doctors. It's clear you as parents have been tireless in seeking help for your child, but the system has failed you. It appears, after a thorough reading of her records, that once a provider heard her declare she was trans, they ceased any real therapeutic care and simply affirmed her identity and the idea that all her problems would resolve once she "transitioned." To safeguard the health of gender confused clients, it is our policy that any co-morbidities must be addressed and resolved first. Our Gender Questioning Care Program is a 2 year long intensive involving therapy, education around the health consequences of cross sex hormones and surgeries, and outdoor service/volunteer work. Participants also listen to testimony from detransitioners. We wish you and your daughter well.

In health,

Planned Parenthood

****

Therapists

Dear L & B,

I am writing to let you know I have resigned from my position as a therapist with the ---.

For the past 5 years, I have advertised my services as a trans therapist practicing an affirmation model, and available to write letters of recommendation for those seeking medical transition. I know this is why S chose me as her therapist.

I am a natal female who transitioned during my college years. I have lived my life as male for over 5 years. It was during my sessions with your family that I began to question the services I was providing.

I want to acknowledge how poorly I served S. The scope of her mental/emotional issues were beyond my skill and training; and I downplayed those issues and only focused on her claim of being trans. I went along with her idea that transitioning was the answer to her mental health issues. This was grossly negligent on my part.

I also failed spectacularly during the family sessions we arranged. I will never forget the moment when you turned to me and asked, "So, is it your view that every young person who walks through your doors and claims to be trans, is trans? What are your criteria for determining who is and isn't? Have you ever turned down a request for a letter approving medical transition? Why or why not? Don't you think the ideal outcome would generally be that a person accepts their sexed body rather than run the risks of surgery and becoming a lifelong medical patient?"

You may remember I was unable to answer any of these questions. You may also remember that I barely spoke 3 words during your fast paced family sessions, and at the end of one session I commented "You sure are a loud family." This was uncalled for. The truth was, my dismal skills as a therapist became glaringly apparent to me. I was not prepared for the complexity and depth you, as S's parents, brought to the sessions. I saw clearly that S had very loving, present, curious, and caring parents; not the villains she had painted you to be.

You may also remember that S ran out of the office repeatedly whenever asked to answer a question or engage in sustained conversation with you. I characterized her outbursts and exits as "a great sign they are learning to take care of themselves." This was a ridiculous spin on what was obvious to you but not to me: S was in no way mature or mentally well enough to even begin discussing such a serious decision as cross-sex hormones or surgery. I ignored every red flag and re-branded S's inability carry on a simple conversation as "setting boundaries." I came home from those sessions filled with doubt and a sense that I was part of something profoundly unethical.

Overall, I believe I helped further confuse and delude S and push her further away from you, which is the opposite of good therapy. I no longer have confidence that I can make good decisions nor be helpful to gender confused young people.

I have written a separate letter to S explaining all this. I have also written a letter retracting my approval of her surgery. I am in no position to help anyone, as I face the unraveling of my own beliefs and come to terms with what I have done to my own body and to the young people I have misled.

With regret,

K

****

Hi L & B,

As S's former therapist, I feel I owe you a long overdue apology.

I had been working with S in a therapeutic capacity for some time when we decided it was time to invite S's parents (you) in for some family sessions. I remember the day I called you to issue that invitation. Your response so shocked me that I thought about it for days afterward: first in anger, then in doubt, then in shame.

I'm sure you remember that call. I told you I was calling on behalf of your then 22-year-old child to invite you to a family therapy session I would facilitate. Your response was not at all what I expected. You said:

"*Of course, we will always show up to work on our relationship with S. But how can we trust that you are a competent therapist, when you start out by perpetuating our daughter's sense of herself as helpless, unable to even make a phone call? How can we trust that you can help S if you do her work for her and enable her to be her lowest functioning self? It doesn't give us any hope that you want S to grow or develop inner strength. If our daughter can't even call us, what evidence is there that she is functional enough to talk to us in therapy? And why are we having to point that out to you, instead of you pointing it out to our daughter?*"

At this point I told you that I was making the phone call for S because of safety issues. You responded:

"*Safety issues? There are no barriers to S calling us except her own discomfort, and discomfort is something a good therapist would be helping their client face and tolerate, not avoid. Are you saying you think we're unsafe?*"

I said I was referring to emotional safety. You responded:

"A good therapist would have asked S, "What's the worst that could happen if you called your parents? Do you have any evidence that they would mistreat you if you called them? And let's say they did respond in anger—couldn't you simply hang up, or tell them you didn't like it? This seems like a growth opportunity for you, S, and if I do your growth work for you, I can't really call myself a therapist."

Well, your words bounced around in my head for weeks. I tried to dismiss it, but the truth is, everything you said is spot on. I have been babying and rescuing many of my trans-identified clients instead of challenging them and helping them grow. Thank you for setting me straight. I have made significant changes in my clinical approach since our conversation.

Again, my apologies,

E (therapist)

****

Hi L & B,

I know you must be worried about S, and though as her new therapist I can't reveal anything to you without her permission, I wanted you to know what my philosophy is regarding young people in distress. My aim is to help my clients be in their bodies and to focus on truth rather than fantasy. My goal is always to guide clients back to their deepest connections- to self, to family, to well-being, to reality. We focus on healing the mind. I want to assist my clients to have a rich variety of relationships rather than placing limitations and demands on others, and I want each client to find their own strength rather than expecting the world to bed to their will. In other words, I am always asking: how can we be our most functional selves? I hope that's helpful to you both during this painful time in your family.

Warmly,

C

59

In the Path of a Hurricane

My daughter is a senior in high school. Under the normal circumstances we would be enthusiastically discussing colleges and careers, planning post-graduation trips, and checking out cute prom dresses. However, the circumstances are far from normal. We are a house in the path of Hurricane T. The thing about hurricanes is that they are unpredictable. It may turn before reaching our house or it may hit it full force and level it to the ground. Or maybe it will cause some damage but not destroy it.

I watch my daughter for the smallest signs of desistance or escalation, like the colors on the hurricane map: Is it red—moving closer my way? Is she wearing her binder again? Is it green? Is she wearing something feminine?

Like mindlessly wiping the dust as you walk through the house, I continue with our daily routine—school, work, chores, driving lessons. However, one does not pick new tiles for the bathroom or start major renovation while waiting to see if a hurricane will hit. Every breeze seems like the first gust—I am always on high alert and can't plan anything.

I have no idea what the next few months will bring. She got accepted in a few colleges and I feel no joy. What difference will it make if she takes the path of self-destruction?

I think about the gap year she should take but how do we plan anything concrete together when I don't know what's in her mind? Is she planning to leave home and start transitioning the day she graduates?

I am not painting the fence, not remodeling the bathrooms. All I do is wait. I wait, frozen in panic, I wait trying desperately to stay close to her. Maybe it will stop or delay the hurricane while I surround my house with sandbags of love. I pray, I obsess, and I wait wait wait ... If the hurricane turns and passes our house, we will paint it pretty cheerful colors and plan everything we can't plan now. We will have so much fun! If the hurricane hits ... Well, I guess I will have to assess the damage and see what can be rebuilt.

I hope and pray that the hurricane turns before reaching our house but if it hits, I hope it will lift up our mighty little house and land right on the transgender cult witch and crush her. And then my girl will find her way back home.

60

The Waves

I've only told a few people that my now 18 year old daughter is somehow convinced she is a boy. My daughter would claim I am embarrassed of her, but honestly it just feels too much. My wounds are raw from the last few years of her mental distress. I am in so much pain I cannot make a sound or I will be dragged under.

My husband and I found out she was self-harming months before lockdown, hiding razors in her shampoo bottles. In January 2020 I was called to pick her up from school because she had made a suicide threat that day. The counselor said I needed to pick her up "as soon as you can or we will take her to the hospital on a 5150 hold". That night, while I thought she was safe in her room and her bed, she texted pictures of her newly-bloodied wrists to a girl who had tormented her. In March of 2020, COVID hit and my already depressed and anxious kid was locked in her room, feeling even more alone and depressed. I still have not come up for air. The waves keep coming. I don't know how much more I can take.

In May 2020, her dad took her to Texas for eating disorder treatment. After three weeks we were told that her eating disorder was secondary to her mood disorder and we had to find her a higher level of care.

At her second inpatient treatment center she lasted two weeks before we were told we needed to take her to a higher level of care.

At her third facility, she stayed for 47 days to stabilize and for testing to find out what her primary mood disorder was. We never saw the words "gender dysphoria" in the 57 page report.

The next stop was a reputable therapeutic boarding school. We were also never told in the 14 months she spent there that she thought she was a boy. In the reports full of references to depression, suicidal ideation, body dysmorphia, anxiety, and self harm, we never saw the words "gender dysphoria".

In December of 2021 she graduated, both from the therapeutic program and from high school. She was wearing a dress and full make-up at her graduation ceremony.

Then, at last, she was finally back home. At first, things were great—full of family jokes and cuddling. She and her brother laughed and made up for lost time together. She filled out eleven college applications and she was accepted to many of them. One would think this should be a happy punctuation mark after almost losing your oldest child. We were wrong, as we were about to find out.

She began seeing a therapist who knew her at her worst from the second facility. I thought I was making the right decision, that my daughter was safe and was working through her mental struggles. She starting wearing her dad's shirts, oversized men's sweatpants, and crocs with socks to therapy, which looks like a depressed kid to me, not a boy. I thought I was paying for someone to get to the root of the depression and body shame and self hatred that began years prior. Actually, my daughter was being affirmed as a boy for months without my knowledge.

This last spring she decided on a fantastic liberal arts college. We sat side by side on our laptops on the couch filling out forms for meal plans, academic interests, housing and classes. With each form that was filled out we both received an automated confirmation email—addressed to a name that was not hers. I gasped in shock and confusion. She quickly changed her name back and left the room.

Next came the housing form, on which she checked "male" without my knowledge. We actually didn't learn she checked male until she was assigned her male roommate in July. She is currently living with an 18 year old boy on a co-ed floor.

I feel so bad for him.

My daughter's side of the room is decorated with anime posters and jewelry organizers. She has at least 10 pairs of shoes and so many items of clothing we had to purchase more shelves on move-in day. She says her roommate smells. She changes in her "man cave" to hide from him, which is a shower curtain under her lifted bed. She says he is hardly in their room. I cannot imagine why.

After she left for college we still feel we are walking on eggshells, afraid of saying something that might upset her so that she yells at us and hangs up. I want to text her some truth, but I'm afraid that, if I do, we won't hear from her again. Our daughter attends a college in a state where it is illegal to get an abortion—but where she can go to a "gender clinic" 35.8 miles away (my we mapped it). We check her location on our phones and go into white hot panic if she is near the city. We scroll in, it's the mall. It's a Walmart. I am loosing my mind.

When she was home for winter break and fell asleep on my lap watching tv. I took a picture of my beautiful girl. I know she is still in there. We had one (ahem) loud conversation after I couldn't bite my tongue anymore. Her dad and I were crying, we were begging her not to start Testosterone. The night did not end well, but the next morning I did what I always do when she is home—I climbed into her bed and spooned her. A week later we had a calm conversation a few nights before she flew back to school, just so I could unemotionally say it all. My husband drove her to the airport and asked her to hold off on anything medical for a while. She may have seen our pain, but she also may have lied to us when she told him that she will wait.

My daughter now sits like she was at her annual exam. She is proud of teaching herself how to burp. She stopped shaving her legs and was actually annoyed by her underarm hair last summer so she piled on the old spice men's deodorant, Swagger. The smell makes me gag when we are in the car listening to her Japanese pop music. The nausea comes in waves.

I feel sick. So unbelievably sick.

61

A Mother's Heartache

My life began the day my beautiful son was born. With his first breath I found my purpose in life and a love that I had never experienced before. He made me a mother. I have other children now besides him, but he always will hold a special place in my heart because he made me who I was meant to be.

He was the sweetest, kindest, cutest thing I had ever met. He was always studying things and learning new things because knowledge was something he craved. From the start, he was trying to figure out how his hands worked, then moved on to taking his toys apart and trying to put them back together. He spent all day outside in the dirt and the mud. We would joke and call him our farm animal because at the end of everyday, that's what he smelled like. He was always into boy things. Boy clothes, boy toys, boy activities. He wrestled, he rode his bike, he loved trucks and cars and heavy equipment. It was in his blood. He was to be my husband's legacy, and we have been damn proud of this boy his entire life.

At 13 my son opened my eyes to the world of politics and activism. I started my journey because of him and did a lot of work in the name of parental rights. I saw this agenda many years ago being weaponized against our children and have been fighting for them ever since. Since then, he has changed his mindset 180 degrees. I know he knows in his heart what is right, but he has been dealt a deceitful and harmful narrative in the name of acceptance.

I vividly remember the first day of freshman year when I dropped him off at high school. He was proud of who he was, he had charisma and a confidence that was unmatched. He has always been a handsome kid too. My boy walked into that school with the biggest smile on his face. This was 5 years ago, and I still remember it like it was yesterday. I sat there thinking how proud I was of him, not only his academics, his abilities and his talents, but his character and the man he was becoming.

That was the last time I can genuinely say I saw my sweet boy that happy. By the middle of his freshman year he was depressed, secluded, miserable and not someone I knew anymore. I asked him what was wrong, gave him the love I thought he needed, put him in counseling and racked my brain every day as to how I could help him. Nothing helped. Little did I know the extent of the damage being done at school to his psyche. At his school if you were not gay or trans, you were not cool. You were referred to as a "breeder" and it was not a good thing. In the middle of his sophomore year, I made a decision some may say this was irresponsible—I pulled him out of school and he never went back. I was doing what I felt like I needed to in order to save my child's life. He ended up testing out of school that summer and started working full time.

I was so proud of his work ethic and his drive to be a better person. It seemed as though this was the right move for him and our family and he was doing better. He wasn't. He was putting on a face for me and biding his time until he moved out.

At 18 he was gone. He moved half way across the country to make a life for himself and that's when I found out all of the things that had actually been going on in my sweet boy's head. He was raised in a stable home, with hardworking parents who were trying to live the American dream. He saw his parents come from nothing, to reaching their lofty goals through great sacrifice and dedication. He was raised by two parents who not only love their children with everything in them, but also love each other. The myth that these children come from unstable broken homes, is just that. The cult has their grip on these children unlike anything I have ever seen or expected.

My son had been taking hormones at home. I had no idea. They were being supplied to him by a friend, not a doctor, not an adult, but a friend. His whole personality changed. He began to cry all of the time, had aches and pains I tried to make go away with solid advice. I had no idea he knew the cause of the pain. My son is against big pharma in a big way, he will not take Tylenol or Motrin, but he was taking hormones. He has been convinced they are safe, with no longterm side effects.

He moved out and started dating a transgirl. His first relationship ever. He was manipulated into paying for things this person tried to steal, lying to his roommates, manipulating people, and doing things he had never done before. In the first two months of living out of our home he would call me every so often and tell me how grateful he was for the life he was given and how grateful he was to be blessed with the parents he had. He would tell his dad how much he admired him for his hard work and dedication to his family, and all of his sacrifices didn't go unnoticed. I found it strange, but at the same time I soaked it in. We have since learned these phone calls were coming from a place of guilt and confusion due to things he had been doing. I know his words were insincere, but they came from a child who was hurting and trying to make sense of everything. He is still struggling.

At the time of this writing I have now talked to him about his choices and what he will do down the road. He says that being transgender is not a mental illness, it is normal. He tells me I am too old to understand what any of this means and I am uneducated on the matter. I have spent countless hours researching this trend, the side effects and the remorse many have gone though when they realized they were lied to about the implications of the treatment and the lifestyle as a whole. I have spoken to trans people who said they knew their whole life this was who they were to be. They had signs very young of something being different. My son has nothing in common with the things they experienced. I told my son that, if this was normal, humanity wouldn't have lasted this long. I explained how hormone replacement and surgery is a multi-billon dollar industry. None of this matters to him. Reason and logic no longer play a role in his normal brain functions.

I have given him resources and contacts to reach out to those who offer different perspectives than those he has been brainwashed with. I don't know if he will utilize any of it. I have extended a hand to help and a heart to love my child. I will not affirm this, I will not support this and I will not play pretend with him while I know there is a mental illness at play and a pressure from the culture that is unmatched.

I share my story because I know there are many other mothers out there struggling with this with very little resources and support. I have searched for it, I have only found websites and forums that tell me that I am the problem and that I need to accept this. I will fight for my child, but I will not buy into a false reality based entirely on feelings and outside negative influences.

62

The Role I Wish She Wouldn't Accept

My daughter was an actress before she even knew it.

I like to say she came out of the womb talking. She was reciting her ABCs at 13 or 14 months of age, reading at age 3, devouring chapter books by 5—always with the flair and flourish of a budding performer.

She lived for dress-up clothes and makeup and princesses. She delighted in the world of fantasy and fairy tale and fearless girls. She didn't just WANT to be the center of attention, she BECAME the center of attention through her sheer charisma, whip-smart humor, mastery of words, and natural leadership.

Having no interest whatsoever in sports, I suggested that maybe she try children's theater. At age 8, she was cast in the ensemble in her first play. By age 9, she was consistently being cast as either the adventurous, fearless girls she read about in stories, or the comedic parts that came so naturally to her due to her sharp wit and impeccable timing.

The next three years were amazing years of growth, with her being busy and happy and our family discussing the possibility of performing arts high schools. We spent a lot of time together, driving to rehearsals or Broadway touring productions, singing musical theater songs in the car. I celebrated each new role she was awarded and delighted in her performances.

She loved every aspect of theater: the ability to take on new clothes, hair, makeup, an accent, a posture, and mannerisms allowed her to become part of the stories she loved so much.

I never imagined that she would decide that the world of story is better than the real world. That playing characters would transcend the stage and overtake her real life. Because now, she wants to permanently live in her own made-up story.

At age 13, depression and anxiety hit our house like a hurricane. Her grades plummeted; she stopped hanging out with her wonderful group of friends and picked up a new group that was into anime and cosplay. She cut her hair off and began dressing like a homeless person. She wouldn't talk to me about her period, which had recently started. She rarely auditioned for plays and lived mostly online, culminating in an announcement at age 14 that she was non-binary. You all know the litany of asks that came thereafter (which we refused), the challenges of navigating therapists and medications, fighting the school's love-bombing and affirmation, etc—but suffice it to say that it was like the tectonic plates of our relationship had shifted—maybe forever.

We're coming up on four years of this now. She's only grown more entrenched, more angry, more masculine. Our once dynamic, hilarious, confident, brilliant girl, raised by two parents in a stable marriage and home, is a dour, self-hating shadow of her former self.

Our culture told her that the real world, and the role she plays in it, is painful and hard sometimes, but not to worry, because she can escape that. She can live in a make believe story and be the central character.

Only this time, she's not that fearless, adventurous girl or the wildly funny comedic sidekick. Her new role is a character who doesn't need to think about puberty or porn or where she doesn't fit in. In this new part, she does not need to learn how to deal with pain or challenges. She can be a victim, part of a special group that is celebrated while claiming it's marginalized. She can have no accountability. She can do or say whatever she wants. This role requires a new name, appearance, costume, way of speaking, mannerisms—and a body to match. And it could be forever.

We are emotionally preparing ourselves for when she turns 18 in a few months—we expect her to come out as full trans, separate herself from us and begin transitioning. Because everyone in her life—except for us and the true friends she left behind—tells her that this story she's written—and the character she can play in it—is real, valid, and worthy. It's celebrated and way better than anything than the role she was born into.

This is the one role I wish she wouldn't accept.

63

Life on a Tightrope

Lose your child or facilitate harm to her. That was my choice when my sixteen year old daughter told me, seemly out of the blue, she was trans. That was a little over a year and half ago. Turns out I was being overly optimistic, as now I know that if I lose her she will still be harmed. I don't even have a Solomon's choice. I would absolutely give her up if it would save her from harm, but it won't. So why shouldn't I affirm? I know parents who do, who have followed their daughters into the trans cult. They don't want to lose them. They put rainbow yard signs out and get their daughters on testosterone. As one friend told me, "I want to be supportive." But really, it is not supportive. It is fear. I understand the fear.

So why don't I affirm my daughter? Why don't I use her pretend male name and pronouns and go along with her belief that she is somehow a boy? Do I love my daughter less than they do? Do I love her more? I don't know. I only know that when she was screaming at me that if I did love her I would be helping her find a surgeon to remove her breasts, I knew I could never do something like that. She made it very clear that she would eventually cut me out of her life if I didn't "get with the program." But I could never forgive myself for participating in hurting her to hang on to her, even if in the end I still lose her and she is still hurt. I would never be able to face myself. I would never be able to face her.

My daughter hated herself and felt like a failure as a girl. She was given the false promise that she could be someone else, could reject the self she found so wanting. I did not give her this option. I did not find her wanting. She found it online, with her peers, teachers and with the GSA at her school. I know it is a fantasy but she does not. She is working very hard to create a new self. Her pretend male self tends to grunt in what I can only assume she believes to be a masculine way. I have four brothers, a father, a stepfather and a husband. None of them grunt. I want to tell her that she is playing a part, a caricature of a boy, but that she is still there, the same person as always behind the mask. I want to tell her that the path to her true self cannot possibly be paved with cosmetic surgery and a lifetime of pharmaceuticals that will destroy her health. I don't because I am trying to walk a tightrope between affirmation and being completely rejected. And that is where we live. We live on a tightrope, trying desperately to maintain connection without facilitating harm.

Living on a tightrope is terrifying and exhausting. I have thought about suicide. There have been days where the only thing tethering me to this life is the pain I would cause my other daughter, my husband and my family of origin if I left it. I also know that my "trans" daughter is going to have a difficult enough time once she realizes that she has damaged her body and health for a lie without having my death to deal with on top of it. But I did formulate a plan and even though I was never going to implement it, it was comforting. I knew that if I absolutely could not go on I had a way out. There were nights when that plan was the only thing that allowed me go to sleep. Sleeping overall has become a challenge. As soon as I lie down in the dark the despair becomes overwhelming. Many nights I just get up and read until four or five in the morning.

Despair ebbs and flows through my days like fog, sometimes light and sometimes heavy. Some days it is a crushing darkness and it is difficult to function at all. Getting out of my head with work, a book or trips with my husband will give me reprieves. The despair is always there and waiting in the wings though. It does not go away, just temporarily recedes. There is no escape from it, not until my daughter is safe. I have a therapist and he perks up when I tell him about those reprieves, as though they could somehow become the rule and not the exception. I humor him because he has been helpful. He sees first hand what is happening in the medical and mental health communities and has been candid about it. He tells me I am having a complex grief response.

I have gone back through my memory trying to identify where I failed her or where I missed an opportunity to protect her. I try to look back for warnings that I missed about trans ideology's growing strength and influence but I was so ignorant and unprepared. I know it is pointless self flagellation, but the pull is so strong. This is where therapy has been most helpful. Therapists generally are not fans of using hindsight to torture yourself. My husband also finds the idea ridiculous that we had any control, any way to prevent something that comes so wholly from outside our family. I have come to understand that whether a child is seduced into this cult is not determined by the parents' political beliefs, religious beliefs, parenting style or family configuration. It is the kids, not the parents, who are the common denominator. They are struggling with one or more of a predictable list of challenges that make them particularly vulnerable.

As difficult as the despair is to manage, it is nothing compared to the anger. The institutions and people I once trusted are either ready to sacrifice my child's body or to look the other way. I don't even know how to describe the rage that inspires. I understand anger and of course have felt it in my life. But this is different. It is visceral. It feels like hatred. I see my liberal friends' faces shutter when I try to explain the medical harms that are being perpetrated against children for reasons of profit and politics. They believe I am just having a difficult time accepting that I have a son now instead of a daughter. One of them actually patted me, trying to comfort me I suppose, in an "It will all be ok" sort of way. I cannot be around them at all. I do not trust myself to control my anger. I treasure the friends and family who understand. The rest I have to keep at a distance.

I live in a very liberal community. I used to love it and now I long to leave. I can't drive five blocks without seeing a "we love our trans youth" sign with the pink and blue trans flag background. I have the school sending me emails using my daughter's pretend male name, talking about how well "he" is doing. It fills me with pain and rage. I had a conversation with her pediatrician once where I was using my daughter's actual name and female pronouns and she was using her pretend male name and male pronouns. Again, it's hard to describe the rage.

I have tried to educate both friends and professionals. I have sent links and articles, including articles written by medical and mental health professionals. I doubt a single person read them. My friends on the political left simply do not want to know. It would be too uncomfortable. Others, I believe, are trying to preserve some sort of plausible deniability. I put pediatricians, mental health providers and educators into that category. These are not stupid people and teachers especially have to be seeing the numbers rising and that they are mostly teenage girls, teenage girls with learning differences or disabilities or mental health diagnoses. They are the socially awkward girls who don't fit in. It is happening right in front of them, in their classrooms.

I believe there will be a reckoning for the institutions and individuals who have perpetuated this atrocity. I don't know what that will look like. It seems to be starting with lawsuits and with states like my own, banning puberty blockers, cross sex hormones and gender surgeries for minors. I listen to lawmakers from what used to be my own party attacking efforts to protect children, to give them time to grow up before making decisions that will lead to sterility, sexual dysfunction and a list of other health problems. It leaves me speechless with rage, the callousness of it.

My daughter's eighteenth birthday is looming. I will not be able to protect her after that. My husband and I will use what power we have to try to give her more time to break free of transgender ideology before she does something that will cause irreparable harm. The only leverage we will have is financial. I am not optimistic. I expect there will be an estrangement at some point. I can only hope it is not permanent.

64

Nightmares: A Child Torn Apart by Ideology

As the transgender trend sweeps the world, young children are suffering too …

Most people cannot fathom what it's like to live in fear of losing your child to an ideology. It is a place where you wake up in the middle of the night with a feeling in your chest that feels as if it could stop your breath cold. A terror as heavy and unyielding as stone. It is the stuff of nightmares and silent screams.

My story started with a divorce from a terribly toxic and damaged woman. We had joint legal and physical custody, but my ex did everything in her power to undermine me and to take complete control over our only child. Our son, only 4 at the time, was attending a progressive preschool in our small New England town. The director of the school had a young trans-identified child and took every opportunity to talk about gender to the 3- and 4-year-olds in her care. The children were taught that they could "switch" genders and that doctors were only guessing at the sex of a baby when it was born. Of course, I learned about all of this much later.

About a month after our traumatic split, the director of my son's school informed me, via a text message, that my son had informed her that he was a girl. This alleged announcement came seemingly out of nowhere but I believe the timing is relevant as my child was experiencing great turmoil in the midst of his parents' breakup. I later found out that my ex and this director were in close contact, positioning themselves as managers of my son's emerging "gender exploration" as well as their perception that I was unaccepting of my son's statement that he was female. At my home, our child manifested no gender dysphoria or confusion whatsoever. This was the beginning of my decent into many nightmares. My reality as our son's other parent, was denied again and again by every legal, therapeutic and educational professional. My ex threatened that I would lose my child if I did not accept "her" as transgender. I was perpetually terrified.

Some of my nightmares:

I am in a nightmare where you scream and scream, but no one notices that your foot is being eaten by a monster.

I told every professional and my ex that I had never witnessed any signs of confusion while our son was with me. He displayed absolutely none of the criteria for Gender Dysphoria (GD). The only thing in question was that he stated—and only to some—that he wanted a girl's name and for people to use female pronouns. Again, that was never a request that I personally heard. From all outward appearances, he was a stereotypical garden-variety boy. He was drawn to playing mostly with boys, loved hitting things with sticks, was obsessed with male superheroes and swords, and was a rough and tumble kid. Incredulously, when I pointed out these facts to the preschool director, she said, "*your daughter is likely a tomboy.*"

This is the nightmare where you reach for something and it dissolves in your hands.

My ex informed me, also via a text, that my son had chosen a girl's name. From that point on, he was only referred to by this name and female pronouns were used exclusively in preschool through the third grade. This declaration occurred about three months after our break-up.

This is the nightmare where you find yourself in a cave with a tiger and your back is against the wall.

I agreed to take our child to a gender clinic with the express hope that they would take my very young son's sudden declaration that he was a girl into careful consideration, along with his inconsistent presentation. I wrongly assumed that the concurrent trauma from the divorce, along with my ex's strident advocacy that our son was trans would be *explored*. I came quickly to understand how naive I was. My son was given a bogus diagnosis of gender dysphoria and the trans train ride began.

This is the nightmare where everyone is speaking another language and no-one understands you.

Early on, we consulted with many therapists. Most stated that they were more concerned with the state of *my* mental health, due to my apparent unwillingness to accept that my preschooler was transgender. If we found a more nuanced therapist who was not as eager to slap a label onto a very young child, my ex refused to work with them. I was told over and over that I needed to celebrate my trans child's identity and to work harder at accepting this reality. My attempts to at least slow down the speed of the train earned me the titles of 'narcissist' and 'transphobe.'

This is the nightmare where you are in a world where nothing is connected to anything real.

On two separate occasions, I was told by the gender clinic we attended that I should start thinking about puberty blockers for our child (he was then 7). This so-called professional advice was offered for a child who had never exhibited any body dysmorphia or gender dysphoria.

This is the nightmare where you want to wake up, but you can't.

I advocated hard for things to simply remain open for my son. To allow for his identity to remain a question while he was so young. Let him play freely, wear whatever he wanted, and continue to use the gorgeous name we had chosen for him at birth (my ex insisted that that name was now his "dead name" and was not to be used). No-one would acknowledge that our son was confused and presented differently with each of us. It was a battle where the adversaries kept on coming.

This is the nightmare where there is no gravity.

Not once were my son's real issues of abandonment and loss ever addressed.

I never gave up. I am not brave, but I knew that I was the only one who could, if possible, find a way to protect my son. I believe I had angels sent to help me. Namely, a woman who came into my life and educated me about what was going on in the dangerous world of trans ideology as it currently relates to children. She stood by me and held me up when I felt I had lost my ability to advocate. She had an unceasing belief that truth and love are ultimately stronger than lies and fear. She asked me repeatedly if I was ready for the fight of our lives. She found story after story about parents like me who were questioning their children's sudden and bewildering change in gender expression, and I began to comprehend that I was actually not as alone as I had once believed. After many false starts, I also found a lawyer who actually took the time to listen to my story and who was willing to fight for my son. I had a retirement fund that almost covered the lawsuit.

After two years of litigation and a trial, I was awarded sole legal custody. My son is no longer in danger of early medicalization in the form of puberty blocking drugs. It is sobering to know that it could so easily have gone the other way. My beautiful child, who has always been very happy in the body he was born with, would have started on puberty blockers right about now. The court could have forced me to comply. Doctors and therapists would have stood by, ready to support this order. My son would have been completely damaged through a completely unproven treatment on vulnerable children that halts the natural process of puberty. I would have been made to live with despair every day of my life, knowing that I had failed to stop this from happening. I also know that many, many others are traveling on that road right now and have been unable to stop the train of medicalization. How is it that there are so many loving and concerned parents who are being systematically shut out from advocating for the kids they know better than anyone else? Is there any other ideology that works to keep parents of minors from being involved in life-altering medical decisions for their young children and teens? The answer to that is no.

My Son Today

My son is now 10 years old. After five years of his other mom affirming him as a girl, his fractured life continues. She still refuses to use his male name and male pronouns, despite the fact that he is very comfortable as a boy everywhere else in his life. One might wonder if a skilled therapist could be helpful in sorting this out and explain how dangerous it is to split a young child in two. I have come to fear therapists—and legitimately so. It is important to understand that when it comes to identity, parents are now at the bottom rung in advocating for their kids, and a therapist's or doctor's role is often to "bring the obstructing parent along" so the child can receive medical treatment. Quietly, in your very own town or city, scores of young children and teens are being taught and groomed to believe that they can change their sex and that this is to be celebrated. Rational, nuanced views from teachers, counselors and doctors are shadowed in fear due to wide acceptance of the affirmation model which has no scientifically proven benefits.

My fervent wish is that my son will grow stronger as he matures in mind and body and be able to pry himself from the insidious tentacles of an ideology that blinded his other mom to who he is and always has been. To be fair, I have no idea where my son will land, but I am certain that he is not a girl and has never wished to be one. The long and painful years of schools and clinicians completely affirming him as a girl child did nothing to bolster his self-confidence. In fact, it had the opposite effect and he learned to cope by shutting down to any and all topics that are emotionally laden. Predictably, the therapist he worked with for three years was never able to break through this wall and help him to feel safe enough to speak. The nightmare continues for our family as it does for so many others. My truth was silenced for years, but as I hope for my son, I will find my voice again. I am always grateful and humbled when someone is willing to listen.

65

What I Think Happened

Our feelings are determined not by what happens, but by the stories we tell ourselves about what happens. This is how I frame my daughter's story, though she would tell it in a much different way.

This story begins in elementary school. Years of being a gifted, highly sensitive kid with autistic characteristics in the area of social interactions has taken its toll on your self-esteem. You are also a late bloomer who still looks and acts like a younger child as your peers begin to go through puberty, emphasizing the already-considerable differences between you and them. One key moment is when some classmates make a list ranking the class in attractiveness, listing you last. You don't understand at the time that this is only because you haven't yet reached maturity and still look like a beautiful child and this moment has a profound effect on your view of yourself. You begin to believe that you are permanently and hopelessly unattractive.

Next, through the admirable cause of teaching acceptance and non-discrimination, kids are taught that not only is being LBGT acceptable, it's cool and better than being straight. Kids who haven't yet been through puberty, and don't really know who they'll be attracted to once they do, encourage each other to declare their orientation and identity and to define themselves by these labels. Any child who declares a non-straight identity gets positive reinforcement from peers and adults who are anxious to prove they are accepting. As a child who doesn't yet comprehend sexual attraction, it's pretty easy to convince yourself you feel about the same way about boys and girls, especially when you know there will be a social reward for doing so. You declare a bisexual identity.

Your peers continue to treat you like a young child and you begin to adopt this as your identity, even when it no longer fits, because you don't know how to break away from the expectations you feel your peers have of you, and you don't know what a more mature version of you would look like.

In this vulnerable state, you start high school. One of the primary developmental goals of teenagers is to find a group to belong to that helps them define who they are outside their families. All teens are highly motivated to do this—it's a normal developmental stage just like a baby learning to walk. You find that your previous peers from elementary school distance themselves and reject you, anxious to be seen as older and not wanting to associate with someone who acts young. You search for another group that will accept you and find the GSA. This seems ok at first and they are kind and accepting but there is a fight among the group and somewhere along the way something goes wrong. I don't know exactly what event triggered your distress—a physical or verbal assault, being exposed to a sexual situation you weren't ready for, or just being exposed to a toxic world view that told you that everything you ever were or believed was wrong and that you were an oppressor.

In the meantime you begin to spend a lot of time in an online community that you were directed to by this real life social group. This community contains people whose goal it is to increase the number of teenagers who identify as transgender. They may have varied reasons—political power, more social acceptance for them as a trans person, a financial stake in the medicalization process, or an attempt to harm western society—but they are very effective. It was presented to you as a fact that a gender is something you are born with, can't be measured but can only be determined based on a feeling, and may be incompatible with your body. If it turns out you were born this way, it would explain all the social problems you've had, and the only way to find happiness is to transition. This is a belief that they promote but it is not a fact. There is no evidence that such a thing exists, although this group will attack anyone who suggests this or suggests there's an element of choice to transitioning.

This community then suggests that if you have trouble fitting in, or feel awkward and uncomfortable with yourself, or reject stereotypes that society might apply to you due to your sex, or even just wonder what gender means, it indicates that you are actually transgender. They say this even though those are very typical teenage experiences that almost everyone has.

Whatever traumatic experience you had earlier has left you without a community you feel you belong to and are accepted in. But you have nowhere else to go, no other group that you feel will accept you. It is extremely important to align yourself with a group and so you begin to adopt their views and styles as your own. It's a toxic community that will easily cast out anyone who disagrees, and so you carefully align your views. It's similar to Stockholm Syndrome, where a victim will begin to align themselves with their captor and take on their views in order to survive.

In this environment, it was very understandable that you (and hundreds of thousands of other teenagers) started to question your gender. It's very important to note that a very high percentage of the teens who identify as transgender are gifted or have autism or other neurological differences. The community has found the most vulnerable of teens to manipulate.

You experiment with identifying yourself as transgender, along with a variety of other labels. At first it seems like casual experimentation and you get a lot of positive reinforcement from the community. But you soon learn that this community doesn't let go easily. Once you've identified this way, they say that if you don't take it far enough or you ever change your mind, it means you were faking it for attention. They demand that you perform actions to prove that you are legitimate, and that you change yourself in ways that make it difficult for you to fit in with any other social group. They convince you that anyone outside the community is hostile toward you and try to alienate you from your family. They convince you that no one but this community will ever accept you, but threaten to cast you out if you don't completely conform to the community and their beliefs. While there are likely a few people in the community that are intentionally orchestrating this culture, it's enforced by other vulnerable teens like you who have become trapped in the culture and don't fully realize that they've become a part of victimizing others.

The community continues to promote negative beliefs that harm its members' self-esteem and keep them trapped. Negative self image, beliefs that something is wrong with you and you are incapable of normal life, beliefs that you are not loved or accepted by anyone outside the community, and beliefs that positive things such as hard work, a positive attitude, a positive self image, scientific truth, and rewarding relationships should be rejected are promoted by the community. Labeling, self-diagnosing, rejecting mainstream society, rejecting family, and presenting yourself as a person who is downtrodden, incapable, and discriminated against will be praised and encouraged by the community.

In this environment, you become extremely depressed. You reject the person that you were previously and try to become someone aligned with the group. You believe that everyone outside the community will reject you. As you become increasingly alienated from everyone else, you become increasingly reliant on the group for positive reinforcement and a sense of identity. Leaving the group or being rejected by it seems unthinkable. Since your real life associates are also somewhat influenced by this culture and accept many of their beliefs, they also may not accept you if you go against the group's beliefs. You feel protected by aligning yourself with this group and so even though their negative beliefs and their impact on your depression are obvious to everyone but you, you are extremely resistant to disengaging from the group.

If you ever did disengage, your personal thoughts and beliefs would begin to return and your self-esteem would begin to recover and you would begin to take actions that are in your best interests and would lead to your happiness. It might be tempting to return to the group in times of stress—it is addictive to have someone else tell you who to be and how to act so that you have no self-doubts—but over time as you gained confidence in yourself those feelings would fade.

You are an amazing, intelligent, creative, capable, and yes, beautiful young woman. You have, and have always had, everything you need to build a happy and fulfilling life and relationships, except for the belief that you do. I hope you can find the courage to be yourself and break free of this.

66

The Heartache of Suicide

In memory of my beloved son Jamie RIP

My son, Jamie, was 32 when he revealed to me out of the blue he was transgender. At the same time he told me he had decided to medically transition and register with the NHS for radical body altering gender surgery. I was blindsided by this revelation. I was never aware that he was unhappy as a boy or as a man. I knew nothing about gender issues at the time and had no idea how to respond. I was just shaken to the core.

At this time my son was severely depressed and undergoing a life crisis following the breakdown of a very difficult relationship. He was making things up about his past, describing people who had been close to him growing up as evil. I was deeply disturbed by and concerned about his mental state. I begged him to get counseling. He became angry and told me he would only get counseling from a trans counselor because no one else was able to understand what it was like being transgender. Then he yelled at me angrily accusing me of being transphobic and told me not to contact him again. I was confused and distressed.

I started to do my own research which did nothing to alleviate my anguish. I wrote to him and tried hard to persuade him not to take this radical action, at the same time letting him know that I would always be there for him. He texted back, asking me to refer to him by his new female name. I couldn't find it in me to do this. Although I tried to maintain contact he never spoke to me again. His mental health continued to deteriorate.

Six months later he took his own life by hanging.

I cannot put into words the continuous and ongoing mental trauma and pain I have suffered. I had to make the arrangements for and attend the funeral of my only son.

Compounding my distress, LGBT activists campaigned to have my son called his chosen female name and pronouns at the service, as well as to have them inscribed on his gravestone and printed on his death certificate. Their representative, whilst pretending to want to support me, intervened and interfered every way possible, going behind my back to the police with his Deed Poll certificate, remonstrating with the funeral director and the funeral operative and drawing up a petition.

My son had lost his way. He was born a boy and died as a man as far as I was concerned. I wanted him to be buried with dignity. The trans activists gathered around the grave, drinking, chanting and throwing things in, one of them shouting his chosen female name angrily. My son's father, who had enthusiastically supported him in his intention to medically transition, was a ring leader. I was confronted and shouted at on two occasions by two of the members at the wake. I wanted my son's friends to be there to share their grief irrespective of their gender identities, but was unprepared for this wall of hostility. To this day, four years later, I am still traumatized. I have suffered two nervous break downs, have not worked since and have frequent nightmares. The 'what ifs' and 'if onlys' haunt me daily. If only I had understood more and realized how cult like and toxic this trans activist movement is I would have done everything to get him out of it.

Growing Up

My son was a typical boy growing up, playing with boys' toys and wearing boys' clothes. He preferred reading books and playing board games over football or sports, as many boys do.

When he was seven we moved to Bangkok where his father had secured a job. When he was nine years old his father started taking methamphetamines. He became verbally abusive and irrational. He was also having affairs with sex trade workers. We rarely saw him. He was not willing to change his ways and we separated.

Jamie was a happy child up to this point but this experience with his father, and the trauma of the resultant separation and family breakdown affected him deeply, and led to behavioral problems. Our life changed dramatically following the separation. I got no financial support from his father and had to work to pay the rent and bills. Trying to cope as a single parent, and to protect my son from his father who was gas-lighting us both, meant I was anxious and stressed. I didn't know how to support my son who had become oppositional and withdrawn.

He spent too much time on his computer in his bedroom. I later found out he was accessing the dark web.

Jamie overdosed at 14, dropped out of school and spent time in psychotherapy, but no amount of psychotherapy and counseling after that was ever able to fix his broken soul.

Adulthood

As a teen and young adult he had girlfriends. I know he was looking for that stable lasting relationship, which he had had in childhood, but sadly it eluded him.

I was proud of Jamie that he did well at sixth form college back in the UK and secured a place at university. In hindsight I think this wasn't the best course for an impressionable young man with low self esteem. His university was in Scotland, 470 miles from my home. I didn't want him to go so far away as I knew it would be hard for me to visit. At the time I was unaware that universities had become liberal, woke establishments. His university, it turned out, is a Stonewall Diversity Champion and LGBTIQ plus aligned.

He did well for his first year and found a nice girlfriend. In his second year he moved into a shared house—but then his father turned up and stayed for several months on his floor. Jamie was unable to cope and dropped out of university, suffering from depression. He joined various political activist groups on campus and started supporting extremist political movements. He tended to be particularly confrontational around ideological issues. When he returned home he was identifying as a Marxist and an anarchist. University was meant to educate him not politically radicalise him. He continued with his studies but had very little contact with me from that time on, and I felt that I personally had become the enemy because his Marxist convictions clashed with my faith. Despite all of these challenges, he graduated with a degree.

The Gender Clinic

I found out that, a few months after his disclosure to me that he was transgender, he attended a private transgender clinic in Edinburgh. He was seen by the medical director, a leading gender specialist in Scotland. I managed to find the presence of mind after the funeral to write to the gender clinic and request their notes.

I found he was advised to change his name by Deed Poll on his first visit. He was also told he would need to live full-time as a woman for two years so that he could change his birth certificate. She offered him a psychiatric evaluation but he declined, saying he would wait for an NHS assessment. This never took place. The gender clinic, interestingly, does not mention psychiatric assessment on their website but just advertises support and help with the entire transitioning process. It would seem that they exist purely to medically transition their clients.

Following his first visit to the clinic, he began socially transitioning and taking three opposite sex hormone prescriptions, which he obtained online, daily. A few months later his gender specialist authorized blood tests to be carried out at the clinic as a means of monitoring his liver and hormone levels. The specialist was aware that Jamie suffered from depression, anxiety, and insomnia. He also told her on his second visit that he had been experiencing mood swings as a result of taking the medication. Ignoring all of this, she stated in her letter to his doctor that he had a typical history of gender dysphoria. Even his close friends and family members were baffled by this diagnosis.

The gender specialist blamed my faith as the reason I could not approve his transitioning—as if any mother in her right mind would be fine with her child taking experimental medication and having healthy body parts amputated. She said that he was in daily contact with his father who was very supportive even though this was a lie—Jamie had not seen his father for two years at that point.

My son did not receive any warnings about the dangers of self medicating, the side effects of experimental opposite sex hormones, and the horrific likely complications from surgeries. If he had, that might have gotten through to him—my son was always sensitive, self conscious and hated hospitals.

There are few or no safety nets for gender dysphoric individuals with suicidal ideation. Doctors who are captive to gender ideology or fearful of trans activists are failing their patients by affirming them in their chosen gender and referring them to gender clinics where they are offered a 'quick fix', ignoring mental health comorbidities. They offer only one possible solution to distress—and it's a path which leads to lifetime dependency on medication and radical surgery with catastrophic complication risks.

Jamie's gender specialist told me that their clinic follows WPATH guidelines—but WPATH is set up and run by transgender activists and is founded, with no scientific basis, on the belief that transitioning is the only path for people with gender dysphoria.

Reflecting

Reflecting on his past, I suspect that a combination of factors—depression, trauma, anxiety, the need for emotional security and acceptance, a crisis of confidence coupled with an addiction to social media and ideological alignments, plus the absence of a suitable male role model growing up, created fertile ground for gender ideology to take hold in my son. Delusional thinking then led Jamie down unhealthy rabbit holes including the belief he was a woman trapped in the wrong body. Whilst I believe Jamie's specialist was well meaning, she was ideologically captured and thus incapable of treating my son with appropriate care. Surely people like my son, with a background of mental health issues, deserve to be treated better and in accordance with rigid, standard medical practice and ethics as they would in any other medical field.

I wish more than anything I had been able to protect my vulnerable adult son. He fell victim to a dangerous cult that separated him from his loved ones. I am sure he could been saved had his difficult past and the root of his unhappiness been explored rationally and had he been able to come to terms with and embrace himself and his natural body. It is too late for my son—but I am compelled to tell my story to raise the alarm along with a growing army of other parents and professionals to expose this abhorrent medical scandal.

Ultimately, no child or adult should suffer my son's fate nor should their families experience the pain and horror of suicide due to this gender ideology movement. My deepest wish is that all medicalising gender clinics be held accountable and closed down. They should be replaced by skilled mental health services where children and adults can be supported to understand the route of their unhappiness and come to terms with their true selves.

67

The Day My Daughter Told Me She Was Not My Daughter

She told me she was not my daughter. I told her she always would be. She was angry and I was crushed. I held it together until after the conversation ended but then I crashed.

When my daughter first announced to me that she was trans, it wasn't a description of an exploration underway but a declaration of a decision already made. She hoped, she said, that she'd never have to talk about it with us, but her personal appearance had been changing over the last months to the extent that it caused me to wonder what was going on. And so one day I asked.

I gently brought it up on a drive and I could see it caused her some anxiety, so we left it for another day. Waiting for that day was not easy. Even as I write about this, one year after it happened, I feel more anxiety than I would like.

We weren't sure what she was preparing to reveal but assumed it had something to do with her sexuality. She wasn't just reticent to share about this, she'd been reluctant to engage at all over the last months. Of course, COVID had made us all that way more than we'd previously been. But for those who already struggled with mental health, as our daughter did pre-COVID, COVID was the perfect catalyst for deeper distress.

The Conversation

The time for the conversation came a few days later at home. We sat in my basement office and I prompted her to speak. This conversation needed to happen at some point, how about now? So she told me... and I was not prepared. I scrambled to explain my understanding of gender, cultural stereotypes, etc.

I used a whiteboard to draw two circles far apart - one I labelled male and the other female. These two circles represented how we often see gender, especially in our theologically conservative Christian circles. We make the distinctions too hard sometimes, I told her, as if men and women are more different than we are similar.

I then drew two circles that had some overlap, explaining that, yes, there are two genders, but that there is a lot in common between the two—that's the overlap. By not too distant societal standards, some women are very feminine and some men are very masculine - and that's fine. Other women are interested in pursuits traditionally considered to be masculine, and vice-versa. This is also fine—I was now looking at the overlap between the two gender circles.

Now, I am not a hyper-masculine man by conservative cultural standards. I do like sports and a few cars, but I also like art and music and other intellectual pursuits. I own no guns, I drive a small car, I love photography... you get the picture. I'm close to the overlap, but no one (I don't think) wonders if I am a woman.

Life in the Overlap

I tried my best to describe her as near the overlap as well, but in truth, I couldn't make the case. There had never been anything remotely masculine about her. As a child and pre-teen she was feminine in every way: no male toys or pretending to be a boy, no expressions of gender confusion or desires to play what are considered masculine sports, etc. Makeup was common, along with feminine jewelry and attire.

Nothing pointed in the current direction... until this, this declaration that she is now male, and wants to be referred to as such.

But it is so obviously and painfully all pretend. In the moments when she is not self-consciously offering a portrayal of this newly imagined identity, she is the normal, expressive young woman who loves cats and babies and books. When we mention this, she realizes she has dropped out of character and the façade comes back. Sometimes it is obvious that she is trying hard to mimic a stereotypical boy her age: talking loud, burping loud, etc.

Back to "The Talk"

Anyway, back to the talk… It was tense and it hurt. She told me she was not my daughter. I told her she always would be. She was angry and I was crushed. I held it together until after the conversation ended but then I crashed.

I sat on our front porch in shock and messaged two of my closest friends: "Please pray for me and keep this between us for now. I won't be telling many people. I'm crushed. I just experienced my worst nightmare. ***** believes she's trans and told me I've been making her hate herself for years because I don't agree that being trans is an option."

68

Swallowed Alive
by the Transgender Medical Industry

My daughter disappeared in college. Save for the first Christmas home, when we celebrated in our usual fashion, we did not see her or hear from her for many years. The manger scene was unboxed and displayed, the tree was cut and trimmed, the cookies were baked and devoured. We volunteered at a local charity wrapping gifts for needy families. We attended services behind wreathed doors, and reminded ourselves of why these days are set aside. She was grateful for the mornings in bed, the home-cooked meals and the family time carved out of busy schedules. Oh, and she was grateful for the new clothes that occupy many a young woman's obsession. There were the usuals - tights, and skirts and a jacket she just had to have. She even 'upgraded' one skirt with her sister's when they decided it was an upgrade for both. And then she left.

Her last Christmas home was like them all. They were family treasures I was certain she would cherish forever. This was not to be. Her memories were erased the following semester in what appears to be one of the biggest psychological operations the world has ever seen. Love became hate, parents became enemies, and siblings became suspicious conspirators. Worst of all, as her mind was corrupted, her body was reduced to a vessel for drugs and the object of a surgeon's knife. What was happening?

The alarm was sounded in a bizarre email. "Mom, I am transgender," followed by nonsensical memories and links to support groups complete with an Orwellian dictionary, which I apparently needed to survive as an 'ally.' I was not looking to survive as an 'ally' but to flourish as a human. Mostly I wanted to know what was now occupying my child's mind. Were her memories of me also erased? Despite it all, she was as steadfast in her newfound convictions as was the university, that her parents could not be trusted. The things that followed should never have happened. Yet they did.

Silence and lack of empathy are among things that stand out from this time. Oh, how I wish I knew to tape the strange interactions I did have with a couple of university employees. The way these degreed and salaried employees had wedged their belief systems between a cherished mother/daughter relationship leave me bewildered to this day. How do you reply when an employee tells you that your own moral values are 'just different'?

Have we met, Mr. University Employee? He no more knew me than did he know my daughter—and he was talking to me about morals! Universities have morphed into political police states where students must adhere to a new paradigm to survive in the new regime. So must the parents and we were not playing.

As for the doctors, it was only silence.

As for the friends…well, most are friends no more.

Great crises arise when empathy dissipates from the human equation. We are here again at this moment of time but perhaps in a bigger way than ever. Without empathy man's body devolves into a mere object. Today evil lurks in social acceptance where empathy is disguised as 'diversity and inclusion'. Uncritical masses become believers rallying for the 'trans' cause unable to see beyond the smokescreen. Power and money make Frankenstein medicine seem palpable where it should be unthinkable.

The signs for all of this were there long ago as scandal after scandal has built a shaky scaffolding to support all manner of horrors across our medical institutions. I was just not privy to all of them yet. The monsters in charge seem destined to carry on no matter what.

My daughter spoke of no diagnosis, only of an alien identity. To receive medical services though there must be that golden goose, the ICD code. I would soon learn that 'gender dysphoria' is that golden goose and one that is abundantly bestowed upon unassuming masses of youth today. 'Gender dysphoria' was a term I had never heard, at least not before finding an article from a rare gender critical therapist back then calling out into the medical wasteland. It was also quite a shock given a childhood, that in a nutshell, leads to tights and skirts on Christmas wish lists!

'Gender dysphoria' is among the tangle of diagnoses offered in the diagnostic manual of the American Psychiatric Association. Medication often accompanies psychiatric diagnoses. They have no magic abilities though and can come at a cost. With a brain disease model of psychiatry, false positives can lead to, what the producer of a documentary on the overuse of prescription medications in psychiatry calls, Medicating Normal. Harm can follow all while drug development and sales can increase to accommodate the new normal.

When the diagnostic offering is 'gender dysphoria' medicine is paired with surgical 'remedies' in an unbelievable concoction. Today the bodies and minds of youth are being swallowed alive by a mental health apparatus that has provided the mechanism to set the transgender medical complex on track for a multi-billion-dollar industry. Please help us make it stop.

Please consider following along at margox.substack.com, *Desexing: Medicine as Means*, for a look behind the smokescreen of the transgender industry.

Parents with Medicalized Children

69

A Father's Anger That Will Not Sleep

It has been two years since my 19 year old son walked into a Planned Parenthood and received HRT drugs on informed consent. His mother and I pleaded with him to not make such a life changing decision at such a young age. But he would not listen to reason and received these drugs without any psychological evaluation or supervision, and little medical supervision.

Since that time I have experienced bouts of intense anger, which have caused my mental health to decline. It's an anger that woke me up at 2 am for nearly a year, and still regularly wakes me up at 4 am. It's has taken a toll on my body, mind, and mood. I experience depression and anhedonia more often than not. I find little to no joy in hobbies I once relished. I take care of the tasks of daily living and not much else.

I honestly did not think it was possible to feel such emotional pain. What am I angry about?

- That society is enabling a cult of self-harm disguised as a fantasy. I am also furious that society sees me as the problem because I'm "transphobic".
- The medical establishment's adoption of euphemisms for mutilating the bodies of teenagers—and calling it "gender affirming care", all while making tidy profits.
- The medical staff that continues to supply my son with wrong sex hormones, even though his mental and physical health is in obvious

decline. At 19 he was thin, and at 21 he is borderline obese. He also reports crying daily. Yet he's unwilling to stop taking drugs that are the source of this harm.

- How the Democratic party (which I used to support) and Biden enable this social contagion. How Biden nominated Judge Jackson who refused to define the word 'woman'. And I'm angry watching Rachel (Richard) Levine saying he was glad he had kids before transition while simultaneously advocating fertility destroying treatments for young people.
- The misogyny of a movement that allows sexual predators to gain access to women's spaces simply by claiming they're a woman.
- The misogyny of a movement that sees women as castrated men, and doesn't value women's ability to bring new life into the world. And that allows males to enter and dominate women's sports (e.g. Lia Thomas), or injure women (e.g. Fallon Fox fracturing Tamikka Brents' skull).
- The media for denying predators exist (e.g. Wi Spa), and not covering physical harms happening to natal women, or when they do for using word salad and intentionally confusing language, like "she raped her with her penis".
- The media for not covering Planned Parenthood's prescribing hormones with only informed consent and no due diligence or following up on the harm to young people who are damaging their bodies (the voices of detransitioners).
- The trans movement's redefinition of words and introducing made up pronouns and trying to enforce their usage and control language.
- My own child for his entitled attitude that he should continue to receive college tuition while destroying his body and mind; his uncaring attitude for the emotional pain of his parents, and the enormous strain that his actions have put on my marriage.
- My own utter powerlessness in the face of these events, and feeling like a failure for not protecting my child from this cult.

I am aging and hoped for the compensation of feeling I had a life well led, and that I successfully launched my children into the world. But my son has stolen that from me and left me feeling like an utter failure. This was a child that I treated with love, compassion, and generosity, and he has selfishly taken all that away.

I am aware of how this anger is harming my mind and body. What am I trying to do about it?

- For the better part of a year I pleaded with my son to stop. His response was to call his mother and I transphobic.
- Every day for the past two years I have restrained myself from sending my son a nasty email telling him what I really think about his narcissistic behavior and misogynistic fantasy.
- I have twice given money to Partners for Ethical Care, hoping their billboard campaigns make a difference.
- I will never vote Democrat again.
- Some days I successfully pretend none of this is happening.
- I enjoy those few moments of morning amnesia where I can't yet recall my current circumstances.
- I saw a therapist for about a year and a half, but it wasn't helpful. Part of me always saw the therapist as part of the profession enabling this social contagion. I also couldn't trust him with my true feelings, as I feared judgment.
- Several times a week I have a crying jag that lasts several minutes. I do it when my wife is out walking the dog so as to not burden her with this.

If I didn't love my son, all of this would be much easier, but I do. And it is my love that causes the grief that feeds my anger.

70

Duct Tape

Despite prolonged effort, my husband and I were not able to help our young adult son find his way out of the trans cult. He believes the lie that he is a she and always has been, that wrong sex hormones are magic pills, and that this absurdity paves the path to his well-being. It's like my son tied himself to a train track, euphoric about the trans train that harms him. It feels like my mouth is sealed by duct tape, which I resist peeling off to implore my son again with reasons to desist. Even the most cogent guidance could prompt my son to tie more ropes around his deteriorating body on the trans train track. I do not tell him how unconvincing he looks as a faux woman, as this could be a catalyst for mutilating surgery. Also, estrangement could be more likely.

Underneath the duct tape is an avalanche of truth. This is what I yearn to share:

After taking hormones, your appearance has diminished: weight gain, unflattering looking clothes, and gynecomastia.

Your anxiety persists, and you've added depression and fatigue on top of that. You were healthier and more mentally balanced just a few years ago in high school.

HRT destroys sexual function and increases the likelihood of heart attack, blood clot, stroke, and dementia. You have likely sacrificed your fertility—but you could restore sexual function and sidestep health risks if you stop wrong sex hormones.

You are being manipulated and treated cruelly by people who are duping you to believe you can change your sex, and these people pad their bank account with you as a lifelong medical patient.

You are also being treated badly by everyone, including those you think of as friends, who sanction putting dangerous hormones into the one healthy body you will ever have.

People who seem accepting of your "transition" when you present yourself in the world are not fooled—and they likely feel sorry for you.

Your autism traits fuel your obsession with being "trans." Aspects of autism, which include feeling weird, having social difficulties, and hyper-focusing have prompted you to fixate on the fantasy of escaping your male body.

You cannot be a woman, only a diminished version of yourself as a man.

You did not have an abusive childhood. You were raised by attentive, caring parents. Your memory and perceptions of the present have been manipulated to separate you from Dad and me, who want to help you sidestep a path that is stealing your health and potential for a happy, fulfilled life.

You have so many strengths, yet you are throwing your best self away with your obsession with the fantasy of being a woman.

You can overcome your actual difficulties with self-esteem, anxiety, and social connection with support from your family and caring others, therapy, and helpful medications.

Time outside can also improve your well-being in a more sustainable way than the trans path: walking, backpacking, cross country skiing, kayaking—it doesn't matter whether you appreciate the earth or trees or a pond or an ocean or a mountain. Time in nature could help you let go of your over focus with gender and embrace your actual body in the actual world. Your father and I pleaded with you to choose non-invasive ways to deal with your feelings until you were at least 25 and your brain matured. We are devastated that you devalue our longstanding love and guidance. Your plowing ahead with transition during college while dependent upon us is callous and self-absorbed. You still have the capacity to reach for real help and restore kindness and respect toward your parents and to yourself.

WAKE UP! WAKE UP! WAKE UP!

Taking the duct tape off to impart again the truth with tact and gentleness would not wake up my son. Online and in the real world, he has been indoctrinated that the "trans" path is optimal and necessary. Many more hands than his own tie my son to the track, where he is assaulted by the trans train with its horrid cargo of hormones and lies. My son suffered a terrible mental health crash. He remains out of reach from the help of his parents, and there is no ambulance.

I yearn for others to wake up, too. At the grocery store, walking my dog, or just about anywhere, I want to shout: Did you know Planned Parenthood prescribes wrong sex hormones to vulnerable young people? Did you know that these hormones sterilize within months and have serious health risks? Did you know families are being shattered while their children are groomed as lifetime medical patients who pretend to be the opposite sex? Please read PITT. Please read the tragic stories of detransitioners. At the ballot box, please vote to end this madness.

In the spirit of sanity, I occasionally allow a duct tape reprieve and share the truth about the trans cult. No one, not even my physician, was aware of Planned Parenthood's evil franchise of prescribing wrong sex hormones. People react with appropriate objection. But even those who hear the truth from under my duct tape may not be concerned that much about the trans cult because it's not their child who has been stolen. Or they may fear being canceled or losing their job.

At the end of another day of loss, the duct tape that seals in my pain is loosened when I try to sleep. Thoughts flood. My 21 year old son is likely sterile in stereotyped awful outfits. I replay him insisting he is a woman with what seems an impenetrable, narcissistic delusion. My husband next to me is sleeping, but when he wakes up, often in the middle of the night, he will grapple with feeling enraged, hurt, and depressed. Insomnia grips. The trans cult's thwarting of my parental instinct to help my son inflicts an unnatural ache. Sometimes I scroll on my phone in the dark through photos that preserve the years of my son's healthy self and our close family. Invariably, this retreat into the past provokes profound sadness, and I need duct tape around my heart if there is any chance of sleep.

The trans cult wraps duct tape around common sense among those it ensnares, and it provides income for the opportunistic. I wish I could wrap duct tape around the trans cult the way one treats a wart. Contain the wart until it's recognized as a virus, and the body sheds it. When will enough people recognize the trans cult as a harmful mass psychosis to be shed?

71

They Want Me to Pretend

They say that the reason she is not doing well is not because of the testosterone or the mastectomy but because I am not trying hard enough to have a better relationship with her.

I don't know what that means anymore. She decided 2 years ago that I was evil. Now anything I say, anything I do, any text I send, any question, any emoji, just confirms for her that I am being "manipulative". It reassures her that her online and real life friends are right when they tell her not to trust me and that if I am "being nice" it's because I'm trying to get her to change.

She believes these things. But she must also be confused. There must be some inner dissonance between these beliefs and the 18 years we spent together. We were close and then, suddenly, one day, she said "you're going to kick me out if I tell you this", followed by, "I am trans". That's how it happened. And in that moment, she was lured away from me by the false beliefs of others. Anything I said simply confirmed for her that I could not be trusted. Anything I said became a threat.

So I am damned either way. I can carry on with my life, try to salvage what's left, hang on to my other child, or I can pretend and pretend and post fake "likes" of her scar photos, like her glitter moms do. I could act out pride and happiness with my child's medically facilitated self-harm. I could try to win her back by putting on a performance. Apparently.

So they want me to pretend. To use male pronouns, even when she's not around, even around my partner. He has been recruited; she has recruited allies within our family, like the Stasi, the thought-police. Even though he says he disagrees with all this, he believes that it's still up to me. That I could make this all better, I could stop her from cutting her arms and her face and turn her into a happier person if I would just give in, surrender.

Of course, there's no such thing as a mother giving in. This is a fundamental truth. Only my dead body is able to give in. So do they all want me dead? Perhaps.

I tried to surrender once, way back. I told her I was glad that she was feeling better (which is what she claimed, after starting testosterone). Then she told me that if anything stopped her from getting a mastectomy she would kill herself. (What surgeon on this planet uses that as an indication for surgery?)

Deep down, I know that no matter how hard I try, no matter what I do, no amount of pretending will improve our relationship. She is on male hormones and other psych meds. She is shut down emotionally, she has made her escape using pharmaceutical tools. It is a losing game to try to "win" her approval, to try to get her to admit to others that I am not evil. Because that would unravel everything. Then the world she knows would truly stop making sense. She would accuse me of pretending. She would play the thought-police. She needs me to be the enemy.

I get all that. I could take all of that. What I can't take is OTHER PEOPLE, like doctors and therapists and my husband telling me I am not trying hard enough to be her mother and that is the root of all our troubles. It always comes back to the mother.

There must be a script somewhere for all of them with all their rules and guiding phrases. And I am the only one refusing to read it or unable to memorize the lines.

I wake up every morning sick, my heart racing, wondering how to get through another day of Failing as a Mother. That's my role. That's the only one I can't pretend.

72

The Standard Clinic Experience—Self-Diagnosis Straight to Hormones in One Day

My family has been hijacked by the transgender movement so, along with my thanks for your bravery, I thought I should share our journey at a pediatric gender clinic.

When my daughter first expressed gender distress, we were encouraged to go to a "prestigious" university pediatric gender clinic.

I still have so much anger/hostility from the day of our appointment. The experience was what I now recognize as boiler plate gender clinic. The intake therapist affirmed my daughter immediately. She did not receive any prior history from her therapist, just took my child's word for it in what we now know is the standard self-diagnosis procedure.

In response to my husbands question about the truth of the suicide statistics, the therapist made a sad face, and just shook her head "yes". My husband broke down sobbing.

The intake therapist offered to get us in to the clinic's medical doctor the very same day so that my then 13-year old daughter could be prescribed Testosterone right away. I asked this therapist, "this doctor would do this? Today?" She said, "Oh yes, they (the gender doctors) do as I say. All told our appointment was only a couple of hours.

Not that day, but eventually, we did go for an appointment with that medical doctor, but my husband and I declined hormones. We went back to this clinic 6-8 times, each time there was a private consult with just my daughter and one with just us parents.

I raised my concerns with the doctor, telling of how I had signed myself into these teen sites as a 14 year old female and seeing all advice and propaganda on how to "pass" with your parents/therapist/gender clinic, etc. Seeing how the 20ish year old "males" promoted testosterone as the only answer. The glorification of mastectomies, the hypnotizing videos, the youtubers and bloggers who secretly messaged these teens with their agendas. It was clear to me that these influences were powerful and that teens were following a playbook. While the doctor seemed interested, she continued to push for my daughter to start T.

Another time I asked the doctor to speak to my child about about any holistic, or dbt, or neutral therapies available as she was depressed and lonely. We pressed this issue at home, and found a neutral therapist—but my child exploded at this. Later she told me the doctor said that the reason she was depressed, sad, and lonely was because of her gender dysphoria and that she needed hormones.

In another private conversation, with only myself and this doctor (who is an MD, not an endocrinologist), she admitted to me that "their clinic is having a harder time distinguishing between 'real' and 'socially influenced' "trans kids".

I also asked this doctor how she could sleep at night, giving young women adult male hormones with with no long term studies available. Her reply with a chuckle, was "it makes them SO HAPPY".

In God's name this is a crime.

73

Dear Doctor,

Letter written to Dr. XXXXX ... no response received

I am the mother of a child who suddenly claimed a transgender identity and became swiftly medicalized—meaning prescribed wrong sex hormones and surgeries to treat gender dysphoria, without any in-depth exploration. I came across your name while researching gender ideology and your background in bioethics seems well-suited to my story and the information that I am here sharing.

I am not seeking your help; sadly I have come to realize there is little to no help available for parents like myself. I am a mere representative of the many thousands of parents who have had their child medicalized in as little as one visit to a gender affirming medical establishment. I have previously spoken with many professionals highly critical of the latest fad in psychiatry of accepting patients' self-diagnosis of 'gender dyspho-ria' and then being ushered into transition. Parents have connected via social media platforms and organizations across the US and internation-ally and we hail from all political and religious affiliations. I am sharing the truth of gender identity medicine today as our family and countless others have experienced it.

Since Lisa Littman's work in 2018 first exposed the possibility that social contagion could be at play in the sky-rocketing numbers of trans-gender identified youth, this topic has been continuously lauded and glorified by the media. Considering there are close to 40k young women wanting 'top surgery' (a euphemism for non-medically necessary breast amputation) today on GoFundMe, it seems that Littman was on to something. Certainly, this is not normal.

The industry today is light years away from the time when anabolic steroids first came on to the market and doctors and patients began to dabble in altering the human body to take on the appearance of the opposite sex. Now, the fact that Paul McHugh shuttered the gender identity clinic at Johns Hopkins in the 1970's because transition did not benefit the patient population has been lost to history.

Fast forward to 2021 and the industry that used to be in back alleyways is exploding like never before. The affirmation model is now the norm and most medical institutions have established guidelines to push patients into the pipeline of gender medicine, while laws are being passed to deter any counseling for gender confused patients. The fact that there is so little help for families like ours does not prove that the affirmation model is sound healthcare. All the parents I have connected to know that it is not. Our children are in harm's way and we are desperately trying to organize to save them from unnecessary mental and physical harm.

I have been experiencing this contagion first hand. My college-aged daughter was prescribed testosterone and, a mere few months later, she had her breasts amputated. There is nothing that could have prepared our family for this tragedy that is still unfolding. To know our daughter would be to think up is down, black is white or that Mickey Mouse is real. She was gender conforming, had mostly female friends her entire life, meets none of the criteria for gender dysphoria as laid out in the DSM-5, and had little interest in stereotypical masculine activities at all. Our daughter was extremely gifted, highly creative, an AP student throughout high school, and involved in countless activities.

Now, she has been indoctrinated to join the cult of gender ideology. She has severed ties with all family members, save for some tenuous contact with a sibling. Can this possibly be medical care? She was encouraged by her like-minded peers, harbored by her university and swiftly led down the rabbit hole of transgender medicine to either be a patient for life or to one day wake up and decide to reconvene in a body that has been harmed for life. And, if she chooses this latter path, no medical assistance will be forthcoming. Gender transition assistance these days is a one-way path.

There are thousands of parents living this nightmare and I've met many of them. Our stories are eerily similar and yet we read lie after lie in the mainstream media that we are bigots, transphobes, 'terfs' and other names, many too despicable to mention. We read that we have disowned our children, when the opposite is often true. We are lied to by educators and the medical community who are hellbent on creating transgender youth. We read the lies that only adults get surgeries or that our children have gone through rigorous psychological counseling. Neither of these is true. Some parents have even lost their children in the court of law when they question this supposed 'care.'

The political and pharmaceutical ties to this narrative are blatant. Our children are seen as specimens for a social experiment. The suicide card that is played has been debunked as many times as it is played and yet the card continues to be played on repeat. We know that the only long-term study ever completed actually shows a 19 times greater risk of suicide AFTER transition. I believe this is likely an underestimation, as the cohort in this study was far different from today's trans-identified patients, who are younger and largely female. It would not be a stretch to say the harms could be far greater.

As parents, we have lobbied Congress, pushed for bills in various states to hold doctors accountable and to quell this gross social contagion. We have pushed for advocacy in schools, churches and the like against the radical indoctrination into gender ideology. We keep our fingers on the pulse of this exploding medical scandal as more and more desisters and detransitioners come forth with their stories, as more and more countries begin to question their practices and pull back the veil on transgender medicine. Here in North America, we are living in the gender medicine capital of the world, with more clinics than any other country. This article speaks accurately of the totalitarian regime I have witnessed under the guise of 'healthcare.'

Imagine how this would turn your personal life upside down if the child you raised suddenly claimed an opposite sex identity? Imagine knowing the actual risk of suicide and having a child who has shut you out of their life? I live in fear for my daughter and other young people across this country where mutilating body parts is increasingly becoming second nature. There are even surgeries and hormones for "non-binary" identifying people now. None of this makes any sense. I fear for families that are as of yet unaware of the dangers that loom. I can say firsthand that this social contagion does not discriminate and, by all appearances, our government is dead set on creating more and more casualties.

While fully realizing the contentious nature of this issue and the work you do, I would be grateful for the opportunity to share my personal story. I have repeatedly witnessed the reactions from parent's firsthand accounts as most people do not realize what is really happening.

Follow up: The author of this letter received NO REPLY.

74

Nevertheless, She Persisted

Persistence. Determination. Perseverance. All good traits. But what is their value when they are used in the service of a harmful, cult-like ideology?

My 22-year-old daughter is trans-identifying. She has been on "T" for three years. Her story is much like many we have all read on this site. She was a very feminine girl, precocious, riven by anxiety, a desire to "fit in" and be part of a large friend group. She was (and is) whip smart. In middle school she set her sights on being admitted to her dream university. She worked towards that goal for years and was successful. She was over the moon when she received her acceptance notification.

Fast forward to a few months after arriving on campus. Having achieved her goal, she finds she is still the same person. She is still anxious and experiencing social issues. She is desperate to know what's "wrong with her". A new college friend suggests the problem is that she's really a boy in a girl's body. Eureka! Like a game of pachinko, all the slots fell into place. This new ideology not only explained *everything*, it provided the answer. Transition and life will be easier. Every problem will be solved. She'd no longer be afraid; she'd be celebrated for being brave. She'd no longer be socially awkward; she'd be the trans-person at the party. She'd no longer feel that being a woman didn't work; she'd be a man.

Within ten months she had totally adopted the trans ideology. She changed her name at school. She stopped communicating with all family members except her parents whom she labelled "transphobes". Aided and abetted by the university healthcare service, (their motto: "one is trans if they think they are"), she started on testosterone. Much happened in the next three years but let's fast forward to where she is now.

She left her dream university before graduating. Although transitioning was to solve all her issues, she developed health issues that prompted her to leave. No doctor could diagnose any malady. Nevertheless, she persisted.

She is currently working menial, hourly jobs. Thanks to the boom economy she's been able to find work with decent pay, but the jobs are in retail and restaurants. Her friends are pursuing careers, exploring graduate schools. She's trying to get a weekend off. Nevertheless, she persisted.

In addition to "T", she is on numerous other medications, many for the side effects of T like vaginal atrophy and bladder infections. Some anti-depressants. And one for hair loss, because she's balding. Nevertheless, she persisted.

What I tell myself to get through the day:

- She is young and can change her mind.
- She hasn't had surgery. Maybe the damage won't be irreversible.
- Her frontal cortex isn't fully developed yet. Perhaps she can reason her way out of this.
- While she had a community of trans folks to greet her and usher her into the new ideology, she also has access to a community of detrans folks who have been down this road and are generous with their own stories and advice (see the detrans reddit of 31k+ members)
- People do foolish things when they are young. Maybe we'll laugh about this someday.
- She's still smart and kind and funny and sweet. Her essential personhood is still there. That transcends gender or sex.

What has this ideology cost her? Education, career, health, dating and social opportunities. What has it added to her life? Nothing. I try to see it, but I can't. Nevertheless, she persisted. Someday, I have to believe, she will come back to herself, and to her family.

75

Dear Concerned Parent,

A comforting letter from the Gender Affirmation Clinic

Dear Concerned Parent,

We are saddened to hear of the depression and anxiety your child is experiencing. But not to worry—you have come to the right place. We are experienced professionals who are equipped to help your child and, by extension, your family.

After months of middling research, we can confidently recommend that your child be placed on a course of medication that will begin immediately and continue for the rest of their lives. The side effects may include weight gain, acne, baldness, sleep apnea, high cholesterol, increased blood pressure, heart disease, irritability, bloating, pelvic cramping, and bladder infections. You and your child can decide to discontinue these medications at any time but, if started pre-puberty, 99% of kids opt to continue on to the next stage of these medications—cross-sex hormones. Talk about a stellar retention rate! Oh, and did we mention infertility? Yes, that is likely to occur but there is no need for concern here. Your child, once they are of age, will likely have a very difficult time finding a romantic partner and sex may be painful in any case.

You can see we don't try to sugarcoat the side effects but it's all worth it. Children know who they are. Our job, as the adults in the room, is to listen to them and give them what they want at that moment. We all know that children who are persistent, consistent, and insistent in their desires rarely change their minds. They know their true sex at a very young age, the same way they can confidently choose their future profession while in grade school.

Once the puberty blockers or cross-sex hormone treatment begins, you can expect to see an elevated mood in your child. They may be euphoric. They are finally living as their true selves! Depending on their age, you can expect a lot of talk in this phase about gendered souls, male and female brains, and a proclivity for stereotypical behavior. Your son will finally be free to wear pink! Of course, that's how we knew he was a girl all along.

It is possible that, after the initial euphoria, your child experiences depression. For FTM transitions, testosterone therapy is associated with depression, suicidality, and intentional self-harm. One study found that puberty blockers did not alleviate negative thoughts in children with gender dysphoria. But we don't really know about all that. After all, this is experimental treatment. Puberty blockers are not FDA approved but they have been used for many years. They've been very effective as chemical castration for men convicted of sex offenses and for poor souls like Alan Turing who was "convicted" of being gay in the 1950s. If they can chemically castrate a grown man, we're confident in the results we can achieve with your child.

Now we should briefly discuss surgery. The less said about this the better, and best to stick to euphemisms. Healthy body parts will need to be removed for your child to better approximate the appearance of their true gender. In most cases we can wait until they are over 18 to operate. We do make exceptions in some cases, however, so please do inquire! For young women, we suggest harvesting eggs before surgery, in the event they ever want to have children and can afford surrogacy.

There are some transphobes out there (also known as TERFs) who insist on robust research and evidence for the efficacy of transitioning children and young adults. Do not be deterred by them! They hate your children and, for reasons unknown, demand proof that these well-established treatments actually work. Gentle suggestion: don't Google any recent gender related news from the following countries: Finland, Sweden, France, the UK, and Norway. These are known to be conservative backwaters run by religious fundamentalists. Probably best to avoid any news out of Europe altogether.

You and your child are about to set off on an exciting new phase of their life—an irreversible, unproven journey. This experience requires courage, faith, and a mind closed off to the exploration of any alternative treatments or explanations for gender dysphoria. Thousands of children have been down this path already. Will yours join them?

Sincerely,

The Gender Affirmation Clinic

Parents on Desistance

76

The Many Months to Desistance

This time last year I wrote my first PITT piece, "This is Not a Desistance Story." It was spring, and I was optimistic and hopeful. "Next May, I'll write an update with a different title," I thought. Yet, I both believed it, and didn't—living in the state of uncertainty and low-grade depression is a surreal experience. My son was 17, and I thought I had a year left. It was spring. I was scared and anxious.

That summer I was on a mission to take as many trips as possible with my teens, and I was joyful and grateful that they were happy to join me. Each week we picked a new destination and I drove for hours. In the car I was in my happy little universe where I was whole, and we were safe. I was selfishly living an ideal homeschooling summer and I was determined to fill it up with ice cream on waffle cones in far-away, half-abandoned towns, sunrises and sunsets on the beach, bonfires and fireflies. I wanted to make sure I would have those memories no matter what. Every day was beautiful and achingly bittersweet.

My son hadn't socially transitioned, he still looked like a boy. By midsummer, his exploratory therapist said that he had a breakthrough. The therapist wasn't worried about him wanting to medicalize, but he was also not sufficiently aware of the immensity of the ideological brainwashing. He thought my son was too smart to be captured. I was aware though—and I was worried. I knew how many smart kids were captured. But my son seemed happy, entirely unconcerned about being called "sir" on occasion. He was growing into a handsome young man. We didn't talk about gender ideology. On Sasha Ayad's advice, gender topics were for him and his therapist to discuss.

Then the too familiar punch in the gut came in the Fall, when he started a part time job and was adored and praised by everyone there—he was still thinking of himself as transgender, and this was not going to change. Ever. He was impatient to socially transition and start taking hormones at 18. On the outside nothing changed. I still saw a happy teen. I had less than 6 months left.

I tried to calm myself with thoughts that this was the often-mentioned Boomerang Effect. My little home-grown, intuition-based "theory", which I wrote about for PITT, was that The Boomerang Phase was actually The Uncertainty Phase, where teens double down on gender ideology to combat fading conviction and a growing sense of cognitive dissonance. It is a difficult, emotional phase, and probably the phase when they are most easily influenced.

I didn't know whether my "theory" was correct, but I also felt I had little choice but to push back during this phase. I wasn't going to stand idly by, watching him being led deeper into the cult by trans influencers. I started to integrate information on the trans ideology into our home-schooling via different podcasts and documentaries by figures including Helen Joyce, Stephanie Davies-Arai, Douglas Murray, Jordan Peterson, Barry Wall, John Uhler, Chloe Cole, Kellie-Jay Keen, etc. It was scary at first, as I was worried about his reaction and our relationship. Some days he would pull his hood over his head, but I saw that he was still listening, and he would perk up within minutes after a podcast or a documentary was over. We watched What is a Woman, and he lived, but we skipped the intro and the ending. Whatever bad mood they caused, it didn't linger. I never made it personal and never asked him where he was at with his own gender identity.

We watched hours of podcasts and the manner of how he was sitting at the table started to change. He didn't cover his face anymore, he sat straighter.

His 18th birthday came and went, with no big announcement, but the uncertainty was still overwhelming. By February I was telling myself that I should stop with the gender critical stuff and we should focus on something else, but then The Affirmation Generation came out, and I just had to show it to him. When I asked what he thought about it, he said there was nothing there that he didn't already know. I was still too anxious to ask what it all meant for him. If he was still thinking of himself as transgender, I didn't want him to verbalize these thoughts to me, thus potentially making them something he needed to defend.

Then at some point in early spring he laughed at a gender critical meme I sent him. Then he made a couple of gender critical jokes. But when I casually said that gender was just a modern and ideological term for personality, he rejected the idea. This made me doubt everything yet again. A month or two later he made fun of the idea that biological sex was nonbinary, and I felt in my bones that this was over. The curse was lifted. I exhaled.

Are we there yet? I wish I knew. From what I've read, some never leave the cult entirely and come back to it in the times of stress. But for now, I won't think about that. I too need a break. In retrospect, he has been incrementally desisting for the last nine months—there were little signs all along, but how do you trust them when you are on a rollercoaster? I'm sure that if I were to ask him about his desistance a year from now, he'd say that he made up his mind entirely on his own and that all the podcasts we listened to didn't matter. Maybe he'd say that he simply grew up, and he would be right. But I would not have been able to live with myself if I didn't make the information about the ideology and biological reality available to him.

The last year went by too slowly and yet too fast. I'm grateful, humbled, empowered, still not entirely back to normal. I know how lucky we are, how, in retrospect, comparatively easy it has been—a mere 21 months, and he hasn't even worn a skirt or a bra. And now it is over, almost like it never happened, like a bad dream you'd rather forget.

77

A Resistance Story

The anxiety that remains after the desistance of my daughter from nearly two years of trans identification is persistent, insistent, and consistent. An identity that was moulded by poor peer relations, bullying, online immersion, and professional grooming. Is she safe from this? Will she be drawn back in? How can we make this all stop? How did we get here?

My sleep is fitful. My thoughts are constantly processing articles, studies, policies, data, and online discourse. I urgently wait for this castle of sand that is the gender industrial complex to be taken by the largest of tides. When will the full moon shine on this darkness. When will this be visible as the pure evil that it is? And when will those who do not completely understand the harm that is being done stop blindly supporting this cause so as not to taint their own sense of virtue. This is not all rainbows and glitter. Surely the elaborate packaging of trans ideology is a red flag?

To preface this piece I will give some personal history for context. Born in the USSR and raised in the USA in the 1980s I lived a life somewhere in between cultures—not quite American enough, not quite Soviet enough, never quite belonging. I was a tomboy, and made to feel shameful for it. My mother was deeply dissatisfied in my presentation and preferences and was sure to let me know it. I wished I could play sports, but that was not considered appropriate for girls by my parents. "Why not ballet?". On the sidelines I watched as my brothers played sports. It seemed life for girls was unfair, full of judgment and limitations set by society.

I am all too familiar with the language and tactics of abusers.

At a young age I was groomed by our neighbors, a father and older son. They tended to all of my tomboy desires and worked to build my trust in them. They eventually seemed like a second family. Then the behaviors started to change. There were the attempts to slip a tongue into my mouth by the father when greeting me with a kiss. The attempt by the son to lock me into a room with him, coaxing me to get into the bed. I did not understand why, but I knew that I needed to get out of that room. I made an excuse and ran. There was an incident where I was out playing in the rain and the son called me over to him. He was masturbating in the driveway. These adults made me fear talking to my parents. I was terrified, betrayed, and unsure of who to speak to. But I eventually spoke to my brother who shared all this with my parents. The son was deemed schizophrenic and was treated at a mental facility for a period of time, then he returned home. At night he would sit on his porch shouting obscenities at my mother and I. The nightmares persist today.

My mother was emotionally and physically abusive all through my childhood. In my teenage years I did not become the unattractive and undesirable person as she had predicted, but quite the opposite. I grew to be a target of more male attention than I was able to process. Eventually I ended up in an abusive relationship far too young and was far too fearful to disclose what was happening with my mother. During this time she had remarried and gotten involved in a religious cult of whom my stepfather was the leader. Her level of judgement and cruelty only grew more volatile. Emotional blackmail was the language of control in both my home and in the toxic relationship. Threatening suicide is an effective way to insure compliance. It is a fear tactic used to deter victims from questioning the intent of their abuser.

In resistance to all of these factors, I developed an extreme case of anorexia. A physical response to all of the trauma I experienced being a girl. My body became a protest, I allowed it to whither away trying to escape the burdens of womanhood. It was a trip to my birth country for a summer that broke the spells of the abusive relationship and the eating disorder. It became apparent in a different social environment that I was ill. I was able to reflect on my deep discomfort with my body and the abuses that lead me to hate it. My true self came through, the defiant, athletic, and bold individual who knew when to escape and when to fight.

What I learned was that abusers lose interest when you start to resist, when you start to ask questions. They cannot be faced with the truth of their actions, therefore they need to dehumanize their subjects. Not everyone makes a good subject. The abusive relationship ended as this person found a new target. I caught my mothers fist as it attempted to land on my face when I returned from that trip. I said "no more!". A year later I was thrown out of her house, kicked out of the cult. The neighbor had nothing but words to sling at us after the court case. He never physically advanced again. Those who don't play by the abusers rules become enemies.

After high school I visited a town regionally renowned for its gay culture and arts scene. I fell in love with the energy of the place and began living there for part of the year. It was a refuge for an outcast. The formative years of my youth were experienced here amongst people of many walks of life, many cultures. This place embodied freedom to express, freedom to love, freedom to just be. It was here that I blossomed and healed from my past. I found my tribe. It was here that I was inspired to see the world and experience life to its fullest. Eventually I would travel, meet my husband and start a family, settling a few towns over. It is here that my two kids have been raised, free to be.

I have a similar story as to how I got here to most parents of trans identifying teens:

My extremely talented artistic, quirky, kind girl, who never showed any interest in anything stereotypically male, suddenly decided she wanted to be perceived as a boy in the spring on 2021. It was the middle of the pandemic and she had been spending lots of time online communicating with other artistic socially awkward kids in various online forums including discord. She had begun puberty in the summer of 2020. The changes were deeply uncomfortable for her and she was consistently moody and withdrawn. School was also difficult as her old friends started to reject her. Bullying set in during middle school. Each day it became more and more challenging to focus on schoolwork due to the online hybrid method that was introduced locally. There was a brewing anger within her and she was not willing to discuss it with us. The family bore the brunt of her bitterness, shouting at her younger brother and lashing out at her mother and father. She would stay up late at night online talking to "friends", while she became increasingly detached from her peers in real life. Hearing her giggle and engage with other youth kept us from prying into her online life. It all seemed so innocent and we were happy to hear some social engagement especially during the isolation periods of the pandemic. But she became highly critical of our parenting, constantly insulting us and comparing her life to those of her online friends. The door slammed consistently, we felt like we did not know this person.

We sought help professionally from her pediatrician of 8 years. We were given a list of therapists to contact, but finding someone available in 2021 proved very difficult. Our daughter had began asking to see a therapist, suddenly eager to talk. The pediatrician offered to start speaking with her until we found someone. They would meet in private, then myself and the pediatrician would speak in private in order to share some insight into my daughters feelings. I trusted this doctor. She advised many things that seemed to be more disruptive and distressing in our house than helpful. But I only realized this in hindsight. At the time I was desperate, My daughter was doing poorly in school, she was depressed. So when the doctor offered her time, I accepted it as a great gesture of kindness. What a mistake this was.

Around the time my daughter started having her monthly checkups with this doctor, she decided to cut all of her hair off. She completely changed her appearance and began wearing bulky oversized clothes, all dark colors chosen from the men's department. All of her more feminine looking clothes and accessories were cast out. The basement was stacked with boxes hastily filled, overflowing with colorful wigs, necklaces, clothing and photographs from elementary school. She took on a new persona.

As the all too familiar tale of the ROGD parent goes, I spent time online trying to learn what I could. As the parent, I could see that this was a reaction to her maturing body and a rejection of her childhood identity. She had always struggled with sensory issues and puberty was deeply distressing and uncomfortable. The online community she was spending time in had trans-identified kids whom she would talk about consistently. I was certain she got the idea online and opted to allow her to pass through this as a phase. We were watchfully waiting.

But those appointments once a month with that doctor were not what I thought they were. I should have noticed the warning signs such as the change in behavior upon entering the doctor's office. The man-spreading, deep voice change, and apathetic character presentation. There was the nurse assistant who kept asking if she had a nickname. The nurse behaved awkwardly before the official doctor meeting would commence, unsure of what to say. This started in spring of 2021 and was intended to be a substitute for actual professional therapy until we connected with a therapist. We found a therapist in early August. Nevertheless the doctor insisted on continuing the meetings. Something seemed strange, I just couldn't put my finger on it.

I will never forget the day that my whole world changed. This pediatrician requested an additional visit in order for us to discuss hygiene. It was just after Christmas. I was invited back into the office after the pediatrician spoke with my daughter for a few minutes. In a brash and hurried manor, I was informed upon re-entering the office that my daughter is not a she but a he and that I should go ahead and start affirming her as such. My daughter was diagnosed with Gender Dysphoria. All the while my daughter was uncontrollably crying. The pediatrician went on to explain that some kid's brains just don't match up with their bodies. This is totally normal and they may go on to transition. She expediently handed me a business card for PFLAG and said maybe I could help convince Dad to get on board. She implied that she had spoken to the therapist and perhaps this could be worked out in sessions with that professional. When I stated that I had noticed a change in my daughter's behavior the past year or so I was immediately spoken over in a condescending way: "She's always felt this way, she was just never able to tell you".

Now she knew my child better than me?

We were to book another appointment in a month. We did not.

There were a couple of conversations with my daughter about all of this after the pediatrician appointment. She blew up on me about not wanting to be a women. I spoke of the idea of transition and how I don't believe altering your body even outside of the context of trans is healthy. She spewed angry rhetoric like:

- "I'd rather die than be who you want me to be!"
- "I thought you would throw me out once you found out I was really a boy!"
- "When I think about being a woman, I just don't want to be one!"
- "I'm just a guy with a vagina, you don't get it!"
- "I've always had gender issues!"

Where was this coming from? She never even wanted to hang out with boys, let alone be one.

My daughter assured me she's been doing research on how to solve this problem, that there were ways to fix her. Transition was something she'd clearly been pondering for months. The pieces were coming together from the whole year. The hints had been dropping for months alluding to her gender transition fantasy and her newly acquired perception of herself as male. I just didn't take it seriously. This was coming from the kid who was stereotypically female in all ways up until recently. All of the ways I was incapable of being as a child, all with no encouragement. There was a performative aspect to her presentation as male; It felt inauthentic, labored, and poorly informed.

She admitted to being same sex attracted, which I already suspected. Nevertheless, she seemed uninterested in the High School LGBTQ club. Apparently her friend group had come up with a new male name for her in a ceremonious way. It seems that in this group everyone chose a letter. But during this conversation on gender and sexuality I was sensing some ambiguity. She was expressing confusion on the topic of gender. There was concern over the term lesbian, it was clear she was not comfortable with this label. She wavered between laughing and crying as we discussed Gender fluid and the slew of other gender identities her friends had acquired. I sensed her foundation in this belief system was fragile. It was as if she was dipping her toes into hot water, reluctant to fully immerse. There had been no name changes at school formally and she used the girls' bathroom. But she admitted to being recognized as a trans kid. Some teachers and most students used the new name.

I told her that I didn't understand all of this but we will try and figure things out. I expressed that I love her no matter what and will learn what I can to help. The next step was for her to discuss this with her Dad and this could happen during therapy if she preferred. She never made that move, and never requested that we formally change her name and pronouns in the house. Yet, her demeanor began to improve at home.

The next month was a blur of tears and panic. I became all too familiar with "Affirmation" and was appalled. I looked up PFLAG and realized that sending my 14 year old to a meeting with a bunch of adults to talk about sexuality and all of the various genders available was inappropriate and potentially confusing. The conversations I had with people I thought were reasonable did not go so well. The therapist seemed shocked by this proclamation and said that she had not spoken to the doctor nor had my daughter ever brought this up. Maybe this was a deception as well? Knowing this person as an acquaintance, I felt I could share my thoughts and concerns. On a lengthy phone conversation I discussed all of the factors I felt led to this conclusion. I shared my instinctual opinion that affirming this identity felt wrong. It felt like an immense lie to my daughter, my child who trusted me as her care taker and advocate. Social transition sounded deeply impactful, a slippery slope towards medicalization. It sounded like solidifying an idea in her head which I was certain was transient. This therapist sent me an email a few days later. It was a forward to PFLAG. It stated:

"My client would like help with his transition, please advise".

I had done my research and was well versed on the advise I would receive.

A few weeks later after another long conversation with this therapist, I was forwarded to a gender clinic. The email expressed concern that if I did not accept this identity I risked "losing my child" and that she is not "abusing substances yet" or "hurting herself yet". All it took was one look at the website homepage to recognize the facility was composed mostly of endocrinologists. I did not call.

Was no one listening to me? What was happening?

I looked to friends for support. What I got was flippant advice and slogans.

I heard things like:

- "If this is her truth you need to support it!"
- "Would you rather have a live son or a dead daughter!"
- "It's no skin off your back to just change your kid's pronouns and name, it's totally harmless!"

- "Don't worry, the surgeries only come later."
- "Just let these kids have gender, it's their revolution!"
- "I'm not sure what you are so worried about, I don't think medicalization is even available for teenagers."

One mother asked me in a bubbly manner after taking a look at my teen … "So is she going to transition or what?"

All parents of trans identifying teens have these experiences.

Moments that pierce through your heart.

There was a fellow parent who advised me on just how poor of a reputation the pediatrician had. Apparently this doctor was infamous in our community for targeting struggling teenage girls and guiding them towards medications. The pediatrician eagerly played therapist in order to diagnose these kids with mental health ailments. This same parent had an incident with her own teen regarding this pediatrician's consultations on anxiety and eating disorders. There were suggestions towards medications that were undisclosed to the parent. The parent ceased to use the pediatrician any longer. Even this person who was completely aware of the misconduct on behalf of the pediatrician was insistent that regardless, in my daughters case this could be her "**truth**".

I spoke with my daughter's best friend's mother. She informed me that her daughter showed her the ropes in the trans arena. My daughter was now trans and had a new name and pronouns. Her old name is a dead name. She also said that my daughter was under the impression that she would start puberty blockers soon. This parent casually remarked that I should discuss my teen's treatment options with her and just do some research. She also noted that of her daughter's class, several identified as trans. Two months later, I got the call from this parent that her daughter now identified as trans.

As I was clearly being seen as the crazy person with all of my questions the next step for me was a therapist for myself. I needed someone to hear me, to actually listen and not solely attempt to persuade. At this point I was in a very bad place, poor sleep, constant tears, nightmares, and suicidal thoughts. I was suffocating. A local parent offered her therapy services to me. This only lasted 2 sessions. In the first I was showered with advise on how to accept the trans identity. This could be a fleeting thing but it could be real I was told. We needed to change the name and pronouns at home to show respect for my child. Doing so would better our relationship! This was not helping me. I slid further into depression and hopelessness. I could not agree with this, it just didn't seem logical.

These sessions ended after the revelation that this therapist also has a trans identifying teen. It came to light that this teen was affirmed, yet her mental condition had been deteriorating. The teen had then accused the therapist parent of transphobia for questioning the chest binder that had been surreptitiously mailed to the house by a "friend". The teen determined her home unsafe and moved in with her father. We did not meet again. Neither of us pursued. It was awkward.

Luckily I had my husband, my father, sister-in-law, and uncle for psychological support. My father was mortified with the whole story and was there to listen to my rants and read the resources I found. My husband and I were both on the same page regarding not affirming and remaining skeptical. He had received similar advice from male friends to affirm (guided by their female partners) but he could not truly accept the advice. He too followed his instincts. We read books including Abigail Shrier's *Irreversible Damage* and Helen Joyce's *Trans When Ideology Meets Reality*. We spent hours sharing articles, thoughts, and fears. Both of us spoke with family overseas and paid great attention to how other countries were handling this phenomenon.

I am deeply grateful that my trans crash course started in late 2021. The resources available through Genspect, 4th Wave Now, and Transgender Trend helped me get out of my misery and back on my feet. It was monumental psychologically to know that it was not just our family going through this. There was advice out there. There were stories, opinions, conversations, and documentaries ready to be consumed and pondered. My husband and I attended a meeting through the Gender Dysphoria Support Network with Stella O'Malley and several other parents of trans identifying teens. Their stories made mine seem so trivial, the magnitude of grief parents were experiencing was awful. But it was hard to ignore just how similar the experiences were in terms of the personality types becoming involved, the rhetoric used, and the treatment received by parents. I realized this trans thing had a far greater reach than my own household or community. It was a global phenomenon of first world proportions.

***The Gender a Wider Lens Podcas*t** helped me solve the puzzle of my teen's personal distress. Through hours of attentive listening I was able to recognize the factors that lead to my own daughter's trans conclusion. Sasha Ayad's Inspired Teen Therapy resources were instrumental assisting in my parenting and understanding of all of the influences and trends in my teen's life.

I found a non affirming therapist through The Gender Exploratory Therapy Association. It was essential to have a therapist to consult with my daughter and allow her to work through her distress without defaulting to thought terminating affirmation.

How we got through this as a family is not a simple journey to explain. I feel we are deeply fortunate to have a daughter who worked a lot of this out on her own. The first step we had to do was sow the seeds of critical thinking and take a deep dive into our own behaviors and family dynamics to understand how this all came to be in our home. Where did the distress originate? The next step was to understand the dynamics of trans ideology and the vast nets cast out to catch distressed youth. Know the perpetrator. We got her to assess her own behaviors regarding technology, to think about the psychological affects it had on her. We discussed influencers, algorithms, social media, marketing strategies and patterns. We put limits on usage and without aggressive enforcement we allowed her to know that we pay the bills for the technology and have a right to know what's she's looking at. I never went through her accounts, I couldn't bear the pain of learning exactly the types of things she was being exposed to. I decided to inform her as best as I could to allow her to critically think about content on her own. The main goal was to improve communication and ultimately allow her to discuss content when she was ready, and she has. The hours of resource consumption fueled me with information and rhetoric to share in the moments when she was receptive to hear. But mostly I tried to make myself available to listen. Gradually the pieces of the story are being told. The puzzle is coming together and it's not a pretty picture.

I could easily fill pages with all of the stories of the past year of my life and how emotionally tumultuous it was. Now that I have reached the other side of this tunnel. I feel relieved yet anxious, angry, and betrayed. The first 8 months of the year I cried at least once a day.

There were even moments when I cried from one eye in the car, the one my daughter could not see. It is a heavy emotional burden to know that my child was swept up in a movement so evil and steeped in hatred right inside my own house, in her doctor's office, and at school. The outside shell of the trans movement is glossy, colorful and full of promise. A wolf in pride clothing. It is no more than an advertisement for a different life, a better future, a rebirth, an escape. I have come to see this a medical construct. A product that the gender industry fuels with direct to consumer marketing to youth online, in school, and in the offices of medical professionals. But on the inside of this product is a dark and deceptive ideology rooted in self hatred and body dysmorphia. There is the predatory medical quackery void of science touting cures. Shrouds of secrecy and deception. The gaslighting of parents who ask appropriate and reasonable questions. These are extreme life changing medical interventions that adults are advising troubled youth to partake in. This is an abusive model and has nothing to do with care.

My daughter's trans identity was a theatric performance of stereotypes. For how can one claim to know the lived experience of another group of people if they have not lived it themselves? Is this not appropriation in the worst way? Never in my life have I heard so many different hate orientated proclamations out of her mouth as in the last year. This identity was based on egregiously sexist stereotypes (in her case of males) which were completely ill informed. It was based on disdain for anyone who disagrees, anyone who misgenders. This movement is happy to knock down women and children in order to win. We are pawns in a game. It is not the concept of trans that is problematic. Adults should be able to choose how they want to live. But adult activists have no business advising youth on how to modify their bodies, their sexual parts in particular! Adult strangers in general have no business discussing sex and gender with children as this leaves the door wide open for abusers. Adult medical professionals have no business suggesting that teens who experience distress around puberty are problematic and require medical and psychological interventions. When did puberty and adolescence become a disease? There are plenty of people living as trans and not proclaiming to know what is best for a child they do not know who is experiencing distress. Pulling families into this debate is like kicking a beehive. Parents will fight back once awareness of what is happening is wide spread. There will be a swarm. Beware of the fury of mothers.

I am plagued daily with a sense of complete betrayal. Betrayal by the institutions that promise to look out for the best interest of our youths. The politicians that close their ears to comment, that would rather be complicit in damaging policies than to admit any form of error. They do not speak for us, they speak for themselves. The medical system and its penchant for profiting from suffering, for targeting weakness. Predatory providers seek to boost their own sense of self worth and virtue by pushing agendas they do not completely understand. Betrayal from society as a whole for not putting the safety of children as a primary concern. Who are we as a society if we cannot protect our children? Instead we eagerly take advice from professionals regardless of whether that advise is harmful. We shame those who do not blindly follow such advise, who ask for proof. How did our children become sacrificial lambs to an ideology? Why are we so "OK" with the idea of administering hormones and surgeries to teens who are different, who are troubled, and who are often just gay?

When will we stop this structure of abuse? When we start asking more questions. When we catch that fist that threatens to silence our protesting mouths—that's when. It's time to say "no more". It's time to listen more. It's time to end the abuse and heal those who have been harmed. It's time to resist.

78

Eastern European Mom

When she was 13, my daughter had a mental meltdown. This came after a few years of cutting, anxiety and depression. She was hospitalized and, while in the hospital, she announced she was a boy. I am a single mom in the US, an immigrant from Eastern Europe with two children, my daughter and a younger son. My very large family still resides in Eastern Europe.

I subsequently learned that my daughter's public middle school had socially transitioned her behind my back. Alarmed at this plot to take my child away, I immediately made plans to return to Eastern Europe. I located a school back home near my family for both of my children. I contacted the school director, explained the situation and was assured that they would not affirm and that they would work with me no matter what struggles my daughter has. So, I sent both kids to Eastern Europe to stay with family and I followed a few weeks later after making arrangements to work remotely.

When I returned to Eastern Europe, I opened up to my very large family about what had happened with my daughter. As opposed to many of the stories I've heard about with US families, where family members are quick to affirm regardless of what the parents see as being in the children's best interest, my family was shocked. They asked how they could jump in to help my daughter distress and mental health struggles. They were also appalled by the gender ideology and their interference in family affairs. Rightfully so, they were shocked that the school in the

US could assume such a major responsibility for someone's child's future and health.

My daughter never disclosed her trans identity to the family our whole time in Eastern Europe.

As a family, we supported my daughter by lavishing her with attention and praise, especially for her beauty. Eastern Europeans are not ones to gush, so this was not natural, but we all praised, all the time, and then we did it again and again and again. Every day we would start with the simple statement "You're such a beautiful girl"! We praised her general beauty, we praised her nose, her chin, her eyes, her smile, her hair, her neck. We also implemented a whole schedule to make sure she was never alone and without family. We organized endless family dinners, gatherings, and celebrations. At every gathering one of us would say "You're such a beautiful girl". And she obviously is—my daughter is perfect in every single possible way. My daughter is a wonder.

I was struck repeatedly and still nearly cry when I pause to think about the doctors who were ready to swoop in and mutilate my beautiful daughter. I still have nightmares of her walking up to me, as an adult, with her breasts cut off, with a deep wound in her arms, with hair on her pretty delicate face, asking why I allowed the doctors to mutilate her.

I told my ex-husband, my daughter's father, about the trip to Eastern Europe and the reason, thinking that he too would support the intervention. He did not; instead, he threatened to take her to the US with him and his new family so that she could transition. At this point, the intervention seemed to be having an effect, my daughter rejected his invitation and stayed with me. But I told my daughter at this time that if she wanted to return to the US, we could do so and that I would bring over as much of our family with us as I could.

She didn't want to stay in Eastern Europe, so as promised we returned to the US, right in time for the new school year.

My daughter had been earning abysmal grades in her large public school. One condition for the return was that she would go to a smaller private school—any school of her choice that we could afford. My daughter picked the smallest, a Catholic school. I spoke freely and very directly to the principal about our story and my fears. He assured me that they didn't focus on gender ideology at the school. However, if my daughter came out and asked to be called "he", the school and teachers (this is California) would have to comply. But the principal said that they would not keep it a secret from me. He also said that they would stay neutral about the trans-identity. They would neither celebrate nor condemn. I thought this was more than a fair offer and enrolled her.

After a few months back in the States, in her new school, my daughter announced, now age 14, that she liked herself as a girl and that she believed she is very pretty. I was so happy, but I tried to play it cool and said that it made me so happy to know that she accepted her healthy body the way it is. And a healthy body is never "wrong"; it is a treasure.

We now talk more freely about gender ideology. She now trusts me more when I say that there is no way to be happy when you reject your body. We are our bodies.

All of my daughter's friends are letters from the LGBQT soup. Lately she started speaking up about how this whole movement seems to be just a narcissistic, attention-seeking ploy. However, she is still sympathetic to the cause. Unlike me. I will never forgive this ideology for what they do to children's brains and to families.

My younger son adores his sister and was horrified and scared when she was confused and ill. In my daughter's dark hours, when she was screaming at us that she was a boy, and that she hated us, he would cry. He would ask me who changed his sister? What happened to her? He was only seven at the time. I yet have to see what, if any, longterm effects all this had on my son.

My son is still young and I work hard to inoculate him. No one can be assumed safe. My son still goes to a public school in the same district that transitioned my daughter. I trained my son to talk to me if anyone at school or outside of the family discusses religion, sex, health, family or political beliefs with him. I told him that these are very dangerous subjects that can be used against our family. This is what my parents taught me while I was growing up in Eastern Europe. They were scientists and anti-communists; we children were not allowed to speak to strangers or teachers about these topics because, if our family was deemed to have problematic beliefs, my parents could be taken away by the KGB. I told my son the same thing could happen here. If he said the wrong thing about gender ideology, CPS could determine that I am a bad mom and take him and his sister away. That has happened to several families where I live. Just read the heartbreaking story of Yaeli.

I consider myself very lucky. Despite the whole ordeal, I am grateful to the hospital that made me realize the double life my daughter was leading which, in retrospect, I believe was the main factor contributing to her depression and cutting. I am grateful to my family that supported and stood by me during the lowest time in my life. I am even grateful to my ex-husband who, while wanting to wedge himself between me and my daughter, only made our relationships stronger.

But I am not ready to lower my guard. I am baffled at this ideology that proudly and openly medicalizes, mutilates and castrates children and all the useful idiots that enable it to do so. What is their end game? A brave new world with cohorts of sick and sterile adults? Generation of girls that are menopausal at 20 or boys that are eunuchs at 18? If you're a doctor that supports this, are you incredibly stupid or incredibly evil?

79

Your Son Is Going to Be a Girl?

I was sitting in the school councillor's office, but I felt like I was on a completely different planet. It was March 2016 and a few days earlier my husband and I had found a well written letter on our 13 year old son's phone stating that he had gender dysphoria and that he was transgender.

I turned to the school for support and when they offered the assistance of a school councillor, I was relieved because I thought would get some sensible answers and advice from a professional. Naturally, I believed, she would question his feelings, ask me about his background, and reassure me that this was maybe a phase.

None of that happened. With no questions asked, she congratulated and affirmed my son right in front of me. Then she gave me the Mermaid's website address to go to for support and advised me to get a referral to the Tavistock clinic so that we could casually pause my son's puberty. I was numb. My son went back into class and I stumbled to my car and collapsed into the driver's seat in tears.

I had never been so confused in my whole entire life. I wondered—had I imagined the last 13 years of my son's life? My son is very clever, loving and funny. As a little boy, he had always been obsessed with Thomas the Tank Engine, Lego and Pokémon. He was happy, and popular at school. The second born of four boys, he loved his three brothers, especially his younger brother who has special needs. They were all really close growing up and they would all spend hours in the garden, play fighting in the summer and building snowmen in the winter. At absolutely no point during his childhood did the thought cross my mind that my little boy was anything but a boy. In fact, he would snub any type of stereotypical girl toys, screwing up his face and pulling his tongue out at the dolls, pushchairs and play kitchens. All of these memories were reeling through my mind as I tried to make sense of what was happening, whilst at the same time battling with the thought that this councillor was a professional, so she must know what she's talking about.

For the next few weeks, I researched gender dysphoria and became even more convinced that it didn't fit my son. He had never shown any signs of being withdrawn, depressed or anxious during his childhood. I wondered if puberty might have been causing him to feel confused about his identity. Or could it be internet influence? He had a phone for his bus journey to school, but that had restrictions as did our internet... I relentlessly searched the internet for an answer, but found nothing.

Maybe I was in denial? I asked him if he wanted to wear different clothes or change his name, but he seemed to panic and had an uncomfortable look on his face. Something didn't sit right with the situation—my son seemed confused and didn't want to talk about it, at all.

As the years went by, he seemed to become more withdrawn and moodier, which could have been just normal teenage behavior... or not? We kept getting what I now call 'the side eye'. He didn't want to talk to us. He stopped wanting to visit family and wanted to spend every waking minute in his room alone playing on his computer. I started to worry about his GCSE's (General Certificate of Secondary Education), as he was hardly doing any revision for them, but he absolutely smashed them, with minimal effort, and got accepted into the best sixth form in our area. Then, shortly after starting sixth form, the pandemic hit and we were locked down.

He stopped wanting to visit family and wanted to spend every waking minute in his room alone playing on his computer. His mental health declined rapidly, he became very moody, anxious and withdrawn. We battled to get him out of his room for daily walks with the other boys, but he aggressively refused. 'Just leave me alone! I am trying to do my school work' was his reply.

A few weeks later we got a call from the school notifying us that, in fact he had done no school work at all. I was stressed—we had been trying to juggle our family business that had been allowed to remain open despite the restrictions and look after the boys, who were now at home full time. In June 2020, our lives were turned upside down when our son announced again, very calmly, at the dinner table that he wanted to be a girl and that he was going to start his transition as soon as he was 18, in four months time.

This time when I searched his internet history on his phone, I was shocked to find a long history of messages on a social platform called Reddit. There were tons of trans-identified teenagers giving my son advice on how to become feminine, which foreign would allow him to buy drugs, how much he should take, how to deceive his parents and lastly how to estrange us.

My heart sank and I started to panic. This Reddit account had been going on since the beginning of 2016 when he was 13 years old. He had been coached on how to circumvent any parental controls. I blamed myself—my son had been groomed online and I was completely and utterly blindsided. The word estrangement broke my heart into a million pieces. I turned to the internet again and now there were 1000s of parents expressing concerns, forums for these parents, and a lady called Lisa Littman who had done a study and coined the phrase "Rapid Onset Gender Dysphoria". This was my son—now it made sense!

I had absolutely no idea how the hell I was going to get my family out of this nightmare. Through stress I stopped working, started researching and connecting with hundreds of other extremely worried, loving and really engaging parents. The more parents I met, the more I found that estrangement was a very common theme, even for the most supportive parents.

I joined a group of mums with trans-identified boys and these mums were on a mission. They had done their research and it was very shocking. Our stories and our sons were almost all identical. Our boys were super intelligent, quirky, awkward, immature and obsessive. None of the boys had any history of being gender non-conforming. One thing they all had in common was the social media platforms and anime. We spoke about how it was like our sons had been taken over and brainwashed. We met with a cult expert who agreed that this gender ideological movement had all the traits of being a cult. So, I started to research cults and only then did I realise what I was up against, and the enormity of the task that I had to take on.

I knew that the internet and the phone had to go. But my son was nearly 18 and I knew that this was going to cause a massive fallout, so I had to be prepared and strategic about it too. I watched a documentary called the Social Dilemma on Netflix and decided that this was how I was going to break the news. I needed to repair my relationship with my son; these people on Reddit had turned him against us all and I needed him to know that we loved him and would always love him no matter what.

The other boys were so worried about their brother and the way he was acting. I sat them down and explained what I was about to do and they agreed it was for the best. I ordered a new router with strong parental controls and got my older son, who was a software engineer to check it out, he confirmed that it couldn't be bypassed. I managed to get my son out of his room for 'family night' and we watched The Social Dilemma together. Afterwards, I announced that I thought it was for the best that all the phone contracts were cancelled and that the internet was restricted for everyone as we all needed to spend more time together as a family. The next day that is what happened. I removed every device from the rooms and into a communal room for educational purposes and I reduced all our phone contracts to the minimal data, even our own. My trans-identified son went into meltdown.

'I need to watch anime' was the argument I heard for the next few weeks. 'We can watch it together on Netflix' I said. 'It's rubbish on Netflix!' What was with this anime? So, I agreed to watch it on the internet with him. I wasn't impressed and remember thinking how depressive and angry the theme was, this kind of viewing wasn't any good for anyone's mental health and I told him. We argued about it and he ended up running away. The police brought him home but things got worse. I very quickly realised he had an addiction to the internet and specifically anime. He was acting like a drug addict whose drugs had been withdrawn. He was extremely agitated, restless and exhausted. I found myself constantly searching for answers, trying to understand what was going on in these kids' heads, especially boys and there was a constant common theme. Anime. Then it dawned on me, as I scrolled though a trans subreddit, boys dressing as anime girls and adopting anime names. My son also wanted to be an anime girl. This phenomenon has recently been best described by detransitioner, magiruvelvet, in his essay "My experience with Anime and how it impacted my life". With this new information, I doubled down on the anime restrictions and I did not hold back my hatred for it either, in just the same way I would for drugs or alcohol if that was what my son was addicted to.

It took a few weeks, but he recovered very quickly and our relationship began to improve. We walked the dogs every day, I took him out for driving lessons and we watched movies as a family—so many movies, funny ones mostly. He started to calm down and to like a normal person. He turned 18 and told me he was going to get a job and get his own phone contract. I told him that was fine however, as it was my house and I paid all the bills, I still was not going to allow any devices in bedrooms. I helped him get a little job in a supermarket. He did get a phone contract and I still stuck to my guns on the rules. He managed to pass his driving test and we helped him get a car, things were really good. Then he went back to school.

My husband and I had already agreed that we would not support a university placement away from home as we did not think he was mentally strong enough. He agreed that he would go to a local university and stay living at home, and he even made the application. Then, one day, I noticed an email come through from one of his teachers with regards to an estrangement application for university! It turned out that my son had been claiming that he was being physically abused at home, his one girl friend was backing up these claims, and the school were going behind our backs to help him make an application for estrangement support with no consultation whatsoever. I was furious and wrote to the headmaster, I even threatened legal action. How could they be so irresponsible? In what other circumstance would a school do this without consulting the police? I mean at least then we could disprove these allegations. They backed down, but we were back to square one. Things were a mess and he continued to tell his friends and their families that we were physically abusing him and eventually they rang the police, who came and removed him from our care.

He messaged me to say he was going to university to transition and he never wanted to see or talk to any of us again. I can't even begin to describe how heartbroken we all were. What followed were nine months of hell. Sleepless nights with worry, numbness, guilt, doubt that I had been wrong. I attempted to stay in touch but I was always met with a barrage of abuse whereby he would make up a history of childhood misery. I would find myself rooting out family photo albums to confirm his happiness as a child and asking my other children if they had happy childhoods. The self-doubt was awful. My oldest son would comfort me and remind me that his brother had been brainwashed by this cult. It had destroyed my family and I would never forgive it.

A few weeks before Christmas I got a text message from him informing me that he was now taking drugs to transition. We already knew that he had socially transitioned, as his older brother had found his social media accounts. I was extremely angry in general and at all those people who had groomed my sensitive boy online, the teachers who had colluded against us, and his friends and their families who had believed we were abusers and facilitated his estrangement. I will never forgive them. My son was now on a pursuit of something that was completely impossible and would destroy his mental and physical health. I stubbornly argued with him about it during this communication, against everyone's advice. But who else was going to tell him the truth? I knew these actions would result in me being blocked but I won't and will never lie to him. He could never become a girl, least of all the anime type!

We found his online anime account and the addiction was clearly obvious. Every day and all night were an anime marathon. It was around five months after he had told us that he had started to transition that he stopped watching anime on this account. I wondered—had he found another platform? Then, out of the blue, shortly after noticing the anime stop, I got a text message. I pushed my luck on the hope that he had come out of the anime trance and asked him to come and visit. He did, on my birthday, and it was the best birthday present I could have ever wished for. He looked as though he had returned from battle, very gaunt and pale. I could also see signs of significant self-harming. I knew I had to do everything I could to get him home. We had the best day together, as a family. His brothers were thrilled to see him, as were we.

Our son came home a few weeks later a completely different person. He wanted to spend time with us. He was thoughtful again, he was back. It was so surreal, it still is, I wonder sometimes if I'm dreaming. All the behaviours stopped dead, the same way the anime did. He's now a world away from that gaunt pale boy who returned to our door back in May. He's happier and much healthier now that he isn't under the mind control of anime and the gender cult.

Gender ideology stole nearly seven years of my son's life, but I am truly grateful that something made him wake up, because a lifetime of medication and pretending to be someone you are not is no life at all. I am petrified of gender ideology and the impact it has on a specific type of kid. It certainly has no place in any school and, as I endeavor to piece back together my own family from this nightmare, I will do my best to help other families who are still caught up in it and, hopefully, bring awareness of this risk to other families too.

80

Seeing an Invisible Elephant

My daughter was identified as 'trans' here in Hong Kong in April 2021 at the age of 11, after two twenty minute sessions with an American school counselor. We were kept largely in the dark for months until we discovered that she was already using a boy's name and pronouns at the school at the same time we were told we must affirm her because she was suicidal.

The year that followed was a long one, during which we felt very afraid and isolated. Fortunately, the law in Hong Kong is clear on the matter of parental authority and, after we felt we understood what was going on, we were able to force the school to cease social transitioning our daughter. We held her very close indeed, and did many of the usual things: we took her largely offline, slowly adjusted her friendship groups and just gently talked to her, drawing her back into family life.

We found in her possession a book given to her by the school counselor with a false cover. This book warned her not to trust us, her parents, and told her to find a 'supportive community' online. It also provided her with the addresses to Reddit forums where I found all manner of horrors: pornography, suicide notes, self harm manuals, advice on how to obtain drugs, and template letters inviting children to tell their bigoted parents to 'fuck off and die'.

My daughter has recently started wearing girls clothes again (at her own instigation) and seems outwardly to have entirely desisted. Throughout that long year following our discovery of her trans identification, I was always mindful that some of her friends were also in trouble over this and I had decided that it was not enough to see her clear of it all, but that I was also obligated to attempt to help others understand the phenomenon, which is why I wrote this account of my experience—to give something back to the forum that really meant an awful lot to us during the dark early days.

In a former life, I was an academic in the world of political theory and once lectured on 'Gender Theory and Feminist Approaches to International Relations' so I had a head start in deciphering the lies, falsehoods and propaganda. I have not come across my thoughts on the anesthetizing effect of identity politics elsewhere, but I think they may help explain how obviously harmful ideology has spread so far and been spread by so many apparently well meaning people.

Identity Politics Has Anesthetized Child Safeguarding and Co-Opted Teachers, Counsellors, Doctors, and Even Parents into the Willing Service of a Castration Cult.

A long time ago a professor of mine explained that the philosopher Michel Foucault had warned everyone to 'mistrust the image'. I have searched for the reference a few times, but never found it, and do not have the sanity to wade through his books, so it will have to remain an indirect reference. Nevertheless, it made sense to me at the time. Reading text, Foucault is alleged to have said or implied, awakens the critical faculties, meaning that when people read they do so at arm's length. They accept what appears true, but fully engage their doubts if something seems implausible or poorly reasoned. Images, on the other hand, bypass the critical faculties entirely, seizing hold of the consciousness in unanticipated ways.

I doubt this is still true. Despite the ubiquity of images in our hyper-media age, the proliferating use of photoshop and the substitution of memes and emojis for actual words suggests people are wise to these tricks and look skeptically at all images now, even to the extent of disbelieving what they can see with their own eyes on the grounds that it is so outrageous it 'can't possibly be true'. Anyone who has been peaked by the catastrophe of gender ideology will recognize the gnawing sense of disbelief as they point out what has become obvious to them but remains opaque to less interested observers, and face blank looks or rolling eyes as the conversation moves swiftly on.

The only way I have found to describe the experience, is to imagine being in a room hosting a large party of apparently intelligent and civilized people and pointing out the dangerous looking elephant crashing around, knocking over the furniture and occasionally squashing the odd unsuspecting child, only to be met with stares of incomprehension as the other guests encourage the wounded child to celebrate the bleeding stump left in place of its leg. They just do not see the elephant. Or if they do occasionally sense a large, foul smelling animal, they believe the fault lies within them, rather than admit the absurdly unlikely existence of a vast, unwelcome pachyderm bellowing and defecating on the carpet.

Suspending Disbelief

A familiar conversation may proceed like this; 'Gender identity', I say, 'makes no sense. 'Gender' derives from '2nd Wave Feminism' and describes that which is imposed on women in order to socialize them as willing subordinates, wives and sex objects. No one 'has' a gender, it is not internal to the person, it is not innate, it is imposed. To speak of 'gender identity' is epistemologically incoherent.' This statement leads to confused looks, 'But gay people I know say it's in their heads.' 'Did I mention gay people?' 'No, but, you know, trans people say it's in their heads, that they are 'born in the wrong body', 'was there an alternative body into which they should have been born?' 'No but that's what they say.' 'But that's madness!' 'Well how do you know? Are you trans? How can you claim to speak for them, when you are not trans?'

Or it might begin like this: 'Children should not be castrated', I argue. 'They are not being castrated' comes the response. They **are** being castrated, but set that aside for a moment. 'Why not?' I ask. 'Because they are too young to understand the consequences.' 'But what about their 'gender identity'? If castration brings their body into alignment with their 'gender identity', why wouldn't you advocate castration for children? Given that they 'know' their 'gender identity' from as young as two years old—why delay the inevitable? What do they need to understand and consent to?' Silence. 'No one is getting castrated before it is medically appropriate.' 'Would you deny them cancer treatment because they can't really know the consequences?' 'No, of course not.' 'But I thought you said this was 'necessary, gender affirming care?' Silence. Rolled eyes.

Gender critical people are always happy to talk about trans issues, yet they are routinely shut down on the grounds that they cannot speak 'for' trans people. The fact that they tend to speak against transgenderism is classed as bigotry warranting cancellation, even though they almost always register concern for people who say they are trans and generally believe adults should be free to live their lives as they wish. So who is speaking about trans issues? Trans people and their allies, and that's it. Some of the most prominent trans medical professionals are themselves trans, Drs Marci Bowers and Erica Anderson among them. Does their 'lived experience' cloud their judgment? Should we trust an alcoholic to treat alcoholism? I can see an argument for it, but it's not compelling. Yet in trans world, the doctor being trans rather dictates the treatment, given that the treatment is to become fully trans. The more important question than 'who is speaking for trans people' is, of course, who is speaking truth about trans issues? Are we entirely sure the 'my truth' that trans people expound is the same thing as 'truth'?

If Gender Is Innate, Why Does It Need Surgery?

And treatment for what? Gender dysphoria? Hmmm. Historically, 'gender dysphoria' merely described the symptom of discomfort with one's sex, implying that if the discomfort dissipates during puberty (30 years of medical research demonstrates this happens in up to 98% of cases, one of the strongest findings in psychiatric medicine) that is surely a positive outcome, you would think. Yet in 2018 the American Academy of Pediatrics redefined gender dysphoria from 'discomfort with one's sex' to 'distress that stems from the incongruence between one's expressed or experienced (affirmed) gender and the gender assigned at birth.' So an 'incongruent gender identity' is now merely assumed without any scientific evidence offered in support of its existence, the nominated symptom is now simply taken to prove the inferred cause. How can you tell if a child is trans? You can't, but they know. Very convenient, diagnostically. Assume the existence of 'gender identity' and the only way out of 'gender incongruence' is castration. Very convenient for well paid surgeons and trans ideologues, if not for the children who will never get their reproductive organs back if they're wrong. You'd want to be sure, right? 'They know,' apparently.

'Diagnostic overshadowing' is the term used by Dr Hilary Cass to describe the process at the UK's Tavistock Gender Identity Development Service by which all further investigation and exploration was curtailed once the question of 'gender identity' was invoked. It might be better termed the retreat of critical judgment. Once a patient is identified as trans, there is nothing for it but to castrate them, and quickly too, as any delay is apparently traumatic and you wouldn't want your unease to harm vulnerable trans kids, would you? All critical inquiry is suspended. Doubts and awkward questions are merely condemned as bigotry. The same pattern happens in schools. A child spends a bit too much time online or picks up the latest playground conversation about 'non binary', this chimes with his or her sense of discomfort at the onset of puberty or feeling attracted to other children of the same sex and they speak to the school counsellor. Immediately they are trans and if their parents don't affirm them they might commit suicide. The child's identity is protected, parents are put on notice, everybody celebrates as another family is shattered, their beloved child sucked into the gender vortex.

Why does 'identity' have this power? Why is a child's claim to be 'trans' not investigated? Why are parents not even asked if the child has ever evinced the slightest discomfort in their sex before? Because that would explode the myth of gender identity premised on the 'lived experience' of the child. It would reassert that discomfort is potentially a symptom of many things, incongruent identity being only the most preposterous. For the truth is, gender identity only ever describes behavior or 'expression' as the term goes. There is nothing inside a boy or a girl that can ever be the wrong sex. Not the mind, not the brain, not the hormones. Gender identity is a phantasm, invented to describe external conditioning, then used by psychologists to describe outward appearances, now attributed to some mythological inner essence. No one is 'born in the wrong body'. Any notion a boy has of being a girl, or vice versa, comes from their understanding of social stereotypes. That's why so many trans women dress like ludicrous parodies of women and speak in erotic terms about menstruation or masochistic sex in which their own violent subjugation is the source of their greatest vicarious joy. Equally girls who imagine themselves to be boys have only the remotest idea of what it is actually like to be a boy. Usually, they are just in retreat at the harrowing thought of becoming a woman.

For anyone to claim that 'gender identity' exists, the onus is on them to demonstrate it with scientific research, not 'lived experience'. Yet this never happens. It never happens because 'gender identity' does not exist independently of the claims made on its behalf. How do you know someone is transgender? Because they say they are. Why do they say they are transgender? Because a helpful TikTok influencer or unqualified school counsellor explained it all to them. You're a boy and you like the color pink? Trans. You're a girl and you like climbing trees? Trans. You don't like the sound of your recorded voice? Trans. No matter the problem, all roads lead to trans heaven, and castration is the key. Puberty blockers (chemical castration) are totally harmless, reversible, give you time to think, like Alice in Wonderland finding the little bottle that says 'Drink Me!' Or Neo choosing the 'red pill' in the Matrix (the directors of The Matrix are trans, if the penny hasn't dropped yet). It is all perfectly timed to just suck the child in. Parents? Don't tell them. And when they find out, warn them that the child will commit suicide if they are not 'affirmed'. Scare the shit out of them. No better way to control people than fear for the life of their child. Yet it is an unconscionable and outrageous lie, quite apart from the malpractice of placing parents under such duress in order to force acquiescence to the castration of their child. No scandal could be more grotesque. That it has gone global, destroying the lives and families of thousands of vulnerable children is an abomination.

The Slow Suffocation of Identity Politics

The whole field of gender medicine is riven with falsehoods, ideology, contradictions, and silence. And on this shaky altar, children's sexual function, fertility and mental health is being sacrificed by the use unlicensed drugs to chemically castrate them, wrong sex hormones to deform their bodies, and surgery to render them eunuchs. It is literally unbelievable, yet it is happening all around the world. What has suspended the critical faculties of so many professional people, who treat this issue unlike any other? No other medical condition would ever be treated using unlicensed drugs with known dangerous consequences and no research to suggest they work. No other body dysmorphia is treated by surgically altering the body. No other identity claim is used to justify overruling the fundamental rights of women to their own sports, toilets and changing rooms. No other identity claim would put rapists in women's prisons or ensure the perpetrators served lower sentences for violent assault. No other identity claim would allow a teacher to wear massive false rubber breasts while teaching a class of children, anymore than would allow a white teacher to show up in black face using a comedy Caribbean accent. And as this elephant continues blundering dangerously around the room, the professionals charged with safeguarding our children scratch their heads at all the shattered bodies and calmly tell the parents they need to be more understanding. Of what, exactly?

None of this should be happening, yet mention the magic words 'gender identity' and critical judgment is suspended, lest it contravene the 'lived experience' of disordered and delusional minds. And here's where we get back to Foucault and his alleged instruction to 'mistrust the image'. His concern was not the image per se, but the suspension of critical faculties that left people extremely vulnerable to manipulation and ideological bias. In today's discursive climate we have subjective truth claims given priority through the auspices of identity politics and the unchallengeable dictums of 'lived experience'. The effect this has on intelligent and highly professional people is the same as for Foucault's image, it visibly anesthetizes their capacity for judgment, such that Supreme Court nominee Ketanji Brown, when asked 'what is a woman' refused to answer, saying instead that she 'is not a biologist'. It didn't escape anyone's notice that Ketanji Brown is, in fact, a woman, even if conditioned into silence on the wider significance of her own sex class.

All of this is the fault of identity politics, but in a subtle and much misunderstood way. Mention identity and people tend to think of the different categories it is applied to; Nationality, religion, ethnicity, sexuality. These categories are recognized and protected to some extent in laws that deal with discrimination. Trans is treated as just another category, even a subset of sexuality, though many have doubts about what it actually means. What those same doubters don't notice is that when they think about 'trans' they are already thinking about identity, and they have already adopted the epistemic framing for matters of identity, which is non-judgmentalism. Whatever anyone's identity is, it is not the business of others to speak for them. And every identity must be afforded respect even if you have doubts. In fact, whatever doubts you have about a specific identity claim you must conceal them, for those doubts fall foul of your duty to treat matters of identity without judgement.

It is, therefore, identity that walls off judgement, and if a trans ally claims the life of a 'trans child' then it is not anyone's place to challenge them, however obvious the danger. So the highly qualified professional, the head of Student Affairs or the dedicated Headteacher meekly steps aside and allows the ideological kidnapping to take place in plain sight. The rhetorical function of identity politics works to deliberately suffocate the critical faculties of anyone who does not share the 'lived experience' of the identity concerned. To understand is to accept identity claims unconditionally.

This is the missing piece of the strangest puzzle, and realizing it makes visible the elephant rampaging through the room. Once the unsuspecting teachers, counsellors and doctors have accepted the existence of 'gender identity' they disarm themselves against its worst abuses. And even the swift, chemical castration of pre-pubescent children cannot rouse in them their protective instincts. Their bargain with 'identity' is already made, and if the child is persuaded that he or she is trans, then any further judgment is forfeit, save how to manipulate the bigoted parents. This is how safeguarding has been subverted, indeed, turned on its head. The gamekeepers have become the poachers. And what of the parents? The first they learn is that their child may commit suicide, and if they don't accept an absurdity, it will be their fault.

The Numbing Truth

Every parent who has fought against this pernicious ideology will recognize the intense dilemmas, the sleepless nights, the minute attention to every aspect of a formerly happy child's life, the desperate hope, the uncontainable anger, the ocean of fear. Every parent who learns about it will recognize the depths of confusion and the scale of disbelief as they try to explain even the most basic insight to people who simply don't have a clue and retreat behind the reassuring indifference of identity oblivion. And they will all understand perfectly well that this must end. None want any other parent ever to experience what we've gone through, yet all will also seek the anonymity that promises their slowly desisting child will not be subject to yet more pressure and abuse.

And it must end. The elephant must be exposed, and all who claim they cannot see it must also be exposed. This is our children, and our future that we are endangering by not speaking up. Sadly, it is also the 'lived experience' of thousands of detransitioners, who now realize what was done to them. Following behind will be all the rest, the supposedly 'happy' transitioners, as they realize they are now the isolated victims of a castration cult. Finally there will be the schoolteachers and the school counsellors who fueled this butchery with their cowardice and confusion, and the doctors who prescribed the poisons and wielded the scalpels. The best of them will be filled with a lifetime of remorse, but at least it will be stopped.

When you strip gender ideology of its protective euphemisms and actually describe what is happening in schools and clinics around the world, you arrive at the astonishing truth. Our schoolteachers, counselors, and pediatric establishments have been deceived by their subordination to the dictates of identity politics into persuading vulnerable children who may be gay, on the autism spectrum, struggling with puberty, or just plain shy, into believing that they are the wrong sex, and that the only solution to this problem is rapid castration, which they are delivering with or without the consent of the child's parents, all across the world.

That is quite an elephant. Do you see it yet?

81

The Gift of Critical Thinking

Life is never easy but you can learn from the cards you were dealt. Parents have learned they need to wait patiently for their kids to return home from the advice of a detransitioner. They can also cherish the gift of critical thinking and use this advice to take care of themselves and create the best life they can. The tide is turning and our children will return home.

If you are a PITT reader, you know the myriad things gender ideology has taken from parents: spousal harmony, trust in professionals, community leaders, and so-called experts (like psychologists, clergy, doctors, journalists, and teachers), friendships, the parent-child bond…since trans destroys everything it comes in contact with and rots our society from within, the list goes on and on.

I'd like to call out the one positive from my own harrowing brush with gender ideology in my home. The trans contagion has given me (back) the gift of critical thinking.

I thought I was a critical thinker. I thought I was informed. Prior to my son's unexpected pronouncement that he was trans, I really felt that I was in tune with current events, and I felt pretty smart about my independent opinions and variety of balanced news sources too.

Actually though, what I had was apathy and, what seems to me in hindsight, an appalling lack of intellectual curiosity. I remember back in high school and college when I was eager to explore every academic and intellectual angle, to open every curiosity door, as that teacher in *Stranger*

Things suggested. What happened to me? It seems like I spent the next 20 years on a treadmill, just doing all the expected things in life, career, money, family, house in the suburbs, blah blah blah. I left it to others—to the "experts"—to think about the rest of it, everything that didn't pertain directly to me.

Then, out of the blue, my family, my child's health and safety, my whole way of life was under attack. This shock—which I would not wish on my worst enemy—jolted me out of complacency. To help my son, I had no choice. I had to open my eyes—and what I learned shook my worldview to the core, dramatically and irreversibly. While I was living my life, queer theory had successfully reframed society and even subconsciously retrained me and my way of thinking, in a way that flew completely below my radar.

Transgender was totally made up, the emperor with no clothes. And, if that was true, what else that I had accepted as fact was based on false premises or completely fabricated?

Now that my son has desisted, I'm able to think about gender about 25% of my day, instead of the 99% of my brain process it consumed for almost two miserable years of my life. But I will never, never go back to my former complacency. I've been backstage now, I've seen the man behind the curtain. And, with my fresh eyes, I saw that gender isn't the only problem that decades of stifled curiosity and free-thinking has created. Pick any area of interest you have and you're sure to find false assumptions treated as facts by a tiny number of self-identified experts who are very happy to tell you what you should think. Maybe the silver lining of our society's mass insanity is the creation of a new generation of skeptics.

So, thank you, gender ideology, for the newly re-discovered gift of critical thinking, and for renewed curiosity, the most human trait of all.

Question everything. I know I will.

82

How to Deprogram a Teen: Parts I, II, and III

This essay is republished with permission from The Glinner Update.

Part I

I am writing this guide in the hope that it will help parents of ROGD teenagers. I see many instances where they are getting very poor advice but mostly, they are getting no advice at all. My belief is that gender ideology goes beyond social contagion and is a cult. My teenager daughter identified as trans for three years but once I realised that gender was a cult, I used deprogramming techniques to successfully rescue her. I will explain why I think that gender is a cult and how I went about deprogramming her. I am an ordinary mother, there is nothing exceptional about me and any parent can do what I did. I rescued my daughter without having to move house or home-school and I did it despite the threatening presence of the hostile professionals out there who encourage and celebrate trans identities against all reason, critical thinking, or good judgement.

There are two main approaches to a child who comes out as trans. Affirmation and watchful waiting. Affirmation is what the professionals would have you believe is the only treatment. It means agreeing with the self-diagnosis of a child without question, ignoring any explanatory factors such as autism and it involves fast tracking ROGD teenagers onto the path of hormones and surgery. Watchful waiting is what responsible therapists advocate but this entails remaining neutral on the question of whether your child is "really" trans. I think that watchful waiting is fine if your child is only flirting with the idea of being trans and if this phase is not destroying their lives and the lives of their families. My daughter was being destroyed in front of my eyes and her life had fallen apart. The impact on our family was devastating and we were only coping by isolating ourselves from the angry, miserable and hateful personality that had come to reside in our daughter's body. She was planning on running away I found out later and the pressure from outside factors made it imperative that I acted decisively in order to save her. I will take you back to how it began but the story will be familiar to many of you.

Sinead has severe attention deficit disorder and attends the local CAMHs for a prescription for Ritalin. She is also on the Autistic spectrum. When she was 11, she experienced a number of sexual assaults by a friend. Her best friend introduced her to the concept of gender and from the age of twelve all the girls in her circle were either non-binary or trans of one flavour or another. I believe that all these factors made her susceptible to the gender cult. She also happens to be a lesbian but, in her case, I don't think that this was a major contributing factor. Not in the way that it was for her best friend who is a butch lesbian and is full of self-loathing, internalised homophobia and misogyny.

The first sign that there was something very wrong was when Sinead was 12 and she became unhappy, withdrawn and angry seemingly overnight. She came out as non-binary and then trans when she was thirteen and a half after first self-diagnosing with everything from BPD (borderline personality disorder) to DID (Dissociative Identity Disorder). She was self-harming and had lost all interest in schoolwork or family life. COVID didn't help and the lockdowns allowed her to spend hours on the internet when she was supposed to be doing online school. I found out later that influencers like Jammie Dodger and Noah Finnce were indoctrinating her into the trans cult and she was also talking to disturbed kids like herself on Discord. I had been turned into a jailor by COVID, checking on her to try and get her to do schoolwork and searching her room for blades to make sure she wasn't cutting. She hated me because I would not agree with her that she was trans and she told me so many times. I hated her too by this point as I did not even recognise the person she had become.

When she did voluntarily talk to me it was to subject me to angry rants about how she had always been a boy and hated dresses etc. I was easily able to refute this invented back story and I never agreed with her that she was trans. However, because she really seemed to be going insane with stress all the family started to use her boy names when at home. I say names because she went through a few before settling on the final ridiculous one let's call it Xavier. She called me transphobic and said that I didn't know anything, and that last part was true. I was strangely reluctant to do any research and I think I only know why now. Firstly, I was afraid that researching it would make the nightmare real and I was full of horror at what was happening to our once happy family. Secondly, I was afraid that the research would tell me that she was indeed trans and there was nothing I could do about it.

Things came to a head after a series of meetings with CAMHs about her autism. Pressure was put on myself and my husband to affirm Sinead in her new identity and her medical records were changed to her new name without our permission. I also felt threatened that if I did not comply that I would be labelled as abusive. I felt that CAMHs were only waiting for an excuse to make life very difficult for our family if we did not affirm. But the psychologists pushed too hard and alarmed me into finally getting on the internet and doing some research.

One of the first things I came across was Lisa Littman's research paper which documents the phenomenon of social contagion among teenage girls with trans identities, followed by the document prepared by the law firm Dentons which reads like a handbook for how to roll out this new religion across Europe. I then ordered Abigail Schrier's book Irreversible Damage on Amazon. Within a few hours I realised that I was looking at a cult. Sinead pretty much ticked every box for risk factors. The sexual abuse I think was the biggest factor and I had just found out about this at the last meeting with CAMHs.

I'm not sure that I realised the reality about gender identity at that time, but I suppose that I never really believed the trans thing in the first place. I had some vague notion that trans peoples' brains were different and of course I was slightly brainwashed by all the one-sided stories in the media. But on the other hand I had been witnessing the carry-on of my daughter's group of friends with all the talk of trans and demi-boys, agender, ace, non-binary and so on. It looked to me like a silly teenage phase, and I was hoping they would grow out of it. I was more concerned about the self-harm, the autism, the anxiety and Sinead's obvious mental distress.

Gender Ideology Is a Cult

So how did I realise so quickly that gender ideology was a cult? It just happened to be an area of interest for me, and I had an old paperback on my shelves about cults with a chapter on deprogramming which I had read with particular interest. Cults are funny things. They all hate and fear other cults and ideologies, but they all have certain traits in common. Sinead had been indoctrinated by the internet and to a lesser degree her peers. Gender ideology now pulled the strings. She was simply a puppet doing as she was told and nothing and no one was going to help her as had been made very clear to me by the appalling moronic behaviour of the CAMHs professionals (and later by my GP and the psychologists at the autism assessment).

Most people jump to the fact that there is no leader in gender ideology and no obvious money motive so how can it be a cult? But they are missing the point. The thing that makes a cult a cult is the level of control over a person. A properly brainwashed person has no free will. Take an ROGD kid. They are controlled by fear. Fear of the transphobic world where they are told trans people are killed and abused every day. Fear of themselves where they are told that they are at high risk of suicide and if they delay transition in any way, they are going to kill themselves. They also fear rejection from their peers if they say anything "transphobic". They are taught to fear their parents who are transphobic, old fashioned and unsafe and they are discouraged from having any interaction with them. A trans kid is coached online and told what to say, what clothes to wear, how to behave and speak. A whole new language is used by insiders and language is distorted to fit the new meanings of the trans community.

Another thing about cults is how they control how a cult member thinks. Critical thinking is forbidden and thought-terminating cliches like "Transwomen are Women" are used to bring the thinking back on track. Any doubt or contradictions are strictly prohibited and labeled as "internalised transphobia". The kids are told that if they are wondering if they are trans then of course they are trans because 'cis' people do not have these thoughts.

Kids are encouraged to ruminate endlessly about their gender identities and their dysphoria in much the same way that prayer or meditation acts in other cults to shut down critical thinking. They are forbidden from listening or watching anything "transphobic". For example, they will be told that JK Rowling hates them and wants them dead, but they will never actually read what she wrote. Instead, they will rely on approved articles that explain why she is so transphobic. You can research this further yourself and I think that a very good analysis and comparison to Scientology is given by Arty Morty.

I am going to be recommending Arty Morty's YouTubes many times because he is excellent at analysing and explaining gender ideology in a concise way. You can save a lot of time by watching his videos and taking notes which will come in handy later.

Part II

It was unthinkable to me that Sinead was 'trans'. A parent's first rule in life is to protect their child and that means that the thought of someone slicing off pieces of her healthy body and destroying her health with hormones sickened me. I would sooner volunteer that I sacrifice bits of myself than that she would do this to herself. Soon after Sinead announced that she was trans she started pestering me for a binder and she had a list of medical steps she was planning to take starting with puberty blockers, testosterone, double mastectomy, and she even planned on metoidioplasty.

I googled the side effects of binders. Constant pain, breathing difficulties and skin irritation were all listed, all unacceptable to me. I later learned that rib deformities and fractures, breast tissue damage, skin stretching, nipple displacement and possible organ damage are all equally likely. I know that this is true because one of her old friends has respiratory problems and a permanently deformed rib cage from wearing a binder. I have seen pictures of severely deformed breasts after years of wearing a binder.

The solution to these issues is to get "top surgery" as quickly as possible.

Puberty blockers were familiar to me as I had a friend who took them as part of IVF treatment. I was under no illusion that they could be reversible or a "pause button". They are powerful, dangerous drugs and I would never dream of giving them to a developing child for a non-medical, unnecessary reason.

Although I did not know it at the time 98% of children who were put on puberty blockers at the Tavistock clinic in the UK went on to take cross-sex hormones. Rather than a pause button, puberty blockers are more akin to a springboard into the deep end of full-medical transition. If they are taken as recommended when puberty starts and followed by cross-sex hormones the child will be infertile and their sex organs will never mature and grow.

In terms of general health, growing bones need sex hormones in order to become strong so brittle bones are a real risk. Brain development is stunted. Another side effect is depression, ironic considering the reason given for prescribing puberty blockers in the first place is to often to prevent suicide.

I knew about testosterone under the old-fashioned label of steroids which medical professionals are quick to condemn when it comes to athletes. However, now it seemed to be ok to give it to teenage girls off-label with no medical studies as to its safety or effectiveness. After an average of three months, a girl's voice will be permanently coarsened and body hair will have started growing. There will be cosmetic changes like fat redistribution and muscle gain, but the real damage is taking place internally. After around four years the changes to the uterus make cancer likely and a hysterectomy is recommended. If this is accompanied by an oophorectomy (removal of the ovaries) then no more oestrogen will be produced. The girl will be dependent for life on external hormones and will be immediately menopausal. There are many more side effects including changes to the heart and taken together, these changes considerably shorten expected lifespan.

Finally, the surgeries. And who better to talk you through them than the patients themselves? TT Exulansic on Odysee shows 'progress videos' of these young girls, providing her own expert commentary. I find it hard to talk about them. I can't watch them for long before I feel my heart constrict with what might have been.

You will not go far on the internet when you start researching top surgery before you come across Dr. Sidhbh Gallagher, the surgeon of choice for very young girls. You can view photos and videos of the results. Row upon row of innocent young faces all smiling into the camera with a thick angry line across their chests where their breasts should be. I imagine that we are supposed to be seeing trans joy but all I see are the self-harm scars along their arms and in one video I could see the girl's little hand trembling violently. Was it pain, shock or horror at what she had done to herself? She was only thirteen.

TT Exulansic describes brilliantly the religious nature of these gruesome operations. They are rites of passage into the trans cult and recruits are encouraged to progress through these operations to demonstrate their worthiness and their "true" transness. Suffering is celebrated and expected. When it comes to bottom surgery, even the archdeacon of the church of trans, Jammie Dodger, was traumatised by the brutality. She nearly died from a haemorrhage but then when it comes to bottom surgery for girls, nearly dying is par for the course. If they pull through, they can look forward to a life of pain and incontinence. Urinary tract infections will become a part of life and regular doses of antibiotics will wreak even more havoc on bodies already ravaged by hormones . It is no surprise that suicide rates for post operative transexuals has been measured in Sweden as 19 times higher than the general population.

This is what parents are afraid of. The complete destruction of the healthy body of their child. When they try to articulate their fears, they are met with incomprehension and gaslighting by professionals. I say professionals here to include all the medical professionals who push affirmation, affirming teachers, LGBT clubs and trans allies of any sort. They all have blood on their hands.

Now, what do professionals believe? I can only say what was said to me and what I have heard said by trans allies and trans charities and it is always the same. They basically believe that we all have a gender identity and that only the child knows their own identity. I was told that there was a medical consensus represented by WPATH that demanded affirmation. Being trans was reeled off in the same breath as being gay as if they were remotely analogous. They really did not seem to think that there was something monstrous about having a secret identity that demanded the total subjugation of a physically healthy body to become an unhealthy simulacrum of the opposite sex. My feeling is that they believe that they are saving the trans child by providing the understanding and support that they are not getting from their ignorant parents. They do not regard the medical side of things with the same horror and fear because it is not their child. They feel like they are demonstrating how liberal and progressive they are, and they do this at no personal cost. Society is telling them that they are heroes for rescuing trans children and defeating their abusive parents or forcing them to comply and affirm.

You have to understand that they are listening to a child who is thoroughly indoctrinated in the cult and has been coached online on what to say. So, the professionals are also being played, even as they are playing the parents. I do not forgive or excuse them, however. How many years of training does it take to become a psychologist or a psychiatrist? And yet they can't recognise when a child is indoctrinated. They do not think that it is strange that all the trans kids say the same thing and make the exact same demands and threats.

But the really strange part is the way that professionals seem to be able to mentally block out the reality of the medical process of transition. I think that they must be indoctrinated as there is some sort of mental short circuit going on there in the same way that trans kids do not seem to notice or question the quite glaring contradictions of gender ideology.

Every time I brought up the drugs and surgery angle, I was assured that it was still far too early to talk about such things. But there was a consistency and preparedness to the response which in hindsight I feel was acting like a thought-terminating cliché.

One final observation here. I am talking mainly about medical professionals because that was my main contact but what about co-morbidities? They knew about Sinead's severe ADD and her autism. Her self-harm was getting worse, not better the more she took on the trans identity. And finally, the sexual abuse. Knowing about that, how could they, as trained professionals, not make a connection to her repudiating her body and her wish to deny her past existence as a girl?

When my husband and I learned about the sexual abuse it made total sense to us that Sinead hated her body and wanted to change it. Again, the only answer I can come up with is that the professionals have been indoctrinated or groomed. Once they hear the magic word trans they react like Pavlov's dog and there is only one possible outcome from then on. Check out the Cass report again on this. It describes the phenomenon perfectly although Dr. Cass does not go so far as to suggest that they have been indoctrinated. She assumes that they are still capable of independent thought. But if that is so, then the only remaining explanation for their eagerness to feed vulnerable children into the trans mutilation factory is that they are either stupid or evil.

Part III

This then was the situation that I faced. I had a daughter who was in a cult and was demanding that she be allowed to permanently damage her health and irrevocably alter her appearance. And the very people who should have been protecting Sinead and trying to help her had betrayed my trust in the most appalling way possible. Clearly, there was no one coming to the rescue. We were on our own. When I realised I was dealing with a cult I was strangely relieved as finally I understood what was going on. And how to fix it.

Here's how I went about it.

Step 1: Preparation and Research

So, what exactly is deprogramming? It is simply removing the programming that your kid has received and allowing them to think for themselves. All you are doing is talking to your teen and telling them or showing them the truth about gender ideology. Or should I say, exposing the lies that they've been told. So firstly, you need to research gender ideology in order to understand exactly what your teen believes. This stage took me two weeks.

Every evening I spent hours late into the night researching gender ideology. I had to understand all the arguments that Sinead had been taught and how to refute them. You must have all arguments covered because you don't know what has made the most impact on your ROGD teen. It's like sitting an exam and revising everything because you don't know what will come up. I also recommend joining a discussion site like Discord to hone your arguments. You need to take on a few TRAs and be confident in your arguments. You must be able to refute whatever your ROGD teen throws at you in a calm and confident manner. Your teenager may come across as an expert in all things trans, but they are no match for an adult who has done their research. As with all cults, gender ideology is completely illogical and absurd and you just need to point this out. We might laugh at the notion in Scientology that there are aliens inhabiting us and directing our actions but similar magical beliefs power the gender movement; The notion that men can become women just by imagining that they are, the notion that we all have a "gender identity" which can be "born into the wrong body". Channel your inner skeptic and don't give an inch of ground. There is no place for "be kind", wishy-washy, half-beliefs. Steel yourself, and trust to the science.

Step 2: Modify Your Parenting Style

Many parents these days are afraid of their teenage children. We have become so used to experts telling us how to parent that I think it has made us distrust out instincts. At the same time parents are undermined in every contact they have with authority from being addressed as "Mum" by the local GP to condescending teachers, journalists, and even public representatives. Maybe this is why so many parents are tiptoeing around their teenagers so as not to incur their disapproval. When things go off the rails with an ROGD teen and you have absolutely no control over them, start by having a look at your parenting style. You need to be respected and have authority before you can even think about deprogramming, and this means an authoritative style of parenting. You should be strict about rules and boundaries while still being approachable and kind. Think Uncle Buck or Nanny McPhee. Don't confuse this with an authoritarian style which will get you nowhere with a rebellious teenager. My parenting style became more authoritative once I realised what was happening with Sinead and I shed the last ounce of respect that I had for the "experts" in CAMHs. If you are reading this, then you have already proved yourselves better parents and experts in your own children's welfare than any therapist. Trust yourselves and the lifetime of experience you have and don't blame yourselves. How could any parent be prepared for a cult that recruits our teenage children through the internet, social contagion and via trusted adults such as teachers and doctors? Secondly, were any of us prepared for the impact of the internet and social media on society and our teenagers? I have been to internet safety sessions organised by my kids' schools and the people who gave those talks were clueless. Half the time was spent talking about the dangers of Grand Theft Auto and the rest about bullying on WhatsApp and Snapchat. This is an adult's view of what kids are up to. What they are actually looking at is far, far worse.

Step 3: Turn off the Poison Tap

Teenagers are sneaky and parental controls over internet access are so weak I wonder if this is on purpose. Parents have no idea what their kids are looking at on the Internet and if they did, they probably wouldn't understand it. Much depends on the mental stability of your teenager that prevents them tumbling down one of the many rabbit holes that are waiting for them such as porn, gender ideology, perverse anime etc. A teenager that has any problem—from lack of friends and struggling in school, all the way to having suffered trauma or some mental condition like Autism—is at risk.

Parents are intimidated by the brave new world of the Internet and the new language of diversity, inclusion and social justice. They want to be liked and so make the mistake of trying to be their teenager's friend. Some even allow themselves to be "educated" by their teenager. I think that laziness or being too busy also comes into it. You need to take the time and get familiar with technology. It is very difficult and time-consuming to block access to each and every App and doing this centrally does not work in my experience. My husband spent a good day locking down access to all Sinead's favourite sites. First, you need to find out what Apps your teen is on and then block them all individually leaving only the bare minimum needed for school. Firstly, get passwords to all devices and then see what Apps they are on. Delete them all apart from school Apps. Then lock down centrally with parental controls all Apps you know about and any others you can think of. Do not leave any App where live chats can take place with strangers (like Pony Town or Roblox.) Put blocks on internet access on the family computer, both time blocks and word searches. You need to become more of an expert on technology and social media and more of an expert on gender than your teen. And you must be vigilant in knowing what your teen is doing at all times. I did not let Sinead out of my sight for months apart from school.

Step 4: Repair Your Relationship with Your ROGD Teen

If you were in my situation this would have seemed impossible. Sinead hated me and saw me as the enemy because the cult had taught her to distrust and hate outsiders, particularly parents. I felt that I had lost all my power as a parent. Don't fool yourself into thinking that you have a good relationship with your own ROGD teen. You only find out what they really think of you when you defy their wishes. See how much they respect and like you when you misgender and deadname them and cut off their internet access. They have been programmed to distrust all 'cis' people, even the allies. Be prepared for how much time and effort this is going to take.

A parent is best placed to deprogram their child because a professional could be accused of conversion therapy, and they simply don't spend enough time with the child to do it. Secondly, a kid wants to like and respect their parents. It is a basic and fundamental need. Even if they act like they hate you, deep down they want a parent they can rely on and respect. They don't want the responsibility of making big decisions and they need boundaries. What you are doing here is just building enough goodwill and trust so that they will listen to you and engage in discussions.

I am in the fortunate position that I only work part-time, and I have complete flexibility so I was able to drop everything and put Sinead's rehabilitation first. Families where both parents work full time are going to struggle with saving their child because it is not something that can be achieved in a few weeks. Although the deprogramming itself is relatively quick it can take a year or even longer to rehabilitate your teen.

As a family, we immediately stopped using the trans name and went back to Sinead's real name. The pronouns had only just started but they too stopped. The constant stream of communication and indoctrination from the internet was switched off. The silly fake trans personality of Xavier must have still been there but I no longer noticed. I spoke to Sinead or what was left of her. She was a broken person and seemed completely worn out by the constant monstrous demands of the cult. I did not hold her responsible for the actions of the trans personality, but I spent hours with her talking with sympathy about what she had been through. She seemed grateful for every cup of tea and every kind word.

I never talked about gender but only about things that were relevant to Sinead. I would have expected her to be furious about the new rules, but she seemed resigned and maybe even a bit relieved that someone else was now making the decisions. Just a warning in case you have not fully understood the previous steps. Do not make the mistake of being kind to the trans personality or relaxing the rules in any way. The trans personality has gone nowhere and is not to be trusted.

Step 5: Deprogramming

I was very scared about making the situation worse but felt that I was ready to start the deprogramming. I had to be very careful initially not to alert the trans personality what was about to happen. I started by asking Sinead to watch a video called Trans kids: It's Time to Talk presented by Stella O'Malley. Sinead put up a bit of resistance, but I had put enough work into the relationship, so she agreed. I think that she might have been a tiny bit curious, and 'Xavier' thought that his faith was strong enough to withstand the blasphemous film. I lurked outside to make sure the video was running, and that she was listening.

She came downstairs and said that maybe, just maybe she wasn't trans. Not much, but I felt that a small chink of doubt had been formed. The following day my husband went away for the weekend, and I brought out my copy of Abigail Shrier's Irreversible Damage. I had underlined what I thought were particularly good points. I would tell Sinead that I had read something interesting and what did she think in order to draw her into a discussion. It was a scattergun approach, and I would try one topic after another.

Every ROGD kid will have their own topic that causes them some doubt or concern. With Sinead, it seemed to be the gruesome surgeries and the awful side effects of cross-sex hormones and puberty blockers. She had been unaware of this as the influencers and all the LGBT websites gloss over these aspects. You must ask questions and force your teen to use critical thinking. Do not use the cult language and they will be forced to explain their understanding in plain language. Often this is enough to demonstrate the irrationality and incoherence of the ideology.

The mantra "Transwomen are women" took about an hour to demolish. But what really helped her to wake up was me telling her firmly that she wasn't trans. No white lies about true trans. Stick to reality and science. Trans people do not have different brains, or hormones or genes. There is nothing that distinguishes a trans person physically. It is a mental disorder, a delusion. As Arty Morty would say "Trans is something you do, not something you are". I also told her that gender was a cult, and she had no problems at all in believing this. In fact, she fell over herself giving me examples of cult behaviour.

Sinead would slip in and out of the belief that she was trans for a couple of months, but the hard work was done in the initial three weeks. When she was with me, and I was hammering away at her trans beliefs she would be nearly convinced but then all her friends were still fully signed up members of the trans church. That initial weekend we spent about six hours at it and the following couple of weeks we would spend one or two hours a day talking and watching videos. We fell into a routine of watching Exulansic who combines brutal reality with sarcastic humour. Her series on Jazz Jennings was a highlight and Skirt go Spinny and The State also did some very memorable and hard hitting YouTubes. I subscribed to Glinner and watched the Mess and generally became obsessed with all things trans. Sinead wanted to talk about gender ideology and she needed to do so for months. After the first few times, I rarely needed to do more than suggest we watch an Exulansic or a Mr Menno or something funny (and gender ideology can be pretty funny). I will put a list of videos that were entertaining and effective below. Teenagers have a short attention span so don't waste it by showing them written reports or boring podcasts.

Step 6: The Following Year

I didn't put any pressure on her to change her boy's haircut or clothes or her friends. I knew that her friends still thought that she was trans and I think that it was embarrassment that prevented her from coming clean. About three months after the initial deprogramming Sinead asked me to phone her friends and ask them to stop using he/him and calling her Xavier. I could tell that they were startled by getting a call from the transphobic abusive monster Sinead had told them all about but in any case, by the end of the year all but one friend was gone. I see the old friends around still and they are all getting more and more entrenched into the trans world. One ex friend deserves a special mention. She is the most dangerous trans ally of all, an active recruiter. She calls herself non-binary but makes absolutely no effort to present as anything other than sexy anime girl. However, she collects all the lost lesbians she can and persuades them that they are trans. She has the most success with the ones who are also autistic.

Deprogramming someone is initially a quick process, but you can't leave them alone or they will slip back into their familiar trans world. Sinead had been trans for nearly three years and had come to depend on that world for support, friends, an answer to her problems and a world-view. It is profoundly shocking for a young person to emerge from that safety and realise that it is all lies. Not only did she have to deal with the real world without her trans safety blanket but now she also had to deal with the real problems that she had avoided for three years. Her autism, the sexual abuse she had suffered and her ADD. Your teenager is very vulnerable in the weeks after deprogramming. Try and get them into a healthy routine again with plenty of sleep because the trans cult teaches kids to neglect their needs. Getting outside to nature is very good for perspective and healing. As Sinead's hair grew and she started to change her clothes, her dysphoria also disappeared. It was obvious that it was trans ideology that gave her dysphoria and not the other way around.

One thing you need to watch out for is floating. This is where the deprogrammed person is triggered by something in their environment, and they feel like they are back in their trans reality. It is supposed to be a very jarring and frightening experience and takes about a year to stop happening. I helped to reassure Sinead when this happened, and we would watch a YouTube or talk about the latest gender nonsense in the news, and she would snap out of it. In fact, the book I read said that it takes about a year to recover from being in a cult and I would agree with this. It takes a long time for critical thinking to be re-established. When you take someone out of a cult you leave them to figure out their understanding of the world themselves. If you were doing conversion therapy, you would be replacing trans ideology with another ideology, but deprogramming just means revealing gender to be the bunch of lies and nonsense that it is. You must be patient and not expect that they will be able to just snap back into real life.

You need to spend a lot of time with your ROGD teen. They are going to lose most of their friends if their friends are caught up in the ideology. You have to keep talking about gender until every last lie has been uncovered and destroyed. And then you have to talk about everything else. You must catch up on years of normal growth and development. And get to know the real person who was hidden for so long in their nightmare trans prison. Even silly things like catching up on what other girls are wearing and interested in. If you have been a transman for that long, you have missed out on a lot of normal activity.

Final Words of Advice

I hope that this account helps other parents. More even than ROGD teens I feel sorry for their parents because I've been there, and I know the rage, panic and fear. I haven't gone into how having an ROGD teenager is so damaging to a family, to other siblings and to the parents' relationship but if you are living through it I'm sure that you are no stranger to the stress.

One last thing and this is very important. Parents must share a common approach in dealing with their trans teenager. When they are trans they cannot be trusted. They will try to turn one parent against the other if it gives them an advantage. The trans personality will lie, steal and cheat in order to keep control of your teen much like an alcoholic will do anything to maintain their habit. I told my husband what I planned to do, and he gave me free rein and supported me. Without that, it wouldn't have had a hope of working.

I know that I did the right thing because Sinead told me so. She has thanked me many times and although I was only doing my duty and it was a pleasure to do it, it is still nice to know that she is grateful. I know that I did the right thing because she is happy again. Without even intending it I am now very good friends with Sinead (while still being the parent). I really enjoy her company and I am so grateful that I am getting the opportunity to get to know her again.

Credits

Introduction

pittparents.com/p/back-from-the-other-side

Parents on Family

1. open.substack.com/pub/pitt/p/maybe-im-suffering-too
2. open.substack.com/pub/pitt/p/who-is-thinking-of-the-parents
3. open.substack.com/pub/pitt/p/the-silence-is-killing-us
4. open.substack.com/pub/pitt/p/in-it-for-the-long-haul
5. open.substack.com/pub/pitt/p/the-opposite-of-love
6. open.substack.com/pub/pitt/p/trans-the-family-destroyer
7. pitt.substack.com/p/i-thought-this-would-be-over-by-now
8. pitt.substack.com/p/i-was-robbed-multiple-times
9. pitt.substack.com/p/from-the-father-of-an-adult-trans

Parents with Estranged Children

10. open.substack.com/pub/pitt/p/the-runaway
11. open.substack.com/pub/pitt/p/the-wolf-at-the-door
12. open.substack.com/pub/pitt/p/trust-transferred-from-parent-to
13. open.substack.com/pub/pitt/p/what-ive-learned-this-year
14. open.substack.com/pub/pitt/p/trauma-that-leads-to-more-trauma
15. open.substack.com/pub/pitt/p/the-crimes-of-the-mother
16. open.substack.com/pub/pitt/p/i-cry-on-the-beach
17. open.substack.com/pub/pitt/p/ill-love-you-forever
18. pitt.substack.com/p/estrangement

Parents on Daily Life

19. open.substack.com/pub/pitt/p/tale-of-two-losses
20. open.substack.com/pub/pitt/p/i-finally-decided-to-tell-the-truth
21. open.substack.com/pub/pitt/p/relationship-as-guru
22. open.substack.com/pub/pitt/p/you-took-my-joy-and-i-want-it-back
23. open.substack.com/pub/pitt/p/to-my-son-i-will-be-your-rock
24. open.substack.com/pub/pitt/p/fighting-for-our-sons-lifeand-our
25. open.substack.com/pub/pitt/p/malevolent-benevolence
26. pitt.substack.com/p/the-gender-party

Parents with Wisdom

27. open.substack.com/pub/pitt/p/this-will-make-me-a-better-parent
28. open.substack.com/pub/pitt/p/sams-story
29. open.substack.com/pub/pitt/p/the-too-too-solid-flesh
30. open.substack.com/pub/pitt/p/close-enough-to-open-my-eyes
31. open.substack.com/pub/pitt/p/one-familys-story
32. open.substack.com/pub/pitt/p/my-sweet-baby-nboy
33. open.substack.com/pub/pitt/p/the-long-game
34. open.substack.com/pub/pitt/p/for-the-parent-of-an-adult-rogd-child
35. open.substack.com/pub/pitt/p/when-two-worlds-collide-part-1-a
36. open.substack.com/pub/pitt/p/when-two-worlds-collide-part-2-a
37. open.substack.com/pub/pitt/p/when-two-worlds-collide-part-3-the

Parents on Schools and Universties

38. open.substack.com/pub/pitt/p/post-pandemic-public-school-propaganda
39. open.substack.com/pub/pitt/p/the-precipice
40. open.substack.com/pub/pitt/p/please-dont
41. open.substack.com/pub/pitt/p/when-you-fear-communicating-with
42. open.substack.com/pub/pitt/p/what-happens-when-schools-follow
43. open.substack.com/pub/pitt/p/how-schools-can-better-support-gender
44. open.substack.com/pub/pitt/p/to-the-administrators-of-my-sons
45. open.substack.com/pub/pitt/p/an-open-letter-to-a-school-board
46. pitt.substack.com/p/the-university-agrees-there-are-no

Parents on Social Contagion and Indoctrination

47. open.substack.com/pub/pitt/p/why-are-we-erasing-neurodiversity
48. open.substack.com/pub/pitt/p/they-need-space-to-grow
49. open.substack.com/pub/pitt/p/we-lost-our-daughter-to-a-cult

50. open.substack.com/pub/pitt/p/culture-of-death
51. open.substack.com/pub/pitt/p/mental-illness-equals-social-credit
52. open.substack.com/pub/pitt/p/my-sons-story-and-the-breakdown-of
53. open.substack.com/pub/pitt/p/forks-in-the-road
54. open.substack.com/pub/pitt/p/there-are-two-phasesa-mothers-intuition
55. open.substack.com/pub/pitt/p/no-contact
56. open.substack.com/pub/pitt/p/when-my-teenager-came-out-as-transgender
57. open.substack.com/pub/pitt/p/the-frantic-search-for-an-identity

Parents on Heartache and Tragedy

58. open.substack.com/pub/pitt/p/letters-we-never-received
59. open.substack.com/pub/pitt/p/in-the-path-of-a-hurricane
60. open.substack.com/pub/pitt/p/the-waves
61. open.substack.com/pub/pitt/p/a-mothers-heartache
62. open.substack.com/pub/pitt/p/the-role-i-wish-she-wouldnt-accept
63. open.substack.com/pub/pitt/p/life-on-a-tightrope
64. open.substack.com/pub/pitt/p/nightmares-a-child-torn-apart-by
65. open.substack.com/pub/pitt/p/what-i-think-happened
66. open.substack.com/pub/pitt/p/daniels-story
67. open.substack.com/pub/pitt/p/the-day-my-daughter-told-me-she-was
68. pitt.substack.com/p/swallowed-alive-by-the-transgender

Parents on Medicalized Children

69. open.substack.com/pub/pitt/p/a-fathers-anger-that-will-not-sleep
70. open.substack.com/pub/pitt/p/duct-tape
71. open.substack.com/pub/pitt/p/they-want-me-to-pretend
72. open.substack.com/pub/pitt/p/the-standard-clinic-experience-self
73. open.substack.com/pub/pitt/p/dear-doctor
74. pitt.substack.com/p/nevertheless-she-persisted
75. pitt.substack.com/p/dear-concerned-parent

Parents on Desistance

76. open.substack.com/pub/pitt/p/the-many-months-to-desistance
77. open.substack.com/pub/pitt/p/a-resistance-story
78. open.substack.com/pub/pitt/p/eastern-european-mom
79. open.substack.com/pub/pitt/p/your-son-is-going-to-be-a-girl
80. open.substack.com/pub/pitt/p/seeing-an-invisible-elephant
81. pitt.substack.com/p/the-gift-of-critical-thinking
82. open.substack.com/pub/pitt/p/how-to-deprogram-a-rogd-teen-parts

About PITT

Parents with Inconvenient Truths about Trans (PITT) publishes stories written and edited exclusively by parents with first-hand experience in the upside-down world of gender ideology.

Founded by Josie A. and Dina S., PITT (pitt.substack.com) is a space for parents who have been impacted by gender ideology to share their uncensored personal stories, experiences, and thoughts, while remaining anonymous to protect themselves and their families. PITT's objective is to inform the public about the devastating impact of gender ideology on families and to end the medicalization of identity for children, teens, and young people.

The essays on PITT are always published anonymously. Any names that might appear on bylines are pseudonyms. Parent authors hail from around the world, including (so far) the United States, the United Kingdom, Australia, Ireland, Canada, Spain, South Africa, France, Italy, Poland, New Zealand, and several countries in Latin America.

PITT is supported, in part, by Genspect, an organization founded by psychotherapist Stella O'Malley that is committed to supporting parents' voices. If you are a parent of a trans-identified child and want a chance to tell your story, you can contact PITT at pitt@genspect. org. Josie A. is a mother and co-founder of Parents with Inconvenient Truths about Trans. She lives on the West Coast. Dina S. is a mother and co-founder of Parents with Inconvenient Truths about Trans. She lives on the East Coast. Florence M. lives on the East Coast and is the mother of a trans-identified young adult. She serves as editor for the PITT Substack, contributes essays, and assisted with the editing of this volume and the first PITT book.